Number Five: Environmental History Series
MARTIN V. MELOSI, *General Editor*

LUMBERJACKS AND LEGISLATORS

LUMBERJACKS

AND

LEGISLATORS

Political Economy of the

U.S. Lumber Industry, 1890–1941

by

WILLIAM G. ROBBINS

Texas A&M University Press

COLLEGE STATION

Library of Congress Cataloging in Publication Data

Robbins, William G., 1935–
    Lumberjacks and legislators.

    (Environmental history series; no. 5)
    Bibliography: p.
    Includes index.
    1. Lumber trade—Government policy—United States—
History. I. Title. II. Series.
HD9756.R6 1982   338.4'7674'0973   81-48375
ISBN 0-89096-129-8

Manufactured in the United States of America
FIRST EDITION

For my father and the memory of my mother

Contents

List of Illustrations

Acknowledgments

THE basic argument in this study was first advanced in an extended essay on the politics and economics of the early conservation movement in Oregon. This, in turn, led to further inquiry into the broader implications and meaning of political economy and its potential for explaining the economics of resource exploitation in the United States. My first ambition was to investigate resource development in the Pacific Northwest, but, through the encouragement of my friend and colleague William Appleman Williams, I was convinced to break beyond the bounds of regional scholarship to the national scene. Oregon State University provided a released-time research appointment in the spring of 1979 and a sabbatical leave for 1979–80. The National Endowment for the Humanities granted me a summer seminar award for 1979, which took me to West Branch, Iowa, and the Herbert Hoover Library Association provided a major fellowship award, which enabled me to complete the research.

I am grateful for the efficient and generous staff assistance at the following institutions: the Oregon State University Library, the Special Collections division of the University of Oregon Library, the Oregon Historical Society manuscripts section, the government documents division of the University of Iowa, the Minnesota Historical Society manuscripts archive, the manuscripts collections in the Cornell University Libraries, the Franklin D. Roosevelt Presidential Library, the Herbert Hoover Presidential Library, and especially the kind and helpful service of the library staff of the Forest History Society.

My thanks to those who read portions of the manuscript: to Thomas R. Cox, San Diego State University; to Ellis Hawley, University of Iowa, for his incisive critique of the chapters on the National Recovery Administration and for the long conversations in the summer of 1979; to William Appleman Williams, whose perceptions of market economics are evident in this study (and who is an equally sharp editorial critic); to Robert Ficken, for suggesting that I take another hard look at the manuscript; and to

Ronald Fahl, the capable editor of the *Journal of Forest History*, for sharing his wealth of bibliographical knowledge.

A very special thank-you to Rita McDonald, engineering librarian emeritus at Oregon State University. Rita volunteered many hours of searching through professional publications, lumber trade journals, and a myriad of primary sources to flesh out the research for this study. She also read the entire manuscript and offered the valuable insights of her lifelong interest in western resource history. A bouquet of roses to you, Rita!

And to Julia Bruce, who typed the manuscript.

And to my friend and companion Karla, for reminding me to keep it all in perspective (and for sharing the meaning of the poem on the wall).

LUMBERJACKS AND LEGISLATORS

Introduction

JIGGER JONES, the larger-than-life logger hero of the Maine woods, first trudged westward to the pineries of the Great Lakes states and then turned back to the great pine forests of the Southeast. His search for the big trees set in motion a folk and cultural movement that scattered tobacco tags and snuff boxes from Bangor, Maine, and Saginaw, Michigan, to Bogalusa, Louisiana, and Portland, Oregon. The movement of the logging frontier west (and south) is the most striking historical aspect of the lumber industry in the United States, at least until the twentieth century. Optimistic and reckless exploitation, economic boom and then disaster, characterized this westward push. When the timber resource was exhausted in one region, there were bigger and taller trees just beyond the ring of the woodsman's ax—in the Great Lakes area beginning in the 1840s and the 1850s, in the great pine forests of the southland in the last quarter of the nineteenth century, and then on to the last great stand, the Douglas fir forests of the North Pacific slope, in the early twentieth century.[1]

Every eyewitness account tells us that these timber stands were impressive, perhaps beyond imagination. One Forest Service study estimates that the original commercial forest in what is now the United States may have contained 5.2 billion board feet. A geographer writing in the 1920s believed that the virgin forest of the United States covered 821,800,000 acres, with the great bulk lying east of the Mississippi River. Forests, in fact, were the predominant feature of colonial America. Clearly, forest re-

[1]The metaphor is borrowed from Stewart Holbrook's informal but informative history of the North American lumber industry, *Holy Old Mackinaw: A Natural History of the American Lumberjack*. Jigger Jones's real name was Jigger Johnson. Holbrook has the name right in a later book (Holbrook, *Yankee Loggers: A Recollection of Woodsmen, Cooks, and River Drivers*, p. 54).

sources—lumber and other wood materials—are more American than any other industrial product. These magnificent stands, recounted in literary classics for at least three centuries, were variously construed as havens for the devil's work, obstacles to agricultural progress, an abundant resource to be turned to profit, and, finally, the setting for the folk and romantic tales of Paul Bunyan.[2]

For hundreds of years before European contact with North America, native Indians skillfully adapted to the woodland environment by using the products of the forest for shelter, weaponry, clothing, and materials for transportation. But these first Americans, while using the timber, did not exploit it for immediate, short-range profit. The European newcomers in the Southwest and on the eastern coast of North America also used forest resources for a variety of purposes. But from the very beginning of their exploitation of timber, a commercial ethic was involved. Europeans used forest products in shipbuilding, as materials for naval stores, and as lumber for the growing number of settlements that persistently and relentlessly forced indigenous peoples further into the interior of the continent.

For well over three hundred years, wood products have been the critical natural resource in the evolution of the American political economy. The forests offered a warehouse of materials for a variety of human needs. They provided a vital energy source for heating and cooking and to power steam engines. Wood was used in housing, for fencing, and in building furniture. Until steel and other substitute construction materials began to replace wood in the late nineteenth century, products from the forest constituted the indispensable raw materials in the growth of the American economy.[3]

A diverse resource of great variety and with broad distribution across the continent, lumber and related wood products were closely linked to the requirements of westward expansion and to the development of the nation's commercial and industrial economy. By the time urban metropolises had spread westward to Chicago in the first half of the nineteenth century, the

---

[2]U.S. Forest Service, *Timber Depletion, Lumber Prices, and Concentration of Timber Ownership*, p. 32; J. Russell Smith, *North America: Its People and the Resources*, p. 630; Roderick Nash, *Wilderness and the American Mind*, pp. 44–66; Samuel Trask Dana, *Forest and Range Policy: Its Development in the United States*, pp. 1–3.

[3]Dana, *Forest and Range Policy*, pp. 2–3. The term *political economy* as it is used throughout this study refers to the interrelationship between political and economic activity and the progressive alterations in those relationships as the economy matured in the late nineteenth and early twentieth centuries.

great pine forests around the Great Lakes were falling to the woodsman's ax. The exploitation and devastation of these forestlands were completed in the last half of the century when the transcontinental rail lines pushed out onto the arid and largely timberless Great Plains.

Despite the significance of timber, the lumber industry has been largely neglected in economic histories and in most discussions of prominent and influential forces in the American political economy. The dispersed nature of the resource, the relative physical isolation of the mills from the centers of population, and, until recently, its keen competitiveness, probably are responsible for its treatment by scholars as a tertiary activity.[4]

The lumber industry provides key insights into the evolution and expansion of industrial capitalism in the nineteenth and twentieth centuries. During its major period of growth, between the end of the Civil War and the first decade of the twentieth century, the industry suffered from dislocation, chronic overproduction, cutthroat competition, and a generally unstable market. Although total lumber production reached its peak about 1905, the industry's difficulties recurred with alarming frequency until the onset of the Second World War. Lumbermen, despite great efforts, were unable either to cope effectively with or to eliminate wildly fluctuating markets. Not until the emergence of a booming demand for war-oriented products in the early 1940s did the lumber industry enjoy any semblance of stability.

Finally, the postwar process of merger and consolidation, which produced national firms like Georgia-Pacific, enabled lumbermen to exercise a greater degree of control over the lumber market. The increasingly stable lumber economy in the years after 1945 evolved in the midst of dramatically altered competitive conditions, the emergence of larger, more efficient and monopolylike operating groups, and the ability of trade leaders to influence the political world to their advantage. But the process by which the industry reached a greater degree of stability was long in the making.

The turbulence of commercial and industrial capitalism and its cyclical gyrations after the Civil War continued unabated into the twentieth century and culminated in the Great Depression of the 1930s. These chaotic conditions were related to mercurial and unstable market forces that capitalists, individually and collectively, were unable to control. In the

---

[4]One earlier writer recognized the neglect of the lumber industry in historical writing (Vernon Jensen, *Lumber and Labor*, p. 18).

case of the lumber industry, improvements in transportation, increasingly sophisticated methods for felling timber, and an even greater revolution in the technology of milling lumber generated a tremendous expansion in the productive capacity of the industry. The consequences were overproduction, glutted markets, and a social-Darwinian struggle for survival that often resulted in extravagant waste, a devastated environment, and decaying communities.

These dynamic productive forces constituted the material substructure that determined the organizational development and the competitive conditions in lumber and in virtually every other industry. As circumstances changed and competition became increasingly destructive, new competitive relations emerged in the form of corporations, pools, trusts, mergers, and trade associations.[5] Some entrepreneurs drifted with the tide, were caught up in periods of economic downturn, and went under. Others tried to anticipate market trends and create the conditions required for economic survival. The critical elements for continued existence and financial success, at least as the progressive entrepreneurs viewed the world, included large-scale operation, corporate organization, cooperation between associations, and effective influence over the political process and the emerging regulatory agencies. Such policies, they hoped, would promote a rationally ordered and stable environment in which technical and investment decisions could be made with fair predictability.[6]

The technological innovations that altered competitive conditions and

[5] For further explication of these ideas, see G. A. Cohen, *Karl Marx's Theory of History: A Defence*, pp. 35–41.

[6] David Noble, *America By Design: Science, Technology and the Rise of Corporate Capitalism*, p. 16. The term *progressive*, employed frequently throughout this study, refers to those capitalists who supported political intervention into economics (as long as they controlled the process) in the interests of stability and order. The view in this book accords with Gabriel Kolko's definition of progressivism as "a movement for the political rationalization of business and industrial conditions, a movement that operated on the assumption that the general welfare of the community could be best served by satisfying the concrete needs of business" (Kolko, *The Triumph of Conservatism: A Reinterpretation of American History, 1900–1916*, p. 3). Progressive lumbermen, in this context, were those lumber entrepreneurs and trade association executives who wanted to use the legislative process and the regulatory powers of the federal government to rationalize and stabilize the lumber industry. They had no qualms about deviating from laissez-faire economic rhetoric as long as the result was stabilization of the lumber trade and maximization of profits. In their effort to achieve order and efficiency, trade executives advocated consolidation of smaller, less efficient units into larger, more efficient ones. These people were rationalizers and modernizers who tried to anticipate the future and act accordingly.

revolutionized lumber production also increased competition because of the availability of capital and resources. These changes contributed to chaotic and excessively competitive markets and convinced the more far-sighted entrepreneurs of the need to rationalize and bring order to these seemingly uncontrollable productive and market tendencies. The modernizers in lumber (and their counterparts in other industries) developed a unique organizational device, the trade association, as a voluntary and cooperative effort to cope with the disorder that permeated the industry.

Trade associations emerged in the more competitive U.S. industries in the 1880s and continued to develop in the twentieth century as an important functional component of a maturing industrial capitalism. The tendency toward commercial and industrial cooperation, expressed largely through the trade association, represented the first major effort by progressive capitalists to infuse a sense of order, stability, and predictability into a chaotic economic environment. The trade association movement attempted to control the extremely competitive tendencies in capitalist industrial development that dominated the latter part of the nineteenth century. Its success or failure is not the major focus of this study. But the attempt of the lumber groups to work through political and regulatory channels to control competition is critical to this undertaking. These cooperative efforts failed, of course, which does suggest that the tensions and contradictions could not be resolved without major structural changes in the social system.

Even when large-scale production units became widespread, the old problems persisted. Large corporations, although seemingly efficient, still required full and constant use of plant and equipment to meet their bonded indebtedness, annual taxes, and other carrying charges. In the lumber industry, large investments in timberland and the need to meet the charges incident to that investment (usually in interest and taxes) compounded such problems and led to periodic overproduction. Efforts to regulate output were never successful, even when a friendly government cooperated with the initiatives of industry in the form of the National Recovery Administration (NRA) in the 1930s.

Where voluntary efforts to curb production seemed to produce some success, the achievement may more accurately be ascribed to a contracting market than to the effectiveness of voluntary controls. During the great heyday of lumber-industry expansion, from the 1880s to 1907, efforts to cooperate through associations, pools, and dividing markets failed miserably. Excessive competition, glutted markets, and falling prices continued to plague lumbermen. Thus the need of capitalist enterprise to expand and consolidate—or perish—placed real limits on attempts to reform the system. Moreover, countering the vagaries of the market always demanded awareness of the needs of the corporate and business world. This emphasizes a critical feature of reform in the United States: its tacit functions are to protect those whose power is threatened and to preserve the status quo.[7]

During most of the twentieth century, major resource industries in the United States have enjoyed congenial and friendly relations with the federal government. The shared objective has been to improve the effectiveness, efficiency, and stability of the existing social order; or, in the rhetoric of industry spokesmen, to work in the national and public interest. Beginning with the establishment of scientific bureaus in the federal government in the late nineteenth century, government bureaucrats viewed related private groups as their natural friends. The industrial organizations, in turn, looked to the bureaus for scientific expertise and marketing information; they also served as effective lobbyists for government agencies seeking increased appropriations for scientific research. These shared interests continued into the twentieth century, with the policy initiatives usually coming from the private groups. Appointments to federal scientific bureaus and to federal regulatory agencies normally had the approval of the business and industrial community.[8]

The close ties between the Forest Service and the lumber industry illustrate this interdependence in classic form. Whether they worked for the federal government, as private consulting professionals, or in the lumber industry, most professional foresters and others closely associated with the forest products business shared a common ideological vision. This made it possible for them to shift easily from the federal government to the private sector or to an academic institution concerned with the welfare of the industry. Although an occasional chief forester like Gifford Pinchot sometimes criticized the evils of business, most of the forestry fraternity did not share that skepticism.[9]

---

[7] James Weinstein, *The Corporate Ideal in the Liberal State*, p. 254. See also Warren Sussman's key essay, "The Persistence of American Reform," in *American Reform: The Ambiguous Legacy*, ed. D. Walden, pp. 94–108.

[8] Robert Wiebe, *The Search for Order, 1877–1920*, p. 298.

[9] Noble, *America by Design*, p. 34. Ralph Nader's contention that the Forest Service has been "the most independent and discretionary agency in Washington" is misleading and promotes the false idea that industrial capitalists and the federal government were naturally antagonistic toward each other (Ralph R. Barney, *The Last Stand: The Nader Study Group*

The values and attitudes of American capitalism dominated the newly emerging professional classes of the late nineteenth and early twentieth centuries. As in other technical fields, economic imperatives guided the work of most of the growing number of professionally trained foresters and of organizations like the American Forestry Association and the Society of American Foresters. Social scientists from the academies who occasionally served as corporate and trade organization managers shared these views. The federal government answered the lumberman's need for specialized knowledge with the research expertise of the Forest Service and with information on the marketing and distribution of lumber products through the Department of Commerce. And from a very early date, the Forest Service provided the industry with rudimentary data that became increasingly more sophisticated as time passed. Such relationships marked the continuing integration of the lumber industry with the national economy.

Several important figures in this study, many of them trained as professional foresters, moved comfortably from public employment to the private sector. In addition, the federal government called on these same individuals during times of crisis—in war and depression—to provide government agencies with expert advice on acceptable and efficient industrial policy. These professionals also gave influential testimony before congressional committees on a wide variety of matters pertaining to lumber and other natural resource industries. Leading lumbermen, usually those prominent in trade association circles, also served the government as appointees on national boards and commissions during emergencies. This remarkably homogeneous group of men understood the prerequisites of the corporate economy and worked to achieve direction and stability for that world. Their inability to cope with the lumberman's broader problems does not imply personal incompetence, lack of effort, or insufficient technical expertise. Rather, the chronic and inherent maladjustments that persisted in the lumber industry up to the Second World War reflected the basic contradictions in a system that promoted the idea of a freely competitive economy but was unable to achieve stability under those conditions. As in other industries and federal bureaus, the problem was defined by a limited vision or imagination—an inability to formulate alternate approaches that offered real autonomy and a sense of socially oriented uses of resources.

Report on the U.S. Forest Service, p. ii). For a discussion of business influence in the professions, see Christopher Lasch, *The Culture of Narcissism: American Life in an Age of Diminishing Expectations*, pp. 218–36.

The controversy over resource policy has often focused on the moralistic and symbolic acts of the crusading Gifford Pinchot, plunging through the blackened stumps with his magic wand, enlarging and creating new federal reserves and fending off the evil and selfish designs of a Binger Hermann or a Richard Ballinger. Others have described the conservation movement as the "fulfillment of American democracy" or as "limited socialism in the public interest." Such rhetoric is captivating and lends an aura of selflessness and sacrifice to the principals involved; it is also a misleading assessment of conservation (as Samuel Hays and others have indicated), because it ignores the economic conditions and political circumstances that shaped conservation ideology.[10]

Other historians have more recently suggested an alternate model. They argue that many resource capitalists supported the conservation movement because these capitalists viewed it as a vehicle to bring order and stability to their respective industries.[11] The evidence is overwhelming that leaders in the lumber industry used conservation propaganda as a tool to achieve stability. Lumbermen supported a broad array of conservation issues in an effort to cope with the industry's persisting problems of overproduction. The real test of any conservation program, in the minds of lumbermen, was its effect on existing economic conditions. Testimony at public hearings and in congressional debates, the results of Forest Service research, trade journal editorials, and articles in scholarly publications concerned with resource issues all point to the intimate association between effective conservation and the economic health of the industry in question.

Conservation policy and public and private forestry measures in the twentieth century have been inescapably political, not merely technical, decisions (as claimed by some industry leaders). The larger-scale lumber industrialists shaped the scope and character of conservation ideology within a sometimes expansive lumber economy, but more often under desperately competitive conditions. To these industrialists, conservation meant industrial stability and controlled production more than it meant a selfless

[10]Elmo Richardson, *The Politics of Conservation: Crusades and Controversies, 1897–1913*, p. vii; J. Leonard Bates, "Fulfilling American Democracy: The Conservation Movement, 1907–1921," *Mississippi Valley Historical Review* 44 (1957): 30. Samuel P. Hays's seminal and revisionist work is *Conservation and the Gospel of Efficiency: The Progressive Conservation Movement, 1890–1920*.

[11]Other studies that follow in the Hays tradition, at least in part, are Kolko, *The Triumph of Conservatism*; Wiebe, *The Search for Order*; and Weinstein, *The Corporate Ideal*.

preserving of trees for future generations. Ideas of preserving natural resources for the public good were directly traceable to the desperate economic plight of the lumber industry and its effort to control erratic market forces through the political process.

Lumbermen and their supporters fought to define their ideologies and to exercise political hegemony over the emerging regulatory and legislative mechanisms affecting their industry. Thus they attempted to direct and shape conservation policy to meet the requirements of a mercurial and unstable market. Indeed, the play of the market was a key determinant that influenced policy at the state and federal levels in the late nineteenth and well into the twentieth centuries. The consequences of an uncontrolled market in lumber, coal, oil, and other natural resource industries were chaotic and unregulated competition, overproduction, and chronic instability. These endemic conditions prompted leaders of the affected industries to seek institutional adjustments to lessen economic stress. In the lumber industry, astute and perceptive spokesmen attempted to link conservation policy to the specific economic requirements for stabilizing the market.[12] To achieve these ends they capitalized upon public appeals for conservation or "forestry" and insisted that any corrective program first meet the industry's need for a stable and rational economic environment.[13]

The conservation movement, therefore, was not removed from the realities of the political economy. The crucial issue was not regaining lost status or preserving social resources for future generations. These impulses were there, to be sure, especially in the grandiloquent rhetoric so characteristic of the movement. But in almost every legislative and regulatory "conservation" measure adopted at the federal level, the Hand of Esau is apparent—the needs of America's expanding industrial economy.

The association between the ideology and practice of conservation and its meaning to the lumber trade is an integral part of this story and is closely related to the industry's perplexing marketing problems. Lumber spokesmen defined conservation as a complex and wide-ranging series of issues all linked to the industry's political economy: prevention of forest fires, equitable taxation and tariff policies, reforestation, standardization of sizes and grades of lumber, and promotion of the more efficient use of

---

[12] Weinstein, *The Corporate Ideal*, p. x; James W. Hurst, *Law and Economic Growth: Legal History of the Lumber Industry in Wisconsin, 1836–1915*, pp. 49–51.

[13] I am indebted to Professor Ellis W. Hawley of the University of Iowa for clarifying many of these ideas.

wood materials. Lumbermen believed these issues were associated with the industry's production and marketing problems. Moreover, they increasingly associated the mercurial nature of the lumber business—its excessive competition, periodically glutted markets, low profits, and cyclical instability—with inefficiency and lack of cooperation. The persistence and constancy of these chronic problems convinced many in the industry to link legislative and regulatory proposals for conservation to the specific material requirements for stabilizing the lumber market.

This study begins with an examination of the lumber industry in the late nineteenth century, its participation in the feverish exploitation of natural resources, and its involvement in the wasteful competitive extremes that characterized most of the natural resource industries. These destructive tendencies prompted farsighted lumbermen to search for orderly, efficient, and rational alternatives to the senseless and ruinous Darwinian world; they feared such instability would threaten stable and predictable economic development—and might even create the conditions for a threat to the social order itself. Such men attempted to rationalize lumber marketing policies through the use of the technical expertise and scientific bureaus of the federal government. Effective cooperation, however, was a slow and complex undertaking because of the scattered nature of the resource, the number of competitors producing different kinds of lumber, and the striking variety in the size of the various operations.

The migratory tendency of the lumber industry further worsened its problems. The opening up of new and cheap virgin stands of timber well into the twentieth century encouraged waste and increased the difficulties of an already excessive mill capacity. Overinvestment in timberland and the need to liquidate standing timber to meet bonded indebtedness and annual taxes created new elements of disorder and additional problems for those trying to forge organizations to meet the crisis of overproduction and downward-spiraling prices. The results led to increasingly turbulent social conditions and prompted the emergence of the Industrial Workers of the World to protest wage cuts, abysmal living conditions, and the itinerant nature of the work force.

Out of the disorder and chaos of unregulated competition, a leadership emerged in the lumber business. These leaders were bent on lessening the industry's propensity toward excessive competition and overproduction through cooperation with trade associations, first on a regional and then on a national level. Lumber trade associations, committed to bringing control to the conduct of market activity, were limited and relatively ineffective in the early years of the twentieth century. The changing nature of the regional associations and widespread uncertainty about the antitrust laws limited the effectiveness of trade associations and restricted their cooperation with the National Lumber Manufacturers Association (NLMA), founded in 1902.

A prolonged period of depression in the lumber industry after 1907 accelerated efforts to strengthen regional associations and to give the national association more authority. Periodically contracting markets and vastly overextended investments in timberland and mill capacity undermined these efforts to control production and prices and to bring an end to the panic liquidation of standing timber. The same associations also sought through the political process to lessen tax burdens, maintain a protective tariff on lumber imports, and gain equitable railroad rates for shipping lumber. In their efforts to stabilize the lumber market, trade associations enjoyed the full cooperation and wholehearted support of the Forest Service.

The great catalyst for meaningful trade association accomplishments was the First World War. Trade executives, including those in the lumber industry, learned the benefits to be reaped through influential government agencies with the power to establish production quotas, order marketing arrangements, and otherwise offer order and predictability to an industry plagued with disorder and instability. The exhilarating experiences of association work during the war carried over into the next decade and received support in high places when Secretary of Commerce Herbert Hoover became the foremost proponent of trade association activity. During this period, organized lumbermen turned back a mild threat to impose regulations limiting cutting on private timberlands, survived a series of antitrust prosecutions, and secured the passage of the first general subsidy to assist states in protecting private forestland against the threat of fire.

Even in the halcyon decade of the 1920s, however, when capitalists were filled with an expansive confidence in the ability of private enterprise to end for all time downswings in the business cycle, the lumber industry's difficulties with overproduction and excessive competition continued unabated. As the decade drew to a close, lumber trade officials proposed ever more radical and coercive solutions to the industry's chronic dilemma of producing beyond the capacity of a steadily decreasing market. The officials wanted to relax the antitrust laws to permit cartellike arrangements to fix prices and limit production, to prohibit the sale of government timber, to reorganize the NLMA, and to appoint a "Lumber Czar" with the power to fix production quotas. They also proposed the consolidation of smaller competing units into larger ones. Some local associations put limited stabilization agreements into effect, and a number of merger talks took place, but timeworn suspicions between competing operators limited such cooperative efforts.

The failure of voluntary proposals to achieve production controls in the economic crisis of the early 1930s convinced many in the industry to see the NRA as a godsend. The NRA, designed to save capitalism from anarchy and social revolution by allocating state authority to the private sector, achieved its broader objective but failed to induce the kind of cooperation that its proponents envisioned. In the lumber industry there were repeated violations of code provisions. Long before the National Industrial Recovery Act was declared unconstitutional in 1935, its Lumber Code Authority was a standing joke throughout the industry. The great experiment was an ignominious failure.

After 1935 the lumber industry groped for a general policy and assurances that the government would continue to support its quest for order and stability. During these years the industry confronted its most serious threat from government regulation in the form of the ambitious proposals of Secretary of Agriculture Henry A. Wallace and Chief Forester Ferdinand A. Silcox. Through a skillful and extensive public relations campaign, the industry staved off federal regulation until the United States was again embroiled in international war. Then trade association executives once again headed for Washington to serve their country (and the industry). During the turmoil of the Second World War, lumbermen achieved much of the legislative program they had sought during the early New Deal years, and they successfully muted further regulation efforts. Although the postwar era is beyond the scope of this study, one must recognize that competitive conditions were altered dramatically, and the economic and political climate was ripe for merger, consolidation, and the increasing dominance of large-scale operations. The number of "gyppo" (small-scale) loggers and mill operators declined in the 1950s, diminished further in the next decade, and by the 1970s was small. In important producing regions like the Pacific Northwest, such shoestring operations were largely obsolete. Now, the corporate units in the industry are dominant in determining market policy.

This book attempts to pierce the mantle of romance and nostalgia that so frequently characterizes histories of the lumber industry. These sometimes ribald and Bunyanesque accounts—even the most readable, such as Stewart Holbrook's *Holy Old Mackinaw*—obscure the character of an industry that was of paramount importance to the rise of industrial capitalism in the United States. Recounting the lusty brawling, the lore of the lumber camp, and the sweat and peril of the loggers' and lumbermen's world does little to sharpen our understanding of the forces that so indelibly shaped policy and forged ideologies. The long and persuasive influence of the lumber industry in national polity is more than the story of courageous river drives and the rise to wealth and power of individual lumber entrepreneurs. It also transcends industry propaganda claiming that lumbermen selflessly and without ulterior motive joined in the crusade to preserve the wilderness and guarantee the perpetuation of the forest resource for future generations. The tale is far more complex.

To understand the political economy of the lumber industry from 1890 to 1941 is to recognize power and influence used in a concerted effort to define and control the future. Lumber capitalists worked strenuously to shape a favorable economic environment. They asserted themselves in legislative halls and in the federal government's scientific bureaus; in these ways they exercised a controlling influence over regulatory policy. Despite this remarkable degree of hegemony, they failed to usher in the millennium they sought. Not only are Jigger Jones and Paul Bunyan far removed from the realities of the contemporary lumber industry, but the dreams of the lumber barons were also incompatible with the social needs of the society.

1

The Great Barbecue and American Forestry

"Let the axe be used judiciously . . ."—*Proceedings of the*
American Forestry Congress (1889)

IN the last decades of the nineteenth century resource entrepreneurs, railroad promoters, lumbermen, mine owners, land speculators, cattlemen,
and farmers indulged in the uninhibited and feverish exploitation of America's natural resources. Urged on by a ruthless and excessively competitive
economic environment, these groups despoiled rivers and streams, devastated timberlands, wasted mineral resources, and overgrazed the western
range. Robert Wiebe calls it "a rape of Gargantuan proportions." This
wasteful pattern of land and resource use was part of the post–Civil War
economy in which entrepreneurs took advantage of rising land values to
liquidate and capitalize on the nation's virgin treasures. The consequences
included eroded mountainsides, parched and desolate rangeland, and rivers
filled with tailings from hydraulic mining outfits.[1]

Westward-pushing railroads, hectic town building, and the country's
rapidly expanding industries created a demand for these resources; entrepreneurs responded with gusto and enthusiasm. An orgy of profit taking
followed, accompanied by the investment of surplus capital to tap still further the bounty of nature. These combined forces polluted and ravaged the
land in a seemingly endless cycle of irrational and disorderly destruction.

But this indifference to the environment did not go unchallenged; tal-
ented and perceptive individuals such as George Perkins Marsh, in his classic *Man and Nature*, brought public attention to the effects of industrial
and commercial activity on natural resources. What is remarkable about
these seminal writings is their incisive political and economic character.

[1] Robert Wiebe, *The Search for Order, 1877–1920*, p. 185; Samuel P. Hays, *Conservation and the Gospel of Efficiency: The Progressive Conservation Movement, 1890–1920*,
p. 263.

People like Marsh reasoned that the negligent attitude toward natural resources was related to the maturing industrial capitalism of the late nineteenth century. Both proponents and opponents of the system argued that many environmental difficulties would be lessened when businessmen resolved issues like overproduction and excessive competition. Lumbermen and the small but growing number of professional foresters insisted that more careful consideration and efficient use of timber depended on stable and equitable markets.

Because capitalism is predicated on assumptions of order, stability, and rational economic activity, the uncertain business and industrial conditions of the late nineteenth century posed serious problems. This extremely competitive and increasingly disorderly world resulted from an economic system whose technology and organization were being continually revolutionized. This disequilibrium[2] contributed to unbalanced growth, a confused and dysfunctional market, rapidly diminishing resources, and decaying communities.

The more modern industrial and finance capitalists realized that progressively greater effort would be required to bring order to this primordial Darwinian world. A few who understood the explosiveness of the situation feared that its continuation would jeopardize stable economic growth and might ultimately threaten the social system itself. Modernists in lumber and other industries adopted a number of strategies to meet this crisis. They effected new organizational structures, increased their efforts to work together through trade associations and other forms of cooperation and supported the conservation movement in an effort to achieve a predictable economic climate. This attempt to reform capitalism involved private cooperation and the support of highly politicized government institutions.

Although the private sector afforded support and initiative to reduce competitive discord, government officials, especially in the scientific bureaus, provided the technical expertise and services essential to stabilize the market. In most instances the increasingly enlarged role of the state served to secure the conditions for economic growth and allowed the power of effective decision making to remain in the hands of industrial and finance capitalists. Businessmen and industrialists worked hard to fend off challenges to their supremacy and to forge a political economy that would

---

[2] Robert Heilbroner uses the term in "The New Economics," *New York Review of Books* 27 (February 21, 1980): 20. See also Gabriel Kolko, *The Triumph of Conservatism: A Reinterpretation of American History, 1900–1916*, pp. 2–4.

lessen social discontent and perpetuate the influence of dominant groups. Historians often are evasive in describing this concerted effort.[3]

The struggle centered on adjusting the legal and political world to the requirements of a maturing industrial system. And a remarkable aspect of this struggle is the effectiveness of the more powerful lumber capitalists in asserting their influence, especially in legislative and regulatory policies that affected their livelihood. Lumbermen and their trade association representatives fought regulatory policies and antitrust measures perceived as harmful, but they also initiated cooperative programs and requested government subsidies when they thought these would resolve their marketing difficulties.

This should not suggest, however, that lumbermen (and other industrialists) moved in regimented concert or in conspiratorial fashion to gain their end, although they did tend to move in one direction. Because of the disparate nature of the industry and the broad distribution and varied types of forestland in the United States, timberland owners and lumber manufacturers maneuvered at cross purposes in seeking solutions to common problems. The size and geographic location of an enterprise and the receptiveness of the individual entrepreneur all contributed to the contradictory swirl of political activity. The initiation of the forest reserves illustrates the point. While the larger-scale lumber capitalists generally supported the reserves because of their stabilizing influence on the industry, smaller-scale operators and those without timberland adjacent to the federal reserves opposed the policy, fearing the increased competition.[4]

A few individuals were aware of the critical importance of lumber to the nation's economic health and understood the industry's dynamic nature, its perpetual quest for virgin timber, and its speculative tendencies and wild market fluctuations. Franklin B. Hough's famous address to the American Association for the Advancement of Science in 1873 directed attention to the "economical value of timber" and emphasized that "our absolute dependence on it for innumerable uses . . . are too obvious for

[3] For a discussion of what Ellis Hawley calls "Neo-institutional History," see Louis Galambos, "The Emerging Organizational Synthesis in Modern American History," *Business History Review* 44 (Autumn, 1970): 279–90; Robert D. Guff, "American Historians and the Organizational Factor," *Canadian Review of American Studies* 4 (Spring, 1973): 19–31; Edwin J. Perkins, ed., *Men and Organizations*; Stephen E. Ambrose, ed., *Institutions in Modern America*.

[4] Henry Gilbert White, "Forest Ownership Research in Historical Perspective," *Journal of Forestry* 48 (April, 1950): 263.

suggestion." When Congress created the Division of Forestry under the commissioner of agriculture two years later, Hough was named to head the new division. The same legislation directed Hough to report on the production and consumption of forest products and to offer an estimate about the future of American forests. Hough's service as head of the Division of Forestry encouraged a community of fellowship between public officials and private lumbermen who shared common views about the lumber industry's difficulties. Hough also was a charter member of the American Forestry Association (AFA).[5]

The importance of private and public forests to a healthy national economy gained wider attention among learned societies and other philanthropic groups in the last twenty-five years of the century. Although scientists and academics dominated the research and public relations apparatus of these organizations, private philanthropists (often associated with industrial capital) supported many of the programs. One example is the AFA, whose activities spanned all aspects of forestry and other areas of interest to conservationists. Founded in 1875, by the turn of the century the association included important lumbermen from every major producing region in the United States. Its policies usually reflected the views of the more forward-looking lumber operators and progressive trade journal editors.

The American Forestry Congress, which eventually merged with the AFA, was another group with scientific leanings and a general concern for the future of America's forests. One of its early leaders, Charles Sprague Sargent, professor of arboriculture at Harvard University, published in 1884 his monumental study *Report on the Forests of North America*. It was the first scientific survey of forestlands in the United States and, among other matters, called attention to the rapidly diminishing stands of white pine in the Great Lakes states. The work was both ominous and suggestive to lumbermen in the great pine stands near the lakes; it attracted them instead to the vast virgin forests along the Pacific coast.[6]

The appointment in 1886 of Bernard E. Fernow, born and trained in Germany, as head of the Division of Forestry (and the attainment of perma-

[5] Ibid.; Franklin B. Hough, "On the Duty of Governments in the Preservation of Forests," in *Conservation in the United States: A Documentary History*, ed. Frank E. Smith, I, 688; Samuel Trask Dana, *Forest and Range Policy: Its Development in the United States*, pp. 80–81; Harold K. Steen, *The U.S. Forest Service: A History*, p. 9.

[6] Steen, *U.S. Forest Service*, p. 9; Ralph W. Hidy, Frank Ernest Hill, and Allan Nevins, *Timber and Men: The Weyerhaeuser Story*, p. 130; U.S. Department of Agriculture, *Report of the Chief of the Forestry Division* (1883): 447–48.

nent statutory rank for the division) indicated a growing federal concern for the future of timber and lumber products in the national economy. Although Fernow directed an understaffed office and was without a forest to manage, he brought to the position an understanding of scientific forest management. He also promoted the establishment of schools of forestry, fostered state legislation for advancing forest practices, and was an active officer in the AFA. Fernow considered the federal forestlands "as practical schools of forestry, as object lessons, as forest experiment stations." Although government control of private forestry was not an issue, he believed the federal government could encourage scientific timber-management practices by successfully managing its own forests. The forester was in the same business as the lumberman, supplying wood to the community. Forestry was therefore linked to practical lumber economics.[7]

Trade journal editors who regarded the forest conservation movement as a "craze" had Fernow's sympathy. Too many amateurs were writing about forestry, betraying little knowledge or appreciation of economic conditions and seeming to oppose the establishment of more rational forest management. Fernow's appreciative understanding of the lumber industry's difficulties set a precedent for friendly and cooperative relations between lumbermen and their principal government agency. As did those who followed him as head of the government's forestry bureaucracy, Fernow believed that economic conditions in the lumber industry determined the extent of timber conservation. "To induce any forest owner to adopt rational and conservative forest management," Fernow wrote in his annual report for 1892, "we should have to show him that it is directly profitable—profit, we must not forget, is the only incentive for private enterprise."[8]

The beginning of instruction in scientific forestry in U.S. colleges and universities during this period was another sign of the growing desire for improved management of the nation's timberlands. Although Charles Sargent at Harvard, Edmund J. James at Pennsylvania, and T. J. Burrill at Illinois all advocated instruction in scientific forestry, the Michigan and Iowa state agricultural colleges were the first to offer courses in forestry.

When Bernard Fernow left the Forestry Division in 1898, he was appointed to direct the first professional school of forestry in the United States, the New York State College of Forestry at Cornell. Fernow, like

[7] Steen, *U.S. Forest Service*, pp. 23–24; Andrew Denny Rodgers, *Bernard Fernow: A Story of North American Forestry*, pp. 113, 196–97.

[8] Rodgers, *Bernard Fernow*, p. 197; USDA, *Report of the Chief* (1892): 314.

many in the industrial world who were concerned with the needs and requirements of private industry, took the lead in promoting scientific and
technical instruction in his specialty. Gifford Pinchot also pushed forestry
as a practical science and contributed substantially to the establishment of
the professional school of forestry at Yale University in 1900. The Weyerhaeuser family matched Pinchot's generosity with a sizable gift to Yale and
later hired many of its graduates. The Yale program and the short-lived one
developed at Cornell were two early examples of practical, scientific, and
technical instruction within the classical colleges.[9]

By the 1890s a broad spectrum of individuals and groups had become
aware of the impact of industry on the nation's timberlands. Between 1880
and 1890 alone, the volume of lumber production rose 94 percent while the
population increased 52 percent. Moreover, substitute building materials
did not yet present a competitive threat to lumbermen. But the boom in
production in the last quarter of the nineteenth century had dramatic consequences—the pineries of the Great Lakes states had been depleted to the
point that they were no longer the most important source of the nation's
saw timber.

Lumbermen then moved south to the savannah forests of the Atlantic
and Gulf states and later westward to the heavily timbered North Pacific
slope—the last great stand of virgin forest, spanning the coast from Hum-
boldt Bay to the Alaskan panhandle. Bonanza speculation in timberland
both in the South and in the Pacific West accompanied this shift. Speculators made huge investments with the idea that they would reap large profits
in the event of a predicted "timber famine." These investments included
extensive purchases that eventually became most influential in twentieth-
century lumber production. To complicate matters, the larger-scale lumbermen were unable to prevent the continued entry of new competitors. A
combination of circumstances persistently attracted new capital investment; these circumstances included rising lumber prices and certain loopholes in state and federal land laws that made alienation of the public domain relatively easy until about 1910. The consequences for the industry
were grave. The number of producers of all descriptions who operated

[9]Dana, *Forest and Range Policy*, pp. 134–36; Hidy, Hill, and Nevins, *Timber and
Men*, p. 133; Henry Clepper, *Professional Forestry in the United States*, pp. 124–25. The
promising Cornell venture ended when the governor vetoed appropriations for the college and
the professional forestry school was dropped. For further insight into the function and purpose of scientific and technical education, see David Noble, *America By Design: Science,
Technology and the Rise of Corporate Capitalism*, pp. 20–32.

with varying degrees of efficiency increased dramatically and worsened the ruthless competition already rampant in the South and the West.[10]

The sharp increase in the demand for lumber and other forest products hastened the development of innovations within the industry and revolutionized the technical capacity of lumbermen to produce more goods. Rising demand also speeded up the process of transporting logs to mill sites and finished products to the nation's burgeoning industrial markets. Charles Mohr informed the American Forestry Congress in 1888 of the vast increase in lumber production and the consequent strain on forest resources in the Great Lakes region and in the South. He warned that heavy capital investments in railroads made it necessary to keep lumber moving steadily until the timber in the entire vicinity was exhausted.

"The resulting production," Mohr cautioned, "is carried on with the sole object of speediest returns, without heed of the future." Because businessmen were transferring considerable investment capital from the "depleted districts" of the North into the South, he urged his audience to remember that "the forces which have led to the depletion of the timber wealth of the North are at present at work with increasing energy in the South." Under these circumstances, he said, "the depletion of the Southern forests will scarcely take a much greater length of time."[11]

Mohr's argument hinted at a theme that later developed into the lumberman's perennial lament—that overspeculation and overstocking in timberland and the investor's need to meet annual carrying charges required the rapid liquidation of commercially valuable stands. According to Mohr, this chain of events fostered excessive competition and the sale of lumber at prices far below its value. "Irreparable are the losses," he argued, "chiefly caused by overproduction."[12]

But he concluded on a note of optimism. The rapid alienation of public timberlands to the private sector and the similar transfer of railroad corporation forests to lumbermen would remove the speculative value of these timberlands from the market. With improved public opinion and with a steady increase in the price of timberlands, Mohr believed owners would greatly benefit by managing their woodland resources on sound economic

[10]Roy E. Appleman, "Timber Empire From the Public Domain," *Mississippi Valley Historical Review* 26 (1939): 193; James E. Fickle, *The New South and the "New Competition": Trade Association Development in the Southern Pine Industry*, pp. 8–9.

[11]Charles Mohr, "The Interest of the Individual in Forestry in View of the Present Condition of the Lumber Interest," *Proceedings of the American Forestry Congress* (1889): 36.

[12]Ibid., p. 37.

principles.[13] This optimism, however, proved misleading. Rapid liquidation and endless overproduction remained the industry's most frustrating dilemma for at least another fifty years.

The attachment of a rider to an agricultural appropriations bill in March, 1891, gave President Benjamin Harrison the authority to withdraw forested land from public entry and to set aside forest reservations. Although seemingly a precipitous measure, hurried through a distracted and inattentive Congress, the new policy represented years of debate and compromise and marked a sharp departure in the land policy of the United States. In 1886 the head of the Forestry Division, Bernard Fernow, drafted legislation that provided for a system of national forest administration and for the withdrawal of all public lands from entry until they were surveyed. Fernow's measure proposed that the lands be held in reservations or sold, depending on the decision of the commissioner of public lands after a careful review of the survey. In 1887 Edward A. Bowers, a lawyer in the General Land Office, collaborated with Fernow to draft what became known as the Hale bill.[14] Although it never became law, the bill helped to shape the forest reserve policy that emerged in the 1890s.

The successful reserve measure of 1891, based on the Hale bill, had the support of the AFA, the American Association for the Advancement of Science, the American Forestry Congress, Secretary of the Interior John W. Noble, and President Harrison. Although chiefly applicable to the region west of the Mississippi River, this new departure in handling the public domain met little initial resistance. President Harrison created six forest reserves in 1891 and 1892 that included more than three million acres, and before he left office he added nine more reserves totaling over thirteen million acres. The lack of controversy over the reserve policy during its first few years can be attributed to the isolated location of the reserves, existence of more abundant and better stands of timber outside the new reserves, and, perhaps, congressional preoccupation with social discontent. Moreover, supporters of the policy argued that the reserves would protect sources of urban water and prevent soil erosion and the siltation of streams.[15]

[13] Ibid.

[14] Rodgers, *Bernard Fernow*, pp. 115–16; Dana, *Forest and Range Policy*, pp. 98–99; Steen, *U.S. Forest Service*, p. 25.

[15] John Ise, *The United States Forest Policy*, pp. 110–15; Hidy, Hill, and Nevins, *Timber and Men*, p. 136; White, "Forest Ownership Research," p. 262; Rodgers, *Bernard Fernow*, p. 199.

The creation of new federal reserves and additions to existing ones between 1891 and 1907 (when Congress rescinded its grant of power to the president) did not end speculation. Indeed, the possibility that additional public forestland would be added to the reserves seemed to stimulate speculation. Thus, lumbermen and speculators engaged in a mad rush for the rest of the unreserved government timberland. John Minto, an opponent of the reserves in Oregon, observed that they were "the chief causes of the rush to secure investments in our timber land by capitalists outside of Oregon." [16]

A mixed bag of motives—rising lumber prices, a fear that large-scale owners would gain a monopoly in timberland ownership, and a general speculative mania—precipitated the scramble for forested land between 1890 and 1910. Annual increases in the total consumption of lumber throughout those years added fuel to an already active land market. The booming market attracted still more speculators to the scene and fostered systematic manipulations and fraudulent practices under both federal and state land laws. Despite the increasing value of standing timber, lumbermen's groups and trade journals generally supported the federal withdrawal policy. Operators in the Great Lakes states and in the South favored the policy, because it put an end to the further alienation of public timberland to private holders. Westerners, especially those representing the larger and more heavily capitalized businesses, favored the reserve system, because it could potentially limit the number of new competitors and stabilize the market. When the national lumber market began to drop off after 1907, major producers became even more vocal in their support for federal control over an increasing share of the nation's forest-growing regions. [17]

The act that empowered the president to create forest reserves failed to specify the function of those reserves. President Grover Cleveland, elected again in 1892, sought congressional appropriations to prevent both theft and fires in the federal reserves. Congress declined to finance guards to police and patrol the federal forests, and the president, in return, refused to create new reserves until Congress set up a system for their administration. In the six years after 1891, supporters of the reserves introduced many bills dealing with the federal forest system, most of them establishing an

---

[16] John Minto to Senator Charles W. Fulton, undated, box 1, John Minto Papers (hereafter cited as Minto Papers), Oregon Historical Society, Portland, Oregon.

[17] Hays, *Conservation and the Gospel of Efficiency*, pp. 263–64.

administrative policy for their use. But Congress dallied in determining a management policy and the issue remained unresolved.[18]

Finally, a group of people interested in planned management moved to end the conflict between the two branches of government, since the dispute seemed to be impeding the proper management of the reserves. The chief of the Forestry Division, Bernard Fernow, and the irrepressible and independently wealthy young graduate from Yale, Gifford Pinchot, expressed the views of professional foresters and probably spoke for many of the more heavily capitalized corporate lumbermen as well. And for a time the beguiling Pinchot even enlisted the support of the crusading preservationist, John Muir.

The move towards a management policy quickened early in 1896 when Charles Sargent and the AFA convinced Cleveland's secretary of the interior, Hoke Smith, to resolve the issue of managing the reserves. At Smith's request the National Academy of Sciences appointed an advisory commission that included Charles Sargent, Gifford Pinchot, Alexander Agassiz of Harvard, geologist Arnold Hague, William H. Brewer of Yale, and Henry L. Abbott of the Army Corps of Engineers. Smith directed the commission to tour the western forests and make recommendations for their management. This set the stage for executive and congressional action the following year.[19]

In a final exercise of executive authority before he left office, President Grover Cleveland set aside more than twenty-one million acres of new forest reserves without specifying how they should be used. Protests from western grazing, mining, and lumber interests poured in upon Congress, because the proper designation and use of the reserves still was not clarified. Fernow thought the president had acted injudiciously in adding such large holdings to the federal forest system. The "storm broke loose," according to Fernow, when western senators and representatives saw a large block of their region withdrawn from private settlement and development.[20]

One of the more ardent western opponents of the emerging reserve system was the prolific Oregon letter writer and Jeffersonian idealist, John

[18] Rodgers, *Bernard Fernow*, p. 222; Dana, *Forest and Range Policy*, pp. 102–103; Steen, *U.S. Forest Service*, pp. 28–30.

[19] Roderick Nash, *Wilderness and the American Mind*, pp. 134–36. The two best sources on Gifford Pinchot are Harold T. Pinkett, *Gifford Pinchot, Private and Public Forester*; and M. Nelson McGreary, *Gifford Pinchot: Forester*.

[20] Rodgers, *Bernard Fernow*, pp. 223–24; Steen, *U.S. Forest Service*, pp. 33–34.

Minto. The self-styled fruit grower and sheepman told Oregon governor William P. Lord that federal policy was a "threat against the dominion of the state over local interests and suspension of the general land laws against landless citizens." Minto viewed the recommendation of the National Academy of Sciences to create more reserves as the beginnings of government by commission, which directly contravened the rights of the states. "The imperious recommendations of the Forestry Commission," he said, infringed on the rights of the citizens. Like many spokesmen for small agriculturists in the West, Minto opposed the reserves because he believed that eastern interests were conspiring to keep forestlands away from westerners.[21]

Supporters of the reserve system feared that the new president, William McKinley, would rescind Cleveland's order and that the whole idea might be in jeopardy. To prevent such a development, the disparate interests supporting the reserves—grazers, miners, lumbermen, preservationists, the AFA, and the National Academy of Sciences—resolved their differences and urged the president to sign the Sundry Appropriations bill, which included the vital Pettigrew amendment for managing the federal reserves. McKinley signed the bill into law on June 4, 1897. Western senators almost unanimously supported the amendment, which opened up the resources in the reserves to managed public use.

The so-called Forest Management Act made it clear that the primary purpose of the federal forests was to provide a steady supply of timber to meet the needs of American citizens. The biographers of Weyerhaeuser company history emphasize that the act boosted the cause of sound public forestry and was significant to Weyerhaeuser and other lumber companies because it ended "western fears that the reserves . . . would lock up valuable wealth, and assured everybody that the formula would be utilization, not hoarding." Bernard Fernow summed up the attitude of those who pushed the act through Congress: the function of the reserves would be one of economics.[22]

Harold F. Steen, author of a recent history of the U.S. Forest Service, underscores the importance of the 1897 management act in his observation

[21] John Minto to Governor William P. Lord, October 25, 1897, box 1, Minto Papers; State of Oregon, *Report of the Secretary of the State Board of Horticulture on Forestry and Arid Land Interests* (1889), copy in box 1, Minto Papers.

[22] Dana, *Forest and Range Policy*, p. 106; Steen, *U.S. Forest Service*, p. 33; Nash, *Wilderness and the American Mind*, p. 137; Hidy, Hill, and Nevins, *Timber and Men*, p. 292; Bernard Fernow, "Letter to the Editor," *American Forests* 2 (1896): 45.

that it became the basis of federal policy on forest reserve management for the next sixty-three years. Samuel Trask Dana, a longtime Forest Service officer and later forestry dean at the University of Michigan, praised the act for proving "in practice to be a statesmanlike piece of legislation . . . a workable and effective instrument." Bernard Fernow, the AFA, Charles Sargent, Pinchot, and the National Academy of Sciences all worked for the passage of the act. However, without the cooperation and support of western congressmen who insisted that the reserves be available for resource users, their efforts would have gone for naught.[23]

While the Congress and other interested parties debated the ultimate function of the reserves, the government's expanding forestry bureaucracy was establishing friendly and sympathetic ties with progressive elements in the lumber industry. The annual reports of the chief of the Division of Forestry reflect the agency's sensitiveness to the importance, as perceived by lumbermen, of the statistical requirements of efficient business practice. When he outlined the division's activities in his fourth annual report, Fernow reasoned that rational action could only "be based upon carefully obtained and digested statistics," whose main function was to aid in "estimating and comparing present supplies and future requirements."[24]

The division's reports and its growing number of publications became increasingly more sophisticated as time passed. The agency disseminated information on mill capacity, production trends, the value of exports, and other tidbits of interest to lumbermen who were looking for long-term trends upon which to base investment decisions. In his public addresses Fernow stressed the need for more accurate statistics about forest resources and lumber production, and he recognized that industries representing large accumulations of capital required accurate data to determine future business trends. After reviewing his frequent statements to trade groups and private business organizations, his published articles in lumber trade journals, and his actions as head of the Forestry Division, Fernow's biographer concluded, "Businessmen had confidence in Fernow."[25]

It is evident from the annual reports of the Division of Forestry that the imperatives of the marketplace guided policy recommendations more than did the science of forestry. In his first report Fernow emphasized the importance of sound forest economics; he deplored overcutting because it

[23] Steen, *U.S. Forest Service*, p. 36; Dana, *Forest and Range Policy*, p. 109.
[24] USDA, *Report of the Chief* (1889): 295.
[25] Ibid. (1892): 303; Rodgers, *Bernard Fernow*, pp. 235–36.

decreased resource capital, contributed to overproduction, and drove lumber prices down. Then, to make matters worse, low-priced lumber had a snowballing effect; it induced timberland owners to increase their cut to meet carrying charges and further saturated an already glutted market. Fernow urged the government to teach by example through the intelligent management of its own reserves and to withhold its timber from the market during periods of depression.[26] The latter practice remained a cornerstone of federal policy through the Second World War.

In 1892 Fernow reported that a few lumbermen had tried to implement rational forest management practices, but because the lumbermen held much of the property for speculation they frequently ended up paying off their debts by sacrificing the timberlands. This speculative spirit bred instability and was devastating to forests, which can require hundreds of years for full growth. Fernow singled out for special criticism those lumbermen who purchased all their stumpage from others. These operators used the most wasteful and reckless methods of exploitation; "after them, fire or the deluge." Forest owners, he argued, did not practice forestry because it was unprofitable, especially when the costs of management were added to harvesting and transportation expenses. Profitable exploitation of timber and forest conservation, Fernow gloomily concluded, "are at present more or less incompatible."[27]

Prominent lumber manufacturers, trade journal editors, and an impressive array of individuals familiar with the forest industries generally were in agreement about the purpose and function of the forest reserves. And they also concurred that the industry's business requirements should determine forest practice and conservation policy. J. E. Defebaugh, the indefatigable editor of the *American Lumberman*, expressed the lumberman's viewpoint to an AFA meeting at the Chicago World's Fair in 1893. Defebaugh bluntly stated that timber owners had no interest in the preservation of the forests purely for the sake of preservation, because these issues were economic and financial. Lumbermen were tied to the capitalist system. When the public domain became private property and, therefore, "the very basis of our political and social organization," Defebaugh observed, it established property rights that could not be disturbed "without a revolution in the accepted order of things." The creation of additional timber reservations in certain parts of the country, he noted, would require the

[26] USDA, *Report of the Chief* (1886): 155–66.
[27] Ibid. (1892): 313–14.

taking of private property. Such a dramatic challenge to property rights would be unlikely "in this generation, if ever." [28]

The Chicago editor argued brilliantly for a material interpretation of lumber politics and economics. Lumbermen, he said, had invested thousands of dollars to purchase government timberland and had made still other large investments in transportation and mill facilities in order to sell a merchantable commodity in great demand. These businessmen, Defebaugh exclaimed, were the backbone of American society, along with the home builder, the railroad entrepreneur, and the frontier settler. The operations of the lumbermen made the settlement of our country possible, and the cultural institutions of America supported and maintained the lumbermen's role. Given the nature of the system, he said, complete government ownership is not possible; therefore, the economics of the private operator must determine the course of practical policy. The threat of fire and disease, the fixed charges of taxes, and the prospect of transporting, milling, and distributing the finished product forced the lumberman to "transfer his forest holdings as rapidly as possible into commercial products. . . . It is evident that little can be expected from the . . . timber owner who depends upon that business for his livelihood in the direction of conserving the forests, simply because it does not pay him." [29]

Finally, Defebaugh told the AFA audience, "No nation can husband a chief resource." Resources like lumber, wheat, and cattle were responsible for the outstanding position of the United States in world markets. The difficulties of establishing an adequate forest policy in the United States, he noted, were financial and political and limited the implementation of progressive forestry practices. It would therefore be impractical to effect a responsible conservation system in the immediate future. [30]

M. L. Saley, editor of the *North Western Lumberman*, echoed Defebaugh's theme at the same conference. "Between the great bulk of the lumbering business and forestry there is at present no actual relation. . . .

[28] J. E. Defebaugh, "Relation of Forestry to Lumbering and the Wood-Working Industries," *Proceedings of the American Forestry Association* (1893): 150–52. For an account of western support for the reserve system, see Lawrence W. Rakestraw, "Uncle Sam's Forest Reserves," *Pacific Northwest Quarterly* 44 (1953): 146–47. Rakestraw concludes that the reserves were created "not as a result of random whim on the part of the executive, but because of a demand for them—either by dwellers in the region, by eastern conservationists, or by land office agents."

[29] Defebaugh, "Relation of Forestry to Lumbering," pp. 153–55.

[30] Ibid., pp. 156–57.

There is no more rushing, pushing business than the manufacture of lumber." The lumberman, Saley recognized, was not in the business for a lifetime or to serve future generations; his operations "are run strictly on business principles and for the purpose of putting the last dollar possible into the pockets of the men who operate them." As with other people in the business world, self-interest guided the timberman to action and encouraged him to disregard long-term considerations in favor of the present. Cooperative relations between the lumber industry and the proponents of forestry would flourish, Saley said, only when the extensive stands of virgin timber were severely diminished.[31]

While the lumber business suffered through cycles of expansion and contraction in the 1890s, the Division of Forestry broadened and expanded its services to the industry and consolidated its position as the most effective custodian of the nation's forestland. An able leadership, a sometimes halting but persistent congressional support, and the backing of powerful forces in the lumber industry made this possible. The laws of 1891 and 1897 set forth the basic features of federal forestry, and in 1898 the energetic Gifford Pinchot replaced Bernard Fernow as head of the division.

Because the Department of the Interior still exercised jurisdiction over the forest reserves, the Forestry Division in the Department of Agriculture was without an acre of forest to manage. The new division head, therefore, focused most of his attention on owners of private timberland in an effort to spread the gospel of practical, scientific forestry. On October 15, 1898, Pinchot and the Division of Forestry published their famous Circular No. 21, which offered assistance to forest owners and practical advice about conservative logging practices. In the succeeding years, applications for advice on forest management flooded the agency. Some of the largest holders of timber—E. H. Harriman, the Great Northern Paper Company, the Kirby Lumber Company in Texas, and the Weyerhaeuser Timber Company —requested information about conservation-oriented forestry practices.

Despite its popularity, Pinchot's program was curtailed after 1905 and formally terminated in 1909. The division's expanded responsibilities after the transfer of the forest reserves to the Department of Agriculture in 1905, coupled with congressional opposition to federal aid for private industry, ended the practice. But the cooperation already achieved established a precedent and a framework for amicable relations with lumbermen. During

[31]M. L. Saley, "Relation of Forestry to the Lumbering Industry," *Proceedings of the American Forestry Association* (1893): 147–50.

his tenure as head of the government's forestry agency, Pinchot fully supported cooperation with the private sector. He argued that lumbering, the nation's fourth-largest industry, was critically important to the national economy and therefore deserved the special consideration of government assistance.[32]

When Congress elevated the Division of Forestry to bureau status in 1901, the agency gained increased prestige and strengthened its position in the federal administrative hierarchy. And with the appointment of the ambitious Pinchot as head, the forestry office launched an aggressive campaign to transfer the forest reserves from the Department of the Interior to the Department of Agriculture. This was not a new idea; in fact, Bernard Fernow had made the recommendation in his final report before leaving government service. But Pinchot's enthusiasm and vigor gave new life to the effort, and when his friend and fellow outdoorsman Theodore Roosevelt was elevated to the presidency in 1901, the prospects brightened for a successful transfer to agriculture.[33]

Both the AFA and the National Board of Trade passed resolutions in 1898 supporting the transfer of the federal forests to the Department of Agriculture, and in later years other groups joined the effort. Presidents William McKinley and Theodore Roosevelt, Secretary of Agriculture James Wilson, and Secretary of the Interior Ethan Hitchcock all backed the move. In his first message to Congress in December, 1901, President Roosevelt recommended the removal of all forestry-related matters to the Department of Agriculture. Two years later, the Roosevelt-appointed Committee on the Organization of Government Scientific Work also urged that all forest work be shifted to agriculture. And Pinchot's heavy hand is evident in much of the committee's work; indeed, he first suggested such a committee to the president, and he later served as its most influential member. Finally, with the prestige and backing of the American Forestry Congress, held in Washington, D.C., in early January, 1905, the Roosevelt administration gained enough leverage to push the transfer bill through Congress.[34]

In part to recognize its new status as the management agency for

[32] Steen, *U.S. Forest Service*, pp. 54–55; Pinkett, *Gifford Pinchot*, pp. 48–50; Dana, *Forest and Range Policy*, pp. 119–21.

[33] Dana, *Forest and Range Policy*, pp. 119–21; Pinkett, *Gifford Pinchot*, pp. 53–54; Steen, *U.S. Forest Service*, pp. 69–70.

[34] "Eighteenth Meeting of the American Forestry Association," *American Forests* 6 (January, 1900): 9; Dana, *Forest and Range Policy*, pp. 121–22; Pinkett, *Gifford Pinchot*, pp. 54–57.

sixty-three million acres of federal forestland, the Bureau of Forestry was renamed the Forest Service in July, 1905. Two years later the reserves were officially designated national forests, thus building an administrative structure that remained intact for several decades. The Forest Service bureaucracy has expanded as need and obligation increased. Although the appointment of a new head and presidential pressures in times of war or economic crisis have caused slight shifts in policy, the basic configuration of the agency has changed very little over the years. The activities and politics of that office and its special relation to the lumber industry are an integral part of this story.[35]

The major lumber centers had shifted to the South and the Far West by the first decade of the twentieth century. This migratory tendency was the historical feature of the nation's economic expansion and the physical press westward to the Pacific. Cheap virgin stands of timber provided the raw material for railroad ties and construction, as a swelling tide of people pushed beyond the Mississippi River. Burgeoning markets like Chicago attracted vast amounts of investment capital and contributed to a dramatic growth in the productive capacity of lumber manufacturers in the Great Lakes states who constructed mills with a capacity far greater than actual requirements. The consequences were overproduction and an intensely competitive and mercurial market for forest products. Then southern and western operators repeated the same pattern of building in excess as over-enthusiastic entrepreneurs scrambled to capitalize on the opening of hitherto inaccessible timberland.

When the most active centers of lumber production shifted to the southern pineries and then west to the Pacific Coast in the last quarter of the nineteenth century, timber values increased, introducing new elements of instability. The investment of capital from the lakes states, the South, and, more importantly, the western logging frontier, began in the mid-1880s and gathered momentum over the next twenty years. A sharp increase in the price of lumber also contributed to the speculative mania in western timberlands during the first decade of the twentieth century and further exacerbated the industry's difficulties.[36] When the price of lumber

[35] Steen, *U.S. Forest Service*, p. 325.

[36] William B. Greeley, *Forests and Men*, pp. 41–42; Greeley, *Some Public and Economic Aspects of the Lumber Industry*, pp. 13–14; Robert E. Ficken, *Lumber and Politics: The Career of Mark Reed*, p. 15.

began to fall after 1907, many of these purchasers found themselves over-extended, because they had acquired forest acreages that far exceeded actual use. To make matters worse, speculators borrowed capital for many of their timber investments and then bonded the newly purchased stands to finance sawmill construction and the building of transportation arterials. From all accounts, these "carrying charges" were extremely high. Because prices normally dropped when the market was glutted, forest owners were in an increasingly precarious stiuation. In order to meet their bonded indebtedness, annual taxes, and, in a few cases, minimal fire-protection costs, lumbermen liquidated their standing timber to pay their bills. This further drove down the price of lumber, encouraged still more liquidation, and introduced greater instability in an industry already plagued with problems common to the management of other natural resources.[37]

The social and human costs of an irregular and fluctuating lumber economy were equally apparent. To lower expenses, lumbermen cut wages and reduced their labor force, and in communities where logging and lumber manufacturing dominated local business, there were no other industries to offset layoffs and underemployment. These recurring depressions demoralized communities and offered little security to the worker. Eventually, the social and economic misery inherent in such circumstances contributed to the formation of the Industrial Workers of the World, a radical union whose roots can be traced to similar social conditions in other industries.[38] Moreover, the propensity to "cut-and-get-out" and move on to the next virgin stand left a devastated and wasted landscape prone to periodic burning and erosion.

Lumbermen responded to these economic difficulties in a variety of ways. The more modern and progressive leaders proposed cooperative, voluntary solutions to their troubles. Mark Reed, a Puget Sound lumberman, symbolized the new breed who believed in more efficient organization, planning, cooperative schemes, and even business mergers to effect a more orderly economic environment. "Mark Reed's most salient charac-

---

[37] Greeley, *Some Public and Economic Aspects*, pp. 4, 61; Greeley, *Forests and Men*, p. 13; Steen, *U.S. Forest Service*, pp. 111–12; Edmund Meany, "The History of the Lumber Industry in the Pacific Northwest to 1917" (Ph.D. diss., Harvard University, 1935), pp. 234–36; Vernon Jensen, *Lumber and Labor*, pp. 26–29.

[38] The best general account of the Industrial Workers of the World is Melvyn Dubofsky, *We Shall Be All: A History of the Industrial Workers of the World*. For a regional view of the union's relation with lumber, consult Robert Tyler, *Rebels of the Woods: The I.W.W. in the Pacific Northwest*.

teristic," his biographer claims, "was his ability to see the big picture."[39] Lumbermen like Reed believed that the industry's problems could be resolved only through cooperative effort and self-discipline. For many of these modernizers the lumber trade association was the great panacea—a vehicle through which lumbermen would resolve the issues of overproduction and excessive competition and return a modicum of stability to the market.

[39] Ficken, *Lumber and Politics*, pp. 3–4.

2

Lumber Trade Associations and the Trust Issue

"Organization is a business necessity."—E.T. Allen

THE trade association movement emerged in the late nineteenth century, expanded and proliferated rapidly in the first two decades of the twentieth century, and then achieved an institutional role in the national political economy during the First World War. These industry-wide organizations represented a stage in the development of capitalism in which modernists tried to cope with economic instability and an increasingly integrated economy through cooperation on a national scale. The trade group represented a voluntary and collective effort to lessen the disruptive strains of competition and to stabilize the lumber market. Social and material changes in the American economy were responsible for the emergence of these organizational and institutional structures. The trade groups also had a correspondingly significant effect on judicial, legislative, and regulatory policy.

Trade associations were a commitment to order in place of competition. The movement represented a concerted business and industrial effort to escape the ravages of the laissez-faire world of the nineteenth century and, through cooperation with the government, to achieve a stable economic environment. The overriding purpose and function of collective trade was to perpetuate the prevailing social system through greater emphasis on organized cooperation as a way to effect a rational, smoothly functioning political economy.[1] The forward-looking entrepreneurs, academics, industrialists, and scientists who led these institutional maneuvers attempted to foresee the future and direct economic action accordingly. The development of cooperative trade associations was their response.

[1] James Weinstein, *The Corporate Ideal in the Liberal State*, p. 252. Louis Galambos, *Competition and Cooperation: The Emergence of a National Trade Association*, is a study of the cotton textile industry but with broader implications.

The expanding trade movement involved a sharing and exchange of knowledge about business transactions, market conditions, pricing information, and other statistical data to help conduct predictable and profitable commercial ventures. The associations, in effect, were part of a broader trend in the evolution of capitalism that witnessed the growth and consolidation of American industry, with the emergence of the pool, the trust, the holding company, and, of course, the large corporation. Trade association officials worked diligently to shape and direct their political and economic environment through mutual cooperation, self-regulation, and a friendly relationship with the federal government. And like other forms of business combination and consolidation, the trade organizations used techniques that continually placed them at odds with the antitrust laws. Anticorporate purists who wished to preserve a freely competing market economy debated the constitutional issue with associations that favored various forms of industrial cartelization. Despite strenuous effort, trade leaders never effectively resolved their differences with the government's antitrust prosecutors.[2]

In 1924 the National Industrial Conference Board, a cooperative research agency, conducted a study of the trade association movement to "describe the development and to test the economic soundness of the laws regulating business organization, trade relationships and market conduct in the United States." The board's report underscored the need for business cooperation, because excessive competition and other aspects of industrial society clearly indicated a need for regulation. The report avowed that, without adequate knowledge of general market conditions, business competition would contribute to miscalculations and periodic imbalances between supply and demand. It concluded that trade associations were the agencies through which industry was able to set forth its position "with marked influence and authority."[3]

The Industrial Conference report traced the early history of these trade groups, which it called "offensive organizations . . . formed for the purpose of enabling their members more effectively to take advantage of

---

[2] John H. Cox, "Trade Associations in the Lumber Industry of the Pacific Northwest, 1899–1914," *Pacific Northwest Quarterly* 41 (1950): 285. The best general discussion of the relation between trade associations and the antitrust issue is Robert Himmelberg, *The Origins of the National Recovery Administration: Business, Government, and the Trade Association Issue, 1921–1933*.

[3] David Noble, *America By Design: Science, Technology and the Rise of Corporate Capitalism*, p. 52; *Trade Associations: Their Economic Significance and Legal Status*, pp. 3, 291, 305.

favorable business conditions." Beginning in the 1890s, these associations had begun to assume the stature of established businesses, with open and regular meetings, elected officials, and a broad scope of activities. The maturing trade movement, therefore, embraced the standardization of products, reduction in litigation, exchange of credit information, compilation of production statistics, stimulation of demand for particular commodities, and encouragement of the passage of favorable legislation.[4]

Association work in the lumber industry probably has gained more scholarly attention than comparable activity in any other trade. The reasons are obvious—the excessive competitiveness of the business, its tendency to overproduce, and the continual entry of new competitors. Moreover, a variety of specialty groups were involved, including timberland owners, logging companies, manufacturers, wholesalers, retailers, and a number of box, shook, shingle, and paper and pulp dealers. Trade leaders directed most of their efforts to controlling production, or "curtailment programs." Lumbermen who had amassed huge acreages in timber and who wanted restrictions on competition to raise prices were the first to experiment with trade associations.[5] Thus, from its inception association work involved legislative and regulatory measures intended to resolve the industry's perplexing difficulties with competition (and to placate public concern for conservation).

The larger-scale lumber manufacturers encouraged the call for greater cooperation, and they wielded their considerable influence through the emerging network of trade associations. Heavy capital investments in timberland and mill equipment and large expenditures in wages, taxes, insurance, and bonded indebtedness made them especially vulnerable to irrational market behavior. The bigger operators also attached great importance to uniform grading and inspection procedures and to reduced railroad rates. Controlled and planned production, they believed, could be achieved through stable and permanent lumber associations, which would help push for necessary laws and regulations.[6] As the industry became more closely integrated into the national economy, lumber trade groups embraced an even broader array of issues important to lumbermen.

The first trade associations in lumber appeared concurrently with sim-

---

[4] *Trade Associations*, pp. 12, 16.
[5] Ibid., p. 15; Cox, "Trade Associations in the Lumber Industry," p. 285; Arthur Robert Burns, *The Decline of Competition: A Study of the Evolution of American Industry*, p. 40.
[6] Cox, "Trade Associations in the Lumber Industry," p. 301.

ilar associations in other industries. A few small local antebellum trade groups sprang up, but these and other lumber trade organizations formed before 1890 did not last long. One disgruntled trade journal editor thought the industry was "rapidly building for itself a national reputation as the parent of commercial organizations that never amount to anything." Despite repeated failure, however, lumbermen persisted, somewhat sporadically but in cooperative fashion, to resolve the uncertainties of their trade. This was particularly true of regions like the Pacific Coast, where productive capacity was expanding rapidly and running well ahead of demand. Under these circumstances of overproduction and reduced demand, submarginal operations went under, and the survivors increasingly sought cooperative approaches to assure themselves a future as producers of lumber.[7]

Manufacturers formed the early trade associations to gain voluntary agreements on standardized grades and sizes and to make their sales operations more efficient. Then, when fixed investments (and competition) increased during the 1880s, cooperation between mills accelerated even more, and gentlemen's agreements to control production or prices gradually merged into formal organizations with an ever-expanding regional and national network. Yet even during prosperous years these new trade groups suffered because of the frequent appearance of new operators. Before 1900, therefore, most efforts at combination came about when the market was demoralized and flooded with lumber.[8]

The turn of the century marked a shift from local and regional trade groups to large-scale national organizations. The increasingly integrated nature of the national economy and the frequent association of producers from different geographic areas convinced many lumbermen to act more aggressively in dealing with the vagaries of the market. These progressive entrepreneurs envisioned an economy in which rational and efficient management, cooperation, merger, and consolidation would eliminate disruptive competition and its associated cycles of boom and bust.[9]

---

[7] James E. Fickle, *The New South and the "New Competition": Trade Association Development in the Southern Pine Industry*; Cox, "Trade Associations in the Lumber Industry," p. 285.

[8] *Northwestern Lumberman* 18 (January 7, 1881): 3, cited in Fickle, "Origins and Development of the Southern Pine Association," chap. 1 of *The New South*, p. 49; Thomas R. Cox, *Mills and Markets: A History of the Pacific Coast Lumber Industry to 1900*, p. 255; M. Browning Carrott, "The Supreme Court and American Trade Associations, 1921–1925," *Business History Review* 44: 320.

[9] Nelson C. Brown, *The American Lumber Industry: Embracing the Principal Features*

The Southern Lumber Manufacturers Association, formed in 1890, was one of the earliest and most aggressive of the regional groups. It set out to establish standard grades and dimensions for lumber products and to implement an inspection service. The southern trade group also adopted legally questionable and compulsory tactics to maintain prices. By 1905 the association had put into effect fifty-two "official price lists" to encourage a healthy market for lumber. After 1905, and on the advice of legal counsel, the organization abandoned price lists and substituted "market reports" in their place. This rhetorical innovation also ran afoul of the law and was dropped.[10]

The first of the national trade associations among the forest manufacturing industries was the American Paper and Pulp Association, founded in 1878. The association influenced legislation, especially tariff policy, and cooperated with the purely lumber-producing sector of the industry on common issues. Finally, the expanding activities of the stronger regional associations, the increasing volume of West Coast lumber shipped to eastern markets, improvements in transportation and communication, and the need for more effective lobbying at the federal level led to the formation of the National Lumber Manufacturers Association (NLMA) in December, 1902.[11]

Lumbermen began working in concert on a broader geographic scale beginning in 1897, when groups from across the country met to discuss strategies to restore the tariff on lumber. The most active were white pine manufacturers from the Great Lakes states who began this early national cooperative effort; the NLMA grew out of a continuing dialogue between several of the larger regional trade groups. The Southern Lumber Manufacturers Association (predecessor to the Southern Pine Association) and the Mississippi Valley Lumbermen's Association (later the Northern Pine Association) were chiefly responsible for the organization of the larger unit. The national group, therefore, originated because of the need to coordinate the work of the regional associations, resolve overlapping jurisdictions, and argue the collective views of lumbermen in government policy.[12]

---

of the Resources, Production, Distribution, and Utilization of Lumber in the United States, p. 232; Cox, *Mills and Markets,* pp. 255, 277.

[10] Charles A. Gillett, "Citizens and Trade Associations Dealing With Forestry," in *Fifty Years of Forestry,* ed. Robert K. Winters, p. 288; *Trade Associations,* pp. 13–14.

[11] Henry Clepper, *Professional Forestry in the United States,* p. 198.

[12] John Ise, *The United States Forest Policy,* p. 336; Brown, *The American Lumber In-*

In one of its early attempts to flex its muscle, the NLMA invited railroad managers to attend its annual meeting in Saint Louis in May, 1904. The letter of invitation reminded the railroad interests that lumbermen were "impelled by the first law of nature, self-preservation . . . to remedy existing evils and promote the welfare of the great lumber industry." The association's first step, therefore, "brings it face to face with car equipment, car shortage, reciprocal demurrage, prompt transportation, claims and other problems." The letter detailed the organization's complaints, cited the critical importance of the industry to the railroads, and finally, in a line reminiscent of a Frank Norris novel, offered both carrot and stick:

> We know not how the Leviathan is created, grows or is built, but we know of the evolution of the lumber manufacturers, and believe that in the National Lumber Manufacturers Association you will find intellect to cope with intellect, and should it come to war, foemen worthy of your steel. But it is not war we wish. By conference, study and intelligent action business problems should be adjusted, and we now ask your suggestions looking to the prompt amelioration and eventual eradication of existing evils.[13]

Railroad-related issues continued to aggravate the lumber industry at least until the end of the First War World. Increases in railroad freight rates and the falling demand for lumber products in traditional markets after 1907 worsened economic difficulties, particularly for western lumbermen. And trade journal editorials continued to ply invective and hurl charges of monopoly at the railroad corporations over inequitable freight rates, car shortages, and inadequate service.[14]

The national association's concerns during these years comprised most perennial trade issues: compilation of statistics, insurance, credits, railroad car service and freight equipment, uniform grades and sizes, the tariff, stumpage prices, and taxes on timbered and cutover lands. Topics

---

dustry, pp. 236–39; *Trade Associations*, p. 15. According to an NLMA memo, a preliminary session in October preceded the formal organization in St. Louis. Three associations, the Georgia Saw Mill Association, the North Carolina Pine Association, and the Southern Lumber Manufacturers Association, set up the initial plans for the national organization (see "Historical Data," November 1, 1937, box 155, National Forest Products Association Records [hereafter cited as NFPA Records], Forest History Society, Santa Cruz, California). The NLMA was renamed the National Forest Products Association in 1965. The record holdings for the association's early years are sparse, and one must infer many of the association's activities through trade journal articles and the comments of contemporaries.

[13] "To The Presidents and General Managers Of The Railroads Of The United States," April 19, 1904, box 138, NFPA Records.

[14] Robert E. Ficken, *Lumber and Politics: The Career of Mark Reed*, p. 21.

at the annual meetings indicated that excessive competition was a major concern of many lumbermen. By 1906 when the Western Pine Manufacturers Association joined, the NLMA included eleven regional and specialty trade groups, who represented a productive total of fifteen million board feet. The association was first headquartered in Saint Louis, then relocated in Chicago in 1913, and finally moved to Washington, D.C., in 1921, as national affairs became increasingly important in the organization's politics.[15]

The shift to the nation's capital came at a time when the trade association movement was reaching its peak of influence, first under Secretary of Commerce Herbert Hoover and later under the short-lived National Recovery Administration. The environment in the capital made more convenient the exercise of the association's considerable power in forging legislative and regulatory policies favorable to lumbermen.

While association activity quickened in the early 1900s, the total annual production of lumber soared to an all-time high in 1906 and 1907. Industrial expansion and the increasing demand for lumber pushed the total output to an annual estimated cut of forty-six billion board feet, most of it coming from the South and the Pacific Northwest. Careless operators ignored rational forest management in the rush to move on to the next stand. Although a few far-sighted lumbermen worked at the state level to form forestry organizations, their sole purpose was to prevent fires from ravaging the virgin forests. Even the optimistic Gifford Pinchot reflected in later years that "the attempt to introduce the practice of Forestry on private lands . . . did not succeed on any general scale." The Forest Service's preoccupation with the national forests after 1905, the increasing availability of substitute building materials, and the sharp drop in stumpage prices and other lumber products after 1907 further inhibited the practice of scientific forestry.[16]

In the first few years after 1900, the burgeoning lumber market and runaway speculation in timberland prompted industry leaders to seek ways to bring order to an economic environment that seemed to be beyond control. Eastern lumbermen, their friends in the American Forestry Association, and several industrial trade associations joined a move to establish

[15] "Historical Data," NFPA Records; U.S. Department of Commerce, Bureau of Corporations, *Report on the Lumber Industry,* pt. 4, p. 53.

[16] Samuel Trask Dana, *Forest and Range Policy: Its Development in the United States,* pp. 171–72; Gifford Pinchot, *Breaking New Ground,* p. 294.

eastern forest preserves in order to assure a perpetual supply of timber, to reforest cutover lands, and to protect the watersheds of streams. In the early 1890s Charles Sargent first suggested the establishment of a reserve in the southern Appalachians for recreational use. By the end of the decade, several groups backed the move to convince Congress to create eastern forest reserves. Theodore Roosevelt expressed his full agreement with the idea shortly after he became president.[17]

None of the early congressional bills to purchase forestland became law. In 1903 the National Wholesale Lumber Dealers Association passed a resolution supporting the creation of an Appalachian forest reserve, which spoke directly to the issue: "The heaviest and most beautiful hardwood forests of the continent are upon these mountains, and for economic reasons their preservation is imperative." The resolution supported the protection of the forests, because it assured a reliable supply of timber and was thus essential to business. Two years later the important American Forest Congress, comprised of leading business, industrial, and lumber people, passed a similar resolution favoring the creation of national forest reserves in the Southern Appalachian Mountains and in the White Mountains of New Hampshire.[18]

When the lumber market began its downward trend after 1907, trade organizations stepped up their support to establish eastern forest reserves. The National Hardwood Lumber Association favored the creation of federal forestlands east of the Mississippi River "in view of the rapid exhaustion of hardwood timber and the importance of these regions for hardwood production.' The NLMA recommended forming large forest reserves in different parts of the country, and the National Association of Box Manufacturers urged the U.S. Congress to create at once national forests in the southern Appalachian and White mountains. The National Association of Cotton Manufacturers and the progressive American Civic Federation joined lumbermen in their support for the eastern reserves. The American Forestry Association considered the Appalachian reserve question a national issue—"The Nation alone can act." The federal government, it said, had granted the West millions of acres of national forests while it had pro-

[17] Harold K. Steen, *The U.S. Forest Service: A History*, pp. 123–24; Dana, *Forest and Range Policy*, pp. 124–25; Pinchot, *Breaking New Ground*, pp. 239–40.

[18] Dana, *Forest and Range Policy*, p. 125; "Lumbermen Favor Forestry," *American Forests* 9 (April, 1903): 204; "American Forest Congress," *American Forests* 11 (January, 1905): 11.

vided none for the East and the South. "In common fairness," the association pleaded, "the Nation cannot afford to slight these sections." Finally, congressional passage of the Weeks Act in 1911 gave the eastern reserves their initial legislative boost.[19]

The first of the great conservation extravaganzas in the twentieth century was the American Forest Congress, which, as mentioned, met in Washington, D.C., in January, 1905. The NLMA and other groups sponsored the gathering "to establish a broader understanding of the forest and its relation to the great industries depending upon it." Before the meeting Frederick E. Weyerhaeuser offered the cooperation and support of western lumbermen to promote enlightened forest practices; later, both Weyerhaeuser and N. W. McLeod, president of the NLMA, emphasized to the congress the practical and profitable value of scientific forestry. President Theodore Roosevelt stressed the economic value of forest preservation in his address, and J. E. Defebaugh, editor of the *American Lumberman*, commended Gifford Pinchot for showing "that direct benefits could be made to result from forestry as a science and as a practice."[20]

The congress passed eighteen resolutions, many of them directed to lumber economic issues; they included reducing timberland taxes to encourage forest conservation and granting the right to export forest reserve timber from the state in which it was cut. The group favored federal support for forest research in agricultural colleges and experiment stations, approved the establishment of eastern forest reserves, and advocated the transfer of all federal forests to the Department of Agriculture. Congress implemented this recommendation when it transferred federal timberlands to the agriculture department on February 1, 1905.[21]

During his reign as chief forester, Gifford Pinchot firmly established a

[19] "Resolution Adopted by the National Hardwood Lumber Association," May 24, 1907, "Resolutions Adopted by the National Lumber Manufacturers Association," June 15, 1907, "Resolutions Adopted by the National Association of Box Manufacturers," August 28, 1907, "Resolutions Adopted by the National Association of Cotton Manufacturers," April, 1906, "Resolution Adopted by the American Civic Federation," November 21, 1907, "Save the Forests in the Appalachian and White Mountains," undated, all in box 61, American Forestry Association Records, Forest History Society, Santa Cruz, California.

[20] Pinchot, *Breaking New Ground*, pp. 254–55; Dana, *Forest and Range Policy*, pp. 140–41; Ralph W. Hidy, Frank Ernest Hill, and Allan Nevins, *Timber and Men: The Weyerhaeuser Story*, p. 297. Defebaugh is quoted in Harold T. Pinkett, *Gifford Pinchot: Private and Public Forester*, p. 56.

[21] "American Forest Congress," p. 9.

sense of reciprocity and mutual interest between the lumber industry and the government's forestry personnel. Pinchot's public relations handiwork filtered down through the ranks of professional foresters in federal employment and set a precedent for the future. When Henry Graves resigned in 1901 from the forestry bureau to become the dean of the new school of forestry at Yale University, the *Lumbermen's Review* praised him for bringing "forest theories . . . into consonance with practical commercial ideas" and for recognizing "the rising tide of practical forest economics." [22]

Two years later Gifford Pinchot emphasized to the National Wholesale Lumber Dealers Association the government's interest in useful forest practices. Before the turn of the century, foresters who had been trained in European schools failed to see "that the lumberman is a business man like other business men." But, he declared, the professional forester now understood that forestry was a business, to be engaged in only when it was practical and profitable to do so. Pinchot told his audience that it was useless to discuss the application of forestry if it did not pay: "This is a business matter. The time has come when it is worth your while to look into it." [23]

In his annual reports, the chief forester frequently mentioned the widespread support for Bureau of Forestry activities. His 1903 summary praised the NLMA for helping to awaken "the great lumber interests to the necessity for practical forestry." Three years later Pinchot organized a Section of Lumber Trade in the growing Forest Service bureaucracy. The new section collected statistics on the annual production of lumber and other forest products, much to the interest of lumbermen, according to the chief forester. Again, in 1909 Pinchot reported that lumbermen were "in hearty sympathy" with the statistical work of the Forest Service. The principal manufacturers and distributors of lumber, he noted, submitted their figures promptly to the Forest Service, realizing that the statistics were very valuable to the service. The data included information on the ownership of forestland, protection, forest taxes, mill operations, fires, planting, production, and the uses of timber. [24] In later years organized lumbermen continued to build on this respect and confidence between government agencies and the forest products industry. Also, federal forestry workers and other public agency officials regularly appeared at lumbermen's meet-

[22] *Lumbermen's Review* is quoted in *American Forests* 7 (June, 1901): 146.
[23] Gifford Pinchot, "The Frontier and the Lumberman," *American Forests* 9 (April, 1903): 176–77.
[24] U.S. Bureau of Forestry, *Annual Report* (1903): 498, (1906): 39, and (1909): 34.

ings to discuss and share common problems in an atmosphere of mutual trust.

Because of Gifford Pinchot's reputation as a critic of timberland devastation, historians have neglected his significant contributions to cooperation between the forestry bureaucracy and the lumber industry. As head of the federal bureau, Pinchot sympathized with the lumberman's difficulties; moreover, his ideas about the economics of forest conservation did not differ appreciably from those of trade journal editors or association spokesmen.

Toward the close of his public career as chief forester, Pinchot wrote an article for the *Annals of the American Academy of Political and Social Science* in which he discussed forest management on private lands. His prognosis was not optimistic. Pinchot reported that the threat of loss from forest fires had "led to the largest progress thus far made in this direction," but that reforestation had only rarely been practiced by private owners, because the conditions were not stable enough to encourage it. Pinchot listed five obstacles to private forestry: (1) low stumpage prices and a low tariff, which tended "to prevent stumpage from selling for enough to cover the cost of producing it"; (2) forestry profits that yielded less than most U.S. investments; (3) the "desire for quick returns"; (4) the constant threat of forest fires, which often pushed private owners to rush their timber to market; and (5) "a faulty system of forest taxation." Pinchot recommended new laws to lessen the risk of fire and to alter burdensome state tax laws. He advised that state regulation of private forest management should move with caution and that property rights should be respected.[25]

Henry Graves, soon to replace Pinchot as head of the forestry division, also contributed an article to the *Annals*. Graves admonished those who unwittingly called for the public regulation of private timberlands, because they proposed solutions "not . . . based on a thorough knowledge of forest conditions or of scientific forestry." In many cases these proposals were unsound in theory, from the point of view of both economics and forestry, and were incapable of accomplishing the desired results. Graves predicted "a policy of state assistance and cooperation with private owners" for protection against fire and to implement a sane system of taxing standing timber.[26]

Trade journal literature during this period expressed most accurately

[25] Gifford Pinchot, "Forestry on Private Lands," *Annals of the American Academy of Political and Social Science* 33 (1909): 488–93, 495–96.

[26] Henry Graves, "Public Regulation of Private Forests," *Annals of the American Academy of Political and Social Science* 33 (1909): 498, 507.

the opinion of organized lumbermen toward the activities and policies of the federal government, and most of the journals held relatively progressive views about forest policy. The trade press published verbatim reports of association activities and the minutes of congressional hearings important to lumbermen. They editorialized on matters vital to the economic health of the forest products business, and all were thoroughly political. The lumber papers, one trade association executive commented, "filled a much needed want in news, exchange of views, and editorial comment upon industry policies and activities. . . . When dissensions manifested themselves, they attempted to harmonize the differences." From all indications, concerned operators kept themselves informed on the issues of the day through the editorials and articles that regularly appeared in the journals.[27]

Trade journals demonstrated a consistent support for federal policy during these years; they approved of the forestry bureau's research and cooperative efforts, supported the creation of eastern forest reserves and additional ones in the West, denounced public land frauds, commended government forestry employees for their studies of deforested lands, praised Congress for advancing the Division of Forestry to bureau status, and discussed in detail a wealth of other concerns vital to the lumber industry. Most of the papers supported Theodore Roosevelt's vast additions to the forest reserves in the spring of 1907 and defended Gifford Pinchot, as did the *Timberman*, for "his absolute disinterestedness and unmercenary motives."[28]

The journals also were aware of the industry's persistent marketing problems. When productive capacity began to outrun demand after 1907, the trade papers addressed themselves to issues related to overproduction. The *Timberman*, published in Portland, Oregon, reported that the government was selling only a small amount of reserve timber because of the large amount of timber in private hands. The *American Lumberman*, an old established journal with a wide circulation, printed a letter from Carl

[27] Brown, *The American Lumber Industry*, pp. 255–56; *Report on the Lumber Industry*, pt. 4, pp. 20, 26; Herbert C. Berckes, "The Pitch in Pine: A Story of the Traditions, Policies and Activities of the Southern Pine Industry and the Men Responsible for Them," undated manuscript, Forest History Society, Santa Cruz, California, p. 22.

[28] *Timberman* 1 (April, 1900): 13, (June, 1900): 12, and 2 (August, 1901): 5, 29. For comments on Roosevelt's creation and additions to the forest reserves, see *Timberman* 8 (March, 1907): 47; *American Lumberman* (March 9, 1907): 24, 28; *Pacific Lumber and Trade Journal* 14 (June, 1908): 22; and *Timberman* 10 (October, 1909): 19.

Schenck, forester at the Biltmore Estate, calling for a curtailment in production. An accompanying editorial insisted that annual cuts should be restricted "with due regard to the consuming capacity of the market." As the depression in the lumber business deepened, the *American Lumberman* called for an acceleration in building construction and criticized conservationists who demanded the preservation of forestland and, at the same time, proceeded "to tax [lumbermen] . . . out of existence." The trade journals were good barometers of the health of the lumber industry, and, according to the exhaustive Bureau of Corporations study completed in 1914, they also were "fairly reliable."[29]

The depression in the lumber market corresponded to the government's increased efforts to curb the illegal activities of trusts and trade associations. This watchdog role frustrated association leaders, who had to keep a wary eye on the government's antitrust ambitions besides helping their membership cope with the vagaries of mercurial market forces. Antitrust suits against lumber trade associations dated from the passage of the Sherman Antitrust Act in 1890 and continued intermittently until 1925. The Justice Department took no important legal actions against association work until the issue emerged again during Franklin D. Roosevelt's second term.[30] The antitrust issue was a critical one for lumber trade leaders, who believed the government was unfairly prosecuting them for acting in restraint of trade. All this while, the excessively competitive lumber market seemed to defy every effort at rationalization.

The legal questions concerning the lumber trade involved association efforts to establish uniform prices, cooperative marketing ventures, and control of production. In order to stabilize the market, regional associations began devising price lists and conducting production control campaigns in the 1890s. Each was related to the other. Trade officials argued that if production were controlled, the price of lumber would be much more manageable. Until 1906 lumber trade associations openly promoted written and oral agreements to maintain uniform prices as a regular part of their work. Most of the associations carried on price and production curtailment without disguise; in support, lumber journals published price lists

---

[29] *Timberman* 8 (March, 1907): 21; *American Lumberman* (November 30, 1907): 27, (June 6, 1908): 35, and (June 27, 1908): 35. The reference to *American Lumberman* is in Brown, *The American Lumber Industry*, p. 256.

[30] Ralph C. Bryant, *Lumber: Its Manufacture and Distribution*, p. 324.

and reported on trade committees attempting to set prices and production controls. These openly conducted ventures came to an abrupt end in 1906.[31]

An unprecedented climb in the price of lumber in 1906 directed the attention of both federal and state justice departments to the lumber industry. Faced with the threat of prosecution, trade associations simply changed the name of the game to conceal their activities; price lists became "market reports," or "statements of market conditions," or compilations of "prevailing prices," or simply "current prices." These reports obviously were subterfuges to allow the associations to pursue their work; trade groups published unofficial lists to avoid the appearance of price fixing. Official and formal committees and gatherings became "unofficial" and "informal," confidential transactions replaced open meetings, and association communication concerning these matters either went underground or was cloaked in vague generalities.[32]

The Congress of the United States finally acted when Senator A. B. Kittredge of South Dakota introduced a resolution that directed the Departments of Commerce and Labor to investigate the lumber industry. The Bureau of Corporations immediately undertook the necessary field work, but despite requests for an early report, the bureau did not publish its results until 1913 and 1914. Because of the charges and countercharges, rumor and innuendo that swirled about the investigation, lumbermen were in a state of apoplexy. Although much of the ranting at association meetings, at conservation congresses, and in the pages of trade journals may well have been a public relations ploy intending to portray the industry as the innocent victim of government prosecution, there was, nevertheless, an element of bitter truth to their argument. Why, association spokesmen asked, were they singled out for investigation when lumber prices were depressed and profits insufficient to meet the costs of production?[33]

Some operators complained that the "lumber trust" rumors hampered their ability to get a fair shake from Congress on tariff rates and other related matters. The *American Lumberman* charged that the government was trying to promote conservation while simultaneously prohibiting produc-

[31] Ibid., pp. 323–24, 327; Ise, *United States Forest Policy*, pp. 335, 338; Cox, "Trade Associations in the Lumber Industry," p. 294.

[32] Cox, "Trade Associations in the Lumber Industry," pp. 294–95; Ise, *United States Forest Policy*, p. 339.

[33] Steen, *U.S. Forest Service*, pp. 110–11; Hidy, Hill, and Nevins, *Timber and Men*, pp. 305–306; Bryant, *Lumber: Its Manufacture and Distribution*, p. 327; Ise, *United States Forest Policy*, p. 343.

tion agreements and banning pricing arrangements as evidence of "combination in restraint of trade." Lumber trade leaders continued to argue that government prohibitions of cooperative enterprise perpetuated chaos and excessive competition, which were the essential features of the forest products trade.[34]

Lumberman Robert A. Long put the case bluntly to the Governor's Conference on the Conservation of Resources, sponsored by Roosevelt in 1908. He urged the government to set a ceiling on the allowable cut, which would raise prices and encourage the more efficient use of forest materials. Then he asked the government to "furnish an incentive, a substantial inducement, to the timber owners to forego present gain for the public good." Long contended that legislation prohibiting business cooperation had contributed to the "demoralizing conditions in our commercial and manufacturing life." Business matters were at a critical stage. "Is it right," he asked, "that a great industry should suffer in order that a prejudice be vindicated and the consumer of today buy his lumber at less than cost?"[35]

Speakers at the 1911 convention of the NLMA repeatedly referred to the Bureau of Corporations study. The association's manager thought the investigation would mislead the public and retard the cause of conservation; he noted, however, that lumbermen should take heart because the American Forestry Association and the National Conservation Association had come to the defense of the industry. Another speaker, Robert Fullerton of Des Moines, Iowa, told the trade representatives that the repeated printing of "lumber trust" articles in newspapers had prejudiced the public mind, prompted the federal investigation, and created a "myth." Fullerton underscored the timber owners' interest in conservation:

Lumbermen from every section of our country have been prominent in advocating conservation from economic as well as altruistic sentiment, and surely no timberowner objects to the government reserving public timberlands for future use and development, as this policy restricts competition, increases the demand, and enhances the value of privately owned stumpage.

Fullerton cited popular ignorance as the reason for many of the charges and "absurd" statements. The "lumber trust and the predatory lumber baron," he said, "are things of the imagination."[36]

---

[34] Hidy, Hill, and Nevins, *Timber and Men*, p. 306; *American Lumberman* (June 6, 1908): 35.

[35] *American Lumberman* (May 16, 1908): 42.

[36] NLMA, *Annual Report* (1911): 54, 183, 185, 188.

At the association's next annual meeting, Everett G. Griggs referred to a "venal press and political factions" that wanted to convince the public that a "lumber trust" was imminent. The idea was ridiculous, Griggs declared, because "the aggravations of the lumber business do not breed this kind of organizer." The association's manager, Leonard Bronson, urged lumbermen to counter the "vicious attacks" against their trade and to bring these false charges to the attention of newspaper publishers. Charles Keith, soon to assume a leading role in the Southern Pine Association, told the convention that the trust issue was a moot point. In order to relieve the depressed condition of the industry, Keith argued, "we must be permitted to enter into reasonable trade agreements under proper and reasonable regulation." The lumber business, he said, must seek to have "constructive economic principles" prevail.[37]

As suspicions about the Bureau of Corporations investigation spread, trade journals became even shriller in their denunciation of the government's antitrust activities. The *Timberman* thought the country had gone "trust mad" and that if the idea was carried to extremes, it would almost preclude the organizing of voluntary associations. The conditions presently existing in the United States, the trade paper contended, made enforcement of the Sherman Antitrust Act "futile and injudicious." The result of unrestricted competition was apparent in the sweatshop, and unrestrained individualism was characterized by impoverished child laborers. But, the *Timberman* noted, "the country has been undergoing a metamorphous [*sic*]. . . . The age of . . . collective organization is upon us." Joint effort and cooperative organization in economic development are "natural and evolutionary."

In a commercial sense we are undergoing a revolution in thought in regard to the method of doing business. It is the battle of cooperation against competition and cooperation must prevail. Competition carried beyond a reasonable point is industrial death. No more striking example of this fact is necessary than in the lumber business of this Coast at the present time.[38]

The NLMA addressed a letter to President Taft asking the government to publish a full report of its investigation into lumber trust and combination activities. Delays in publishing the full report, the letter noted, had caused apprehension and heaped undeserved abuse upon the industry.

[37] Ibid. (1912), pp. 21, 38, 116.
[38] *Timberman* 13 (November, 1911): 19.

Moreover, economic conditions proved "the absurdity of even the faintest intimation that any combination exists between manufacturers of lumber." Retailers also joined with the national association in spoofing "the Mythical Lumber Trust." John W. Barry, an Iowa lumber dealer, told the Western Retail Lumbermen's Association that in four years of extensive study the Bureau of Corporations had discovered nothing and could find no evidence of a combination among lumbermen to raise prices."

Edward T. Allen, who was beginning a long and distinguished career as forester with the Western Forestry and Conservation Association, told the Western Retailers that when forest economics was better understood, "mystery will no longer manifest itself against lumber trusts, timber barons and mill magnates on general principles." The lack of understanding of the forest industry's economic problems, according to Allen, had contributed to the government's "illogical" activities against the lumber business. A country that applauded the systematic grading and marketing practices of the citrus growers in California and the apple growers of Hood River, Oregon, and offered government experts to help improve their orchards would not penalize lumbermen for similarly trying to cooperate with each other and thereby improve their business. Allen recommended collective effort to promote the welfare of the lumberman, because "we are more trusted organized than unorganized," as he put it. He urged trade association leaders to teach people about the intricacies of the industry's activities and to recognize that "organization is a business necessity."[40]

While lumber trade spokesmen fumed about the "muckraking" charges that appeared in the press and the pending publication of the Bureau of Corporations study, the Forest Service, at the suggestion of the young William B. Greeley, proposed a "constructive" study to examine the lumberman's problems. The secretary of agriculture later directed an investigation of taxes, market conditions, forest fire destruction, and other factors that contributed to waste and inefficiency in the industry.[41] In the meantime, the Bureau of Corporations published in four parts its massive *Report on the Lumber Industry.*

[39] Griggs's letter to Taft is printed, in part, in the *Timberman* 13 (April, 1912): 19.

[40] *Timberman* 13 (February, 1912): 32J.

[41] Two of the more strident articles on the lumber industry are Charles P. Norcross, "Weyerhaeuser—Richer than John D. Rockefeller," *Cosmopolitan* 42 (January, 1907): 252–59; and Charles Edward Russell, "The Mysterious Octopus: Story of the Strange and Powerful Organization That Controls the American Lumber Trade," *World Today* 21 (1912): 1735–50. Steen, *U.S. Forest Service*, pp. 111–12.

The first part of the bureau study dealt with standing timber, its potential value, the control and concentration of ownership, and the process by which privately owned timberlands were alienated from the public domain. An introductory statement listed the "foremost facts" in the findings of the report:

(1) the amassing and coordination of forest lands in a few enormous holdings.
(2) vast speculative purchases and holdings "far in advance of any use thereof."
(3) a big increase in value of this standing timber with great profits to owners who had neither created its value, nor substantially enhanced it.[42]

The second part of the report focused on the concentration of timber ownership, how individuals and corporations amassed these large holdings, and the relative marketing power of private and public timber in selected regions. And "control" of timberland went beyond mere ownership. "A timber company, by owning the land which gives the only practicable outlet for other timberland lying back of it, may be said to 'control' that other land." Because a few large corporations owned great acreages within the national forests, they controlled much of the adjacent timber resource.[43]

Part three of the study assessed the large acreages of some timber owners and their potential long-term effects on the economic, social, and political realities of America. The tendency toward concentration ensured efficient and economic mill operations, because "lumbermen would hesitate to put up a large thoroughly equipped mill unless they had or could secure enough timber tributary to it to last 15 or 20 years." But the amassing of immense timbered areas into a few large holdings conveyed great power over regional industrial development. Furthermore, the bureau study suggested, those who exercised this economic control were also prone to seek political control in order to extend their power and to make their position more secure. Large-scale owners already exercised considerable political influence in tax policy, "one of the evils accompanying great concentrations in the ownership of land."[44]

The last part of the report—the most neglected in scholarly studies—discussed lumber organizations and their influence on the lumber trade. The investigators noted that lumber organizations regularly "advanced" prices and thereby increased profits, that the trade activities of lumbermen

[42] *Report on the Lumber Industry*, pt. 1, p. 1.
[43] Ibid., pt. 2, pp. 4, 10, 16.
[44] Ibid., pt. 3, pp. 155, 182–83, 187.

contributed to higher lumber prices, that these practices were carried on through subterfuge, and that the NLMA had been active in efforts to shape legislation.[45]

In a more detailed explanation, the study concluded that the threat of antitrust prosecutions in 1906 had caused the associations to go underground. Then the following conjecture: one of the main goals of associations was a standard product—after that, uniform price quotations would follow. The first step to effective price fixing, therefore, was the standardization of grades and sizes of lumber. Finally, the bureau presented the grandiose conclusion that lumbermen had effected control of the market. Lumber manufacturers, it charged, adjusted readily to changes in supply and demand and made a practice of basing "their action upon a comprehensive knowledge of market conditions."[46]

The Bureau of Corporations study has been criticized for making loud noises but coming up empty-handed on the lumber trust issue. Moreover, contemporaries familiar with the lumber industry pointed out that the investigation produced no court proceedings or restrictive legislation. Most scholarly references accept this appraisal and ignore the important implications suggested throughout the study.[47]

Certainly by comparison with other industrial combinations at the time, the lumber trade did not effectively restrain trade, even though associations strived mightily to do so. The charge that lumbermen's organizations exercised real control over the forces of supply and demand assuredly is an erroneous one. Despite this truth, the bureau's report still needs to be examined for its long-range political and economic implications. Thirty years after its publication, many of the industrial trends described in the study began to materialize. This suggests, in fact, that its authors had a highly sophisticated understanding of the potential for concentration, economic monopoly, and political influence.

Trade journals printed restrained accounts of the Bureau of Corporations report. The *West Coast Lumberman* noted that "price control was and is impossible in that vast dissimilar ownership of individual enterprise" and challenged the bureau's contention that "standardization of grades is

[45] Ibid., pt. 4, p. xvii.

[46] Ibid., pt. 4, pp. xvii–xx, 4–6, 10.

[47] Bryant, *Lumber: Its Manufacture and Distribution*, p. 328; Hidy, Hill, and Nevins, *Timber and Men*, pp. 308–309; Ise, *United States Forest Policy*, pp. 343, 353; Dana, *Forest and Range Policy*, pp. 191–93.

the first step to price fixing." Standardized grades between producing sections, it argued, were impossible, although they might be very advan-
tageous. In a later issue the *West Coast Lumberman* charged that the delayed printing of the reports was "a deliberate attempt to create political
capital . . . at the expense of a great but disorganized industry." It likened
the fourth volume of the report to "a literary dreadnought . . . but in-
wardly merely illustrating the folly of promiscuous letter writing."[48]

During this time of economic depression and legal confusion, the
state of Missouri began proceedings in 1907 against the Yellow Pine Manufacturers Association for its alleged attempt to establish production controls and to stabilize prices through the circulation of price lists. The Missouri attorney general's writ sought to prevent the companies from doing
business in the state and to levy fines against them. The "Missouri Ouster
Case" dragged on until 1913, when the Missouri Supreme Court found
members of the Yellow Pine Manufacturers Association guilty of conspiracy to limit the production of yellow pine and to fix prices.[49]

Wilson Compton, who would soon become the most important figure
in the NLMA, called the "Missouri Ouster Case" one of the most significant legal cases dealing with the issue of price control by trade associations. Compton noted that part of the problem was traceable to the association's secretary, who raised the price of lumber when he thought such
action justified by the market. Although this was against the trade organization's policy, the court contended that it had the effect of raising prices
above the level that would have prevailed under free competition. Although Compton questioned the court's decision, it remained in his estimation "an apt statement of the standing law as to the publication and circulation of price and market statistics."[50]

Three lumbermen, Charles A. Keith, Robert A. Long, and J. B.
White, finally resolved the yellow pine legal conflict and reincorporated its
membership as the Southern Pine Association. A young officer of the new
association remembered the period as one in which lumbermen "were jit-
tery, wary, fearsome and suspicious—of themselves and of their neigh-

[48] *West Coast Lumberman* 26 (May, 1914): 19–20, (July, 1914): 19, and (August,
1914): 19.

[49] Bryant, *Lumber: Its Manufacture and Distribution*, pp. 328–29; Fickle, *The New
South*, pp. 41–42; Ise, *United States Forest Policy*, p. 336.

[50] Wilson Compton, "Trade Association Activities in Relation to the Law," reprinted
from *American Lumberman*, July 19 and 26, 1919, box 155, NFPA Records.

bors." In spite of such anxiety, the restructured trade group continued to instruct its members on a variety of strategies to stabilize the market. Also, regional trade journals published a commercial barometer and urged members to regulate production accordingly.[51] But the newly formed organization continued to tread a narrow path on the trust issue and periodically attracted the attention of progressive reformers. Although trade organizations continued to run afoul of the antitrust laws, the legal barriers to cooperation certainly were less destructive to controlled corporate activity than were the mounting pressures of the lumber industry's economic problems.

As war raged through Europe in 1914 and 1915, lumber trade officials continued to seek techniques and arrangements to lessen the competitive rivalries that plagued the industry. Association work represented only one of the cooperative attempts that lumbermen pursued to meet the exigencies of chronic overproduction and chaotic market forces. Heavy investments in timber holdings during a period of large-scale speculation in forestlands had contributed to the formation of trade associations. Then when the storm of speculation ended, the heavily capitalized and overburdened industry faced a period of depression and declining prosperity. Operators who had amassed excessive acreages of standing timber were extremely vulnerable to price fluctuations. To counter these developments, trade association representatives engaged in intensive political activity at the state and federal levels to encourage government agencies to establish favorable regulatory policies.

---

[51] *Trade Associations*, p. 14; Fickle, *The New South*, pp. 44–47; Berckes, "The Pitch in Pine," p. 14; U.S. Federal Trade Commission, *Report on Lumber Manufacturers Trade Associations* (1922), pp. 57–59.

3

Lumber Politics and Conservation

"The cupidity of capital will only be curbed by the assurance to the
long time investor that the Government is behind the investor."
—Everett G. Griggs, President, National Lumber Manufacturers
Association, 1912

ALTHOUGH lumbermen experienced legal difficulties with the antitrust
laws after 1906, they had more success with their legislative and regulatory
objectives. They vigorously pursued state and federal aid for fire protection, established good relations with the Forest Service, and molded the
conservation movement to suit their economic needs. Bernard Fernow recognized the relationship between competitive conditions in the industry
and conservation-related issues, as did trade association officials and individuals like J. E. Defebaugh. Supporters of the national forest system
made the same essential link between lumber economics and conservation
in the first two decades of the twentieth century. R. S. Kellogg, an early
Forest Service officer and later a prominent spokesman for lumber interests, thought lumbermen had "operated as economically as they could under prevailing conditions." They destroyed the forests "because of economic demand. . . . The forest[s] will not be handled rationally until they
become valuable."[1]

Organized lumbermen, trade association editors, and Forest Service
personnel like Kellogg and Gifford Pinchot cooperated on a number of related issues besides their support for the federal reserve policy. When the
Forest Service came under attack over the "lumber trust" issue, the American Forestry Association (AFA) denied that the government agency "has

[1]John H. Cox, "Trade Associations in the Lumber Industry of the Pacific Northwest,
1899–1914," *Pacific Northwest Quarterly* 41: 307; R. S. Kellogg, "The Rise in Lumber
Prices," *American Forests* 12 (February, 1906): 68–69.

gone practically into the lumber business . . . to make money out of its forest reservation." According to the association, the Forest Service confined its cutting to mature stock and managed its lands on a "sustained annual yield" basis. When critics accused the service of favoring the great lumber corporations with its sales policies, the AFA issued a memorandum absolving the agency of selling primarily to large companies, which held timber for speculation. Virtually all sales, the memo claimed, were to small local operators, because the government's timber sales policy "is directly opposed to the establishment of a monopoly by a combination of lumber companies."[2]

William L. Hall, another early Forest Service employee, thought the government was "helping to make conditions favorable for all industries to produce to their greatest capacity" by not flooding the market with cheap timber. The *Timberman* observed that the government had sold very little, because of the large amount of untouched timber in private hands. A federal forestry official told the Portland trade journal that "the future will demonstrate the wisdom of the forest reserve policy." When the state of Oregon sued the Southern Pacific Railroad Company for violating the terms of the original Oregon and California land grant, the *Timberman* demanded that the grant be revested to the federal government.[3] Modernizers like George Cornwall of the *Timberman* were aware that such action might curb speculation in the lush timberlands of the Oregon and California grant, because a friendly government agency then would regulate the cut in accordance with market demand.

Forest Service officials, the AFA, and lumbermen were responding, in part, to the charges of Idaho's Senator Weldon E. Heyburn, a leading opponent of the federal reserve system, who accused the Forest Service of acting in collusion with the major lumber interests. This "vicious system of forest reserves," Heyburn proclaimed on the eve of Roosevelt's 1907 withdrawals, "is so unfair, as to encounter the antagonism of every American citizen." The government, he said, was creating a monopoly, because those who already had large holdings wanted the remaining public stands

[2] "Timber Sales," undated paper, and memo no. 1770, both in box 61, American Forestry Association Records, Forest History Society, Santa Cruz, California.

[3] William L. Hall, "Some Comments on the Government Timber Sale Policy," 1906, p. 8, vol. 1, box 1, Western Forestry and Conservation Association Records (hereafter cited as WFCA Records), Oregon Historical Society, Portland, Oregon; *Timberman* 8 (March, 1907): 21, 47, and 9 (March, 1908): 19.

of timber withdrawn from the market; they wished to eliminate competition by closing off all other forestland. Heyburn accused the AFA of cooperating with the Weyerhaeuser interests and the Forest Service to the detriment of the common people, who opposed such concentrations of land. The Idaho senator's erratic, but sometimes telling, remarks caused one supporter of federal forest policy to conclude that Heyburn possessed "a vivid imagination" and lacked "judicial poise."[4]

When President Theodore Roosevelt expanded the federal reserves in his famed midnight rendezvous with Gifford Pinchot, lumber trade journals and many of the nation's foremost lumbermen praised the president's action. The *American Lumberman* called Roosevelt's decision "wise and . . . the people at large will stand back of the President in the matter." The new reserves, it claimed, would provide timber for future generations and protect watersheds and irrigation projects. The *Pacific Lumber Trade Journal* joined the chorus backing the federal withdrawal policy. Frank Lamb, an important Washington operator, argued that executive proclamations had been mainly responsible for forest conservation. Previous government land policy, he said, had contributed to a "lottery-like disposition of our resources," which had "bred a specie of subsidy seeking graft." In later issues, the *Journal* continued to defend the Forest Service and its "intelligent policy" of harvesting timber.[5]

According to the *Timberman*, the Roosevelt withdrawals found enthusiastic and almost complete endorsement. The "vast timber interests" supported the conservation movement, the Portland paper contended, "not from sentimental reasons . . . but . . . because they realize its deep economic significance and its important bearing on the continuity of the lumber industry." The *West Coast Lumberman*, the leading lumber journal on the Pacific Coast, concluded that federal policy would help steady the forest industry and would preclude overproduction and the demoralization of the lumber business. Joseph B. Knapp, manager of the Northwestern Association of Box Manufacturers, recommended the further concentration of timber ownership because it was economical and efficient. Moreover, the timber sales policy of the Forest Service was "entirely fair." The same logic moved R. L. McCormick, secretary of the Weyerhaeuser Tim-

[4]U.S. Congress, *Congressional Record*, 60th Cong., 1st sess., January 30 and February 4, 1907, pp. 2020–21, 2200; John Ise, *The United States Forest Policy*, pp. 292–93.

[5]*American Lumberman* (March 9, 1907): 24; *Pacific Lumber and Trade Journal* 14 (June, 1908): 22, and 15 (January, 1910): 81.

ber Company, to see curtailed Forest Service timber sales as "the best business policy for their management."[6]

When the lumber supply regularly exceeded demand after 1907, industry and federal forestry officials paid more attention to the relation between profitable lumbering and implementing conservation practices. The *American Lumberman* contended that conservation would come to the forest only when the market guaranteed lumbermen sufficient profit "to cover the administrative charges during a long period of years while the timber left is maturing."[7]

The *Timberman* associated good forest management with the control of production, with preventing and guarding resources. It cautioned against putting more timber on the market and noted that "we are entering a saner and more just appreciation of the real viewpoint of the conservation movement in regard to our National Forests." On another occasion, the *Timberman* observed that "conservation means the most complete utilization of any product. . . . Lumbermen everywhere were deeply interested in the outcome . . . as it means the market will not be glutted and gorged with a tremendous output." Edward T. Allen, a man with a growing reputation in forest economics, was convinced that the disposal of government timber profoundly affected the management of private timberlands. Finally, a writer to the Portland *Oregonian* observed that large-scale owners opposed the opening of the reserves because it "would depress the price of lumber."[8]

For many lumbermen, burdensome timberland taxes provided the most cogent explanation for the depressed state of the lumber market. Trade leaders contended that unreasonably high taxes on commercial timber caused owners to liquidate their stands to meet taxes and other carrying charges. When Theodore Roosevelt and Gifford Pinchot sponsored a series of conservation congresses, lumbermen argued that high annual taxes were responsible for the failure to implement forest conservation.

In 1903, Ernest Bruncken wrote one of the first published reports crit-

[6] *Timberman* 10 (October, 1909): 19; *West Coast Lumberman* 25 (December, 1913): 23. The McCormick statement is quoted in John Minto, "What is to be his Relation to the State and the Nation," undated manuscript, box 2, John Minto Papers, Oregon Historical Society, Portland, Oregon.

[7] *Timberman* 9 (December, 1908): 40G; *American Lumberman* (September 28, 1908): 29.

[8] *Timberman* 11 (September, 1910): 19, and 11 (July, 1910): 19; E. T. Allen, "The Economics of National Forest Timber Sales," ca. 1909–10, vol. 1, box 1, WFCA Records; *Portland Oregonian*, January 30, 1911.

ical of the "faulty system of taxing woodland property." He considered wrong-headed state tax policies one of the greatest barriers to private forestry; the tax system had produced the "grossest discrimination" against forest property. Tax reform efforts, he contended, "must be directed towards abolishing this inequality." The Forest Service also showed a receptiveness to the tax issue when the agency established its Division of State and Private Forestry in 1908. As one of its first assignments, the new office assisted states in legislative studies of tax policies. And the later annual reports of the chief forester reflected the continuing commitment of the division to help revise state timber taxes. One Forest Service officer told the fledgling Society of American Foresters in 1906 that private owners would make little real progress in keeping up their forests until the tax situation was improved. Moreover, the tax burden was greatest in the older states, where "the tax levied upon the standing timber is often a warning to the owner that he must cut it or run the risk of great loss."[9]

When the crisis of overproduction persisted, the topic of timberland taxation gained more attention. At the organizational meeting of the Western Forestry and Conservation Association in 1909, the two key items of discussion were fire protection and the taxation of forests. The organization's Committee on Taxation suggested a program of public education to create "a healthy public sentiment . . . that an unjust . . . burden of taxation on timber lands stimulates the removal of timber and consequently decreases the taxable valuation of the counties."[10]

E. T. Allen, the association's secretary until his retirement in the late 1930s, was one of the earliest industry representatives to call attention to the relation between conservation, reforestation, and timberland taxes. Allen told the second Pacific Logging Congress in 1910 that forest taxation penalized conservative forest management; that the yield of the timber crop should be taxed, not the ownership of the land. The *West Coast Lumberman* also proposed adjusting state tax laws in Oregon and Washington as one solution to the problem of overproduction: "The present system of taxing the same crop year after year . . . is a sacrifice of the Pacific North-

[9]Ernest Bruncken, "Private Forestry and Taxation," *American Forests* 9 (October, 1903): 509; Harold K. Steen, *The U.S. Forest Service: A History*, pp. 92, 130; Alfred Gaskill, "How Shall Forests Be Taxed?" *American Forests* 12 (January, 1906): 119. *American Forests* went through several changes in title, one of which was *Forestry and Irrigation*.

[10]*Forty Years of Western Forestry: A History of the Movement to Conserve Forest Resources By Cooperative Effort, 1909–1949*, pp.8–10.

west's greatest natural asset." The fault, the *Lumberman* argued, rested with voters and legislators.[11]

Edward Hines, president of the National Lumber Manufacturers Association (NLMA), joined discussion of the tax and conservation issues at the association's 1910 convention. Timberland taxation, he insisted, "must be considered with the national conservation movement." He considered lumber manufacturers as active in conservation as professional foresters, but stressed the need to handle conservation along "enlightened and practical lines." Hines urged that the direction of the conservation movement "be controlled and practical ideas . . . be insisted upon. . . . Let the tax follow the saw." Two years later, association president Everett G. Griggs warned that reforestation would come only with properly adjusted tax laws. The chairman of the association's Committee on Conservation, J. B. White, told the 1913 convention that "in conservation . . . we have the cure for all of the ills that the lumbermen are afflicted with today." But, he cautioned, "we cannot afford, with the present rate of taxation . . . to let our trees stand."[12]

A broad spectrum of individuals supported the industry's argument that forest taxes and conservation were related issues. A contributor to *American Forests* asserted that unjust taxation of timberland was the main reason trees were heedlessly cut. Also, if state and federal governments relieved lumbermen from taxes on deforested land, 90 percent of them would reforest their cutover areas. An *American Forests* editorial cheered in support: "Take off the Taxes." Moreover, the editorial continued, if it was worthwhile "to establish National Forests and for the states to plant trees, . . . it is preposterous to leave the system of taxation in such condition that trees which are already growing must be cut."[13]

Chief Forester Gifford Pinchot shared the industry's belief that inequitable taxation was the chief obstacle to conservative forest practices. State tax laws discouraged holding either standing timber or cutover lands, he observed, and fear of excessive taxation was a powerful stimulus for premature cutting and the later revestment of much cutover land to the states. Pinchot believed that tax assessors often had been lenient; there-

---

[11] *Timberman* 11 (August, 1910): 35; *West Coast Lumberman* 25 (February, 1914): 19.

[12] NLMA, *Annual Report* (1910): 15–17, (1912): 21, 25, and (1913): 111.

[13] C. H. Goetz, "Why Americans Cut Their Forests," *American Forests* 13 (July, 1907): 282; "Lumberman's Views on Reforestation," *American Forests* 14 (January, 1908): 35; "Take Off The Taxes," *American Forests* 14 (March, 1908): 122.

fore, "the effect of existing laws has not always been without mitigation." But the states had failed to provide long-range assurances for the timberland investor, and this was "a powerful deterrent to the practice of forestry, which requires a long term investment."[14]

Henry Graves, who replaced Gifford Pinchot as chief forester in 1910, urged the states to adjust taxes on forestland "to encourage the private owner to cut his timber conservatively." When he rejoined the Forest Service after a nine-year leave, Graves observed that little change had occurred and that if the present system of taxation continued, it would help ensure the destruction of forests. Assistant Forester William B. Greeley repeated the same theme a few years later in his Forest Service study, *Some Public and Economic Aspects of the Lumber Industry.* "Uncertainty as to the future extent of this burden is a menace to the stability of timber ownership," Greeley claimed. Lumbermen with too much timberland had to liquidate to pay the carrying costs and thereby were handicapped in successfully competing in the marketplace.[15]

Finally, Wilson Compton warned in an article in the *Journal of Political Economy* in 1915 that timberland owners were in a state of crisis, because their land holdings were subject to an unmodified general property tax. He recommended a tax reform whose social purpose would be "the encouragement of both reforestation of non-agricultural land and the reasonable use of the present stock of virgin timber." Because timber presently was subject to the general property tax, Compton argued that an increase in the value of timberland would always prompt the owner to harvest. He called the common taxation of forestland "one of the most potent limitations to the withholding of timber from sale." Like William Greeley in the Forest Service, Compton held tenaciously to these views in his long career as secretary-manager for the NLMA.[16]

Although there was some support for timberland tax reform, a few informed individuals like Fred Rogers Fairchild, professor of political economy at Yale University, were more skeptical. Fairchild was beginning

---

[14] Gifford Pinchot, "Forestry on Private Lands," *Annals of the American Academy of Political and Social Science* 33 (1909): 493.

[15] Henry Graves, "The Advance of Forestry in the United States," *American Review of Reviews* 41 (1910): 464, 466; William B. Greeley, *Some Public and Economic Aspects of the Lumber Industry*, pp. 16–17.

[16] Wilson Compton, "Recent Tendencies in the Reform of Forest Taxation," *Journal of Political Economy* 23 (December, 1915): 973, 975–76; Compton, *The Organization of the Lumber Industry*, p. 6.

a long and distinguished career, in which he served occasionally as the federal government's expert witness on the taxation of private timberlands. His views invariably clashed with those of Wilson Compton, and the two argued over timber tax matters from the early twentieth century until the Great Depression.[17]

Fairchild authored a report on timberland taxation for the National Conservation Commission and also participated with Bernard Fernow in an International Conference on State and Local Taxation held in Toronto, Canada, in 1908. At the Toronto gathering, he summarized the lumberman's story "of forests prematurely cut on account of taxes, of wasteful and destructive 'skinning' of timber land, of cut-over lands not reforested, but abandoned because of taxation." A sad lament, Fairchild observed, but mistaken, because in most instances no evidence supported the claim that forests had been damaged by taxation. In his opinion, the large volume, the waste, and the failure to reforest cutover lands could not be attributed to excessive taxation. "The recent heavy and wasteful cutting of our forests," Fairchild argued, "has been due to various economic influences, among which taxation has played a small role." Adjusting the tax laws, therefore, would do little to advance progressive forest management practices.[18]

Despite these reservations, Fairchild recommended changes in state tax laws so that the tax burden fell on the yield of harvested timber. This suggestion struck at the lumberman's vital need—assurance to the investor that there would be no sudden application of the general property tax to timberland. Forest owners wanted greater reliability and predictability for their future tax responsibilities. "It is not the excessive nature of taxation," Fairchild noted, "but rather the uncertainty that bothers most timber men."[19]

Fairchild drew similar conclusions in a statement to the National Conservation Commission. The collection of timber taxes by county officials, he said, was haphazard and in most cases underestimated. Excessive taxation occasionally surfaced in Michigan, Wisconsin, Minnesota, and along

[17] For example, see Wilson Compton to Fred Fairchild, November 4, 1931, box 77, National Forest Products Association Records (hereafter cited as NFPA Records), Forest History Society, Santa Cruz, California. Compton chided Fairchild for his "astonishing" report to the Timber Conservation Board, which claimed timber taxation was not a substantial factor in forcing timber owners to cut, or to refrain from cutting.

[18] Fred Rogers Fairchild, A. C. Shaw, and B. E. Fernow, *Forest Taxation*, pp. 1–2, 5–6.

[19] Ibid., p. 6.

the Pacific Coast, Fairchild reported, but "it is safe to say that in general timber land, like most other property, is grossly undervalued by the assessors." The Yale economist again warned that investors in "forestry" wanted enough financial stability to make future calculations safely. But if the current system were strictly enforced, Fairchild believed, the consequences would be burdensome, and the investor would feel insecure about the future. A timber tax should be based on yield; "It is equitable and certain." [20]

A later Forest Service study of timberland taxation in Michigan concluded that taxes were not uniform among counties and that cutover areas were taxed much higher than lands with standing timber. But the study found that taxation was not strictly enforced, that timberlands were traditionally underassessed, and that the state's tax situation was arbitrary and uncertain. [21]

Bernard Fernow, like Fairchild, believed that forest destruction had not been hastened and that forest management had not "been advanced by over or under-taxation." But the system should be rational and predictable: the fault with timber tax policy in the United States, he said, was lack of uniformity. [22]

Fairchild, Fernow, and Gifford Pinchot addressed the essence of the tax issue, especially as it might influence those entrepreneurs who took the long view of matters. The future, not the present or the past, was the basis of their critique. Lumbermen wanted a rational and predictable system, removed from legislative meddling, and their recommendations that states reform their forest tax systems were in accord with the lumber industry's broader quest for order and stability. But difficulties lay ahead. The effort to alleviate the "tax burden" placed the lumber industry in perpetual conflict with progressive tax reformers. Lumbermen never resolved the issue to their satisfaction and continued to blame burdensome timberland taxes both for overproduction and for the industry's failure to practice effective forest conservation.

[20] Fred Rogers Fairchild, "Taxation of Timberlands," in *Report of the National Conservation Commission*, vol. 2, pp. 591, 611–12, 631–32.

[21] Alfred K. Chittenden, *The Taxation of Forest Lands in Wisconsin*, pp. 7, 62. The study was carried out in cooperation with the Forest Service.

[22] Bernard E. Fernow, "Principles Underlying the Taxation of Forests," in *Taxation of Forests*, pp. 7–9.

Lumbermen also linked the tariff on the importation of lumber to the conservation of forest resources. Early in the twentieth century, Congress threatened to place lumber on the duty-free list after more than a century of protection (except for the period between 1894 and 1897, when there was free trade in sawed timber). A few early foresters had also recommended abolishing the tariff on lumber, reasoning that such action would lower lumber prices and conserve timberlands. A U.S. Reclamation Service official added that the tariff virtually offered "a pecuniary bounty on the destruction of our forests." But the free introduction of lumber from Canada and Latin America, the official noted, would help stop the ravaging of forestland.[23] These early disclaimers, however, came full circle in the great tariff fight of late 1908 and 1909, when most organized lumbermen supported protection. In that struggle, the industry flexed its collective-lobbying muscle and maintained the substance of a protective tariff for lumber.

Conservationists who wanted to protect the nation's forest resources and a few lumbermen with operations in Canada had mobilized considerable support to remove the lumber duties. The regional trade associations (especially those in the West) and their trade journal counterparts skillfully argued that the introduction of tariff-exempt lumber from Canada would lower the price of lumber and thereby perpetuate waste, because it would be unprofitable to haul anything except the best logs to the mill. Forest owners contended that they needed a fair return before the country's timberlands would be preserved. The *American Lumberman* set the standard for the tariff debate: "The idea that cheap lumber would tend to conserve the forest resources of the United States certainly is absurd." Forest conservation could never thrive until it was commercially feasible and ensured greater profits. The journal denounced the "ill-considered and fallacious arguments" calling for the removal of the duty as a conservation measure. Lower prices, it claimed, would mean less conservation, while higher prices would raise the value of standing timber and lead to the "practice of conservative logging methods."[24]

[23] Samuel Trask Dana, *Forest and Range Policy: Its Development in the United States*, p. 174; Steen, *U.S. Forest Service*, p. 93; "Letter from J. Sterling Morton," *Proceedings of the American Forestry Congress* (1888): 12–13; Arthur P. Davis, "Suggestions for Forest Policy," *American Forests* 12 (January, 1906): 39.

[24] Cox, "Trade Associations in the Lumber Industry," p. 308; *American Lumberman* (September 12, 1908): 29, and (December 5, 1908): 31.

When the House Committee on Ways and Means held its first hearings on the tariff schedule in late 1908, the *Timberman* commended lumbermen for their "strong showing" in favor of protection. Most of the testimony on the question of conservation, the journal observed, supported the industry's position that free trade would not promote conservation of American forests, but would disturb the home market and add to the already large inventories on hand. A representative of the Yellow Pine Manufacturers Association told the House committee that removing the tariff would hurt southern lumber operators. Moreover, regional trade leaders argued that other factors were responsible for the rise in lumber prices rather than the existing duty, which was a very modest one.[25]

Association spokesmen, including the most important producers from all sections of the country, trekked to Washington to testify against tariff revision. Frank Lamb, a prominent Washington lumberman and log broker, favored retaining the tariff "until the time comes when it . . . is profitable to grow [trees]." Until then, he argued, "you will have no forestry or forest conservation on the private lands of the United States." Edward Hines, an important man in the future Southern Pine Association, led southern opposition to "cheap" Canadian lumber. Some operators were more desperate: a Washington shingle manufacturer told the committee that the tariff meant survival or failure to those in the shingle business. Removing the duty on shingles, he said, "is going to destroy our business. . . . It is a question of market. If we lose our market, we have to close our mills." The *Pacific Lumber and Trade Journal* reprimanded "the statesmen" in Washington who would contribute to the waste of the last great expanse of timber in the United States. The effort to revise the tariff, the trade paper declared, "is radically, absolutely and fatally wrong."[26]

George Emerson, another Washington lumberman, told the congressional committee that the current duty on lumber provided only "a little wall" around low-grade lumber. Remove this protection, he cautioned, and the low-quality stuff would be left in the woods, resulting in an enormous waste of forest resources. The remedy was a better price for low-grade material, which would eliminate waste in the woods and reduce the fire hazard. "The preservation of our forests is the only question in lumber tariff

---

[25] *Timberman* 10 (December, 1908): 19; James E. Fickle, *The New South and the "New Competition": Trade Association Development in the Southern Pine Industry*, pp. 36–37.

[26] Testimony printed in *Pacific Lumber and Trade Journal* 14 (December, 1908): 22, 24; Fickle, *The New South*, p. 37; *Pacific Lumber and Trade Journal* 14 (January, 1909): 17.

protection," Emerson observed, and this depended on "good markets for low grades." The tariff would directly affect what happened in the woods.[27]

Trade journals and lumbermen's associations hammered away at the relation between the tariff and the practice of conservation. The Western Forestry and Conservation Association forwarded resolutions to Congress and Chief Forester Gifford Pinchot stating that lowering the tariff would destroy conservation and threaten reforestation. The *Pacific Lumber and Trade Journal* feared that the lumber industry "would suffer irreparably if this unintelligent clamor for free forest products" led to a removal of the tariff. And the trade press exulted when Gifford Pinchot supported the tariff in testimony to the House Ways and Means Committee. The *Timberman* observed that Pinchot's support for a lumber duty made him "a decided success as head of the Forest Service."[28]

Congress subsequently retained the duty on lumber, albeit at a reduced rate. The NLMA claimed credit for the partial victory, and the association's manager praised the industry for uniting on the tariff issue. In succeeding years, industrial leaders continued to criticize the idea that forest conservation could be achieved by encouraging competition with Canadian lumber. Even with a relatively mild tariff, they argued, most mills used only "choice logs," because there was no market for low-grade lumber. But the limited tariff victory of 1909 was short-lived. Enactment of the Underwood Tariff in 1913 removed all lumber except cabinet woods from the protected list, a situation that prevailed until 1930. The act also removed the duty on the importation of shingles as well.[29]

But the real significance of the tariff fight was to demonstrate the ability of lumber organizations to shape public opinion and to direct a skillful and concerted lobbying campaign. Washington's Governor Marion E. Hay accused lumbermen of maintaining a large and powerful lobby "for the purpose of preventing any reduction in the Dingley rates on lumber." Also, the Bureau of Corporations, in its extensive report on the lumber industry,

[27] *Pacific Lumber and Trade Journal* 14 (January, 1909): 23.

[28] "Transcript of organizing meeting of WFCA," box 1, WFCA Records; *Pacific Lumber and Trade Journal* 14 (February, 1909): 17; *American Lumberman* (March 13, 1909): 35; *Pacific Lumber and Trade Journal* 14 (February, 1909): 19; and 15 (September, 1909): 17. When Gifford Pinchot was fired from the Forest Service, the *Timberman* called his dismissal a "national loss." The lumber industry "never had a better friend," especially during the "dark days of the tariff discussion" (*Timberman* 11 [January, 1910]: 19).

[29] Steen, *U.S. Forest Service*, p. 94; NLMA, *Annual Report* (1910): 26, 34, and (1912): 135; Dana, *Forest and Range Policy*, p. 175.

charged the NLMA with "political intrigues" during the tariff controversy. The trade group's committee-packing efforts and other schemes, the bureau charged, constituted an "earnest and insidious lobby." [30]

In the game of broker politics, of course, not everyone gets a fair cut, and this seems to have plagued lumbermen in the battles over the tariff. Shortly after the passage of the Underwood Tariff Act, the West Coast Lumber Manufacturers Association complained that the increasingly "demoralized and unprofitable" conditions in the lumber industry resulted directly from the new tariff act. A shingle manufacturer argued that the removal of the duty on shingles required remedy, or "the time will soon come when our shingle mills will be the home of bats and owls." [31] In the ensuing decades the tariff issue continued to be a source of disappointment, especially in times of depressed prices.

The lumber industry continued to be a target of controversy in congressional debates over agricultural appropriations for the Forest Service. Muckraker writers like Charles Edward Russell added to the persisting suspicions of monopoly and collusion between the private sector and government agencies. One insurgent western progressive, Elias Ammons, contended that the Forest Service "has been a willing tool in the hands of the lumber trust. . . . It feeds upon our industries, thwarts our development, and hinders our growth." It was unprofitable, unwelcome, and, Ammons charged, "makes a miserable misfit amongst our free institutions." Idaho's Senator Heyburn again rankled the defenders of the Forest Service when he demanded a cut in its 1911 appropriations. The service, he said, sent its foresters to gather seed to "plant in the nurseries, and the seeds were gathered by robbing the squirrels' nests." [32]

Oregon's Senator George Chamberlain defended Forest Service appropriations because they involved "great economic questions." He praised the work of Gifford Pinchot and insisted that the national forests had kept the nation's timberland from control by a monopoly. Chamberlain defended

---

[30] Cox, "Trade Associations in the Lumber Industry," p. 311; *Timberman* 11 (October, 1910): 45; U.S. Department of Commerce, Bureau of Corporations, *Report on the Lumber Industry*, pt. 4, pp. xx, 69–70.

[31] *West Coast Lumberman* 25 (March, 1914): 39, and 28 (August, 1915): 25.

[32] Charles Edward Russell, "The Mysterious Octopus: Story of the Strange and Powerful Organization That Controls the American Lumber Trade," *World Today* 21 (1912): 1735–50; "Speech of Elias M. Ammons Before the Colorado Assembly in Reply to Mr. Pinchot," in *Congressional Record*, 61st Cong., 2d sess., May 19, 1910, p. 6530; *Congressional Record*, 61st Cong., 3rd sess., March 1, 1911, p. 3774.

Forest Service sales policy against the charge that its decisions favored the larger operators.[33]

The severest critic of the Forest Service was Congressman William E. Humphrey, from Washington's First District. His attacks, which coincided with the publication of the Bureau of Corporations study, marked the high point in the opposition to the federal forest system. Humphrey was convinced that the federal forests were "the greatest public wrong ever permitted in this country." He contended that the original reserves, designed to prevent private monopoly, were working in the opposite direction. Through the lieu land system, the Forest Service had promoted the formation of large acreages that were transferred first to railroad interests and later to large companies like Weyerhaeuser. Federal timber-sales policy in the state of Washington, according to Humphrey, encouraged monopoly and strengthened those who owned land adjacent to the national forests. This practice, he noted, worked to the advantage of the Northern Pacific Railroad and the Weyerhaeuser interests, because the Forest Service kept its timber off the market unless it could obtain "the prices fixed by the Weyerhaeuser syndicate."[34]

Representative Humphrey directed his sharpest criticism at the conservation movement and the AFA, whose membership, he declared, "is like calling the sinister roll of the great vested 'interests' of the Nation." It included railroad barons, timber kings, and wood-pulp and paper magnates, who used their influence and cash to promote conservation in the name of the people. Humphrey hinted that even he had been duped at first.

For several years I could not understand the interest or the motive of these men in this conservation movement. I saw "as through a glass darkly." But since I have come face to face with the facts I see clearly, as I trace the transfer of millions of acres of the public domain from the people to the "interests" represented in this great "conservation" movement. . . . The railroad interests and those interested in the forest products of this country have furnished the brains and the money . . . that have made conservation what it is in the Pacific Northwest today, and these gentlemen have reaped their reward. Associated with these men were the dreamers and the impractical and the unintelligent educated theorists.[35]

Humphrey recommended increasing the federal timber cut rather than allowing it to rot in the forest, and he urged that the reserves be removed

[33] *Congressional Record*, 62d Cong., 2d sess., May 16, 1912, pp. 6531, 6539, 6544, 6547.

[34] Ise, *United States Forest Policy*, p. 298; *Congressional Record*, 63rd Cong., 1st sess., June 2, 1913, pp. 1862–66.

[35] *Congressional Record*, 63rd Cong., 1st sess., June 2, 1913, p. 1866.

from the control of philosophers and academics and given to businessmen and practical lumbermen. The national forest, he said, "is largely the plaything of a bunch of theorists and schoolboys." In another lengthy and censorious speech, Humphrey read into the record the names of influential members of the AFA, who, he said, constituted "a sordid commercial body."[36]

Despite the sometimes harsh language and the charges of collusion and political inveigling, the Forest Service weathered the storm. Its success must be attributed, in part, to the enthusiastic support and cooperation of the lumber industry. The objective of the Forest Service, Henry Graves informed the annual meeting of the Western Forestry and Conservation Association in 1911, was to cooperate with timber owners in various parts of the country. Assistant Forester Earle W. Clapp told the same audience, "It is extremely gratifying to members of the Forest Service that we can be a party to the kind of co-operation that now exists in the Northwest." And George S. Long, associated with the Weyerhaeuser interests, paid tribute to the influence of Gifford Pinchot, who "has drawn to him the very best class of bright, keen, earnest, trained young men."[37]

A broad array of groups associated with the industry emphasized this cooperative spirit. Chief Forester Graves, speaking in 1912 to a joint conference of lumbermen and federal forest officials in California, called upon the two groups to harmonize their differences. The editor of the *Timberman*, George Cornwall, informed the same audience that it was "idle and futile . . . to ignore or belittle this important branch of the National Government." One year later the National Conservation Congress recommended a federal forest policy to steady the forest industry in order to prevent overproduction and the demoralization of the industry. The *West Coast Lumberman* called the recommendations "the most practical report ever made under the name of conservation." E. T. Allen, the author of the report, argued that lumbermen had to sell at market quotations to pay their carrying costs. Therefore, widespread selling of government timber would immediately lower the price of stumpage, which would wipe out the majority of manufacturers who needed to cut their own stands.[38]

[36] Ibid., p. 1867; *Congressional Record*, 63rd Cong., 2d sess., March 10, 1914, pp. 4623–25.

[37] *Timberman* 13 (December, 1911): 47, 52–53.

[38] Ibid. 13 (February, 1912): 18, and 15 (December, 1913): 26–27; *West Coast Lumberman* 25 (December, 1913): 23; E. T. Allen, "Economics of Timber Supply in Relation to Production and Consumption," in *Proceedings of the Fifth National Conservation Congress* (1913): 345, 348.

Despite these complaints, the annual harvest from the national forests remained small until after World War Two. Moreover, when the lumber market was glutted, the Forest Service refused to sell except when local communities relied solely on the national forests for economic survival. Henry Graves reported in 1911 that the Forest Service, "at the cost of considerable sacrifice of receipts," had declined to make timber sales since the beginning of the general depression in the lumber market in 1907. Two years later, Graves again recommended against flooding the market with cheap Forest Service timber, because it would drive down the price of lumber. He noted that the annual federal cut was too small (one-half of 1 percent) to appreciably affect the price of lumber. Limiting the harvest from the national forests, he believed, would restrict the availability of timber and promote conservation.[39]

No one did more to associate conservation with the material requirements of the lumber industry than William Buckhout Greeley, who succeeded Henry Graves as chief forester. Greeley, like Edward T. Allen, provided a link between the forest conservation movement of the Progressive Era and forestry politics after the First World War. Both began their professional work as government foresters in the Pacific Northwest under Gifford Pinchot, and their active careers spanned the first fifty years of the twentieth century. Much of their work was opposed to the policies of their former chief. Both Greeley and Allen shifted from the Forest Service to management positions with trade associations, where they devoted much of their time and energy as expert witnesses for organized lumbermen. Their lifelong effort in working for legislative and regulatory policies favorable to the industry has gained them a prominent place in forest history.[40]

In 1913 Greeley assured the NLMA that Forest Service timber would not threaten the already glutted lumber market. If lumbermen could control production, Greeley told the trade group, the value of the government stands would appreciate and help to perpetuate competition. The Forest Service was gratified, he observed, because it had been "helped at nearly every turn by the assistance and cooperation of broad-gauge lumbermen." Greeley also initiated and drafted the Forest Service response to the Bureau of Corporations *Report on the Lumber Industry*. His study absolved corporations and trade associations of trust activity and directed attention

---

[39] U.S. Forest Service, *Annual Report* (1911): 20, and (1913): 16.

[40] E. T. Allen's career still awaits a biographic article, even though information about his public life is plentiful. For Greeley's career, see his autobiography, *Forests and Men*; and George T. Morgan's *William B. Greeley, A Practical Forester*.

to the peculiar economic conditions of the lumber trade. The cause of instability and the chief deterrent to conservation, according to Greeley, was "the great burden of timberland investments, . . . excessive mill capacity, poor financing, and low average efficiency in manufacturing and merchandising." The experiences of the past several years clearly revealed the relation between economic conditions and forest conservation.[41]

The Forest Service study, a cooperative venture with the Federal Trade Commission, was important to trade association leaders. E. T. Allen suggested that lumbermen should review the report so that changes could be made "before passing it on." Allen told Royal S. Kellogg, Secretary to the NLMA, that "the industry was promised such an opportunity," and he feared that Greeley might be avoiding the original arrangement. Kellogg assured Allen that he had seen a preliminary copy of the report: "I don't think the lumbermen will find much to object to in it," he said, "even though it goes to the Federal Trade Commission before they see it."[42] In the future E. T. Allen would be more trustful of Greeley.

Most trade leaders expressed sympathy for the Forest Service, which had to walk hat-in-hand before each congressional session to obtain the appropriations necessary to support its work. The service, Allen complained, was unable to establish a clear-cut, dependable national policy, because Congress failed to support and finance the necessary planning programs. "Every congressional session," Allen grumbled, "sees the whole subject debated from a dozen viewpoints, chiefly political, with a marked lack of statesman-like treatment based on any real knowledge of forest economies." Occasionally trade groups protested reductions in Forest Service appropriations for the protection and prevention of fires. A. W. Laird, associated with the Weyerhaeuser interests, told a Federal Trade Commission hearing in 1915 that lumbermen in the Pacific Northwest enjoyed splendid rapport with the Forest Service and that the cooperation was mutually beneficial. But, like other industrial leaders, Laird deplored congressional demands on the Forest Service to secure revenue commensurate with its expenses. Excessive political pressure, Laird said, would place government and private timber in competition in an already saturated market.[43]

Assurances of cooperation and good will between the Forest Service

[41] NLMA, *Annual Report* (1913): 129, 134; Steen, *U.S. Forest Service*, pp. 111–12; Greeley, *Some Public and Economic Aspects*, pp. 3–4.

[42] E. T. Allen to R. S. Kellogg, May 3, 1916, and Kellogg to Allen, May 8, 1916, both in box 110, NFPA Records.

[43] *West Coast Lumberman* 29 (December, 1915): 42; "Reports of Officers and Commit-

and the lumber industry persisted throughout the second decade of the twentieth century. Government workers like Chief Forester Henry Graves and Assistant Forester William Greeley provided much of the stimulus for that atmosphere. The two men repeatedly emphasized that government-industry cooperation would redound to the public benefit. The prosperity of private industry and the public welfare, according to Graves, were one and the same. In the absence of trust and good feeling, he noted, the public stood to lose. The chief forester told a San Francisco forest conference in 1915 that "one of the provinces of the government is to aid constructively in solving industrial problems." The government, he said, understood the complexity of economic conditions and realized the futility of dividing "the country into armed camps." The Forest Service, he concluded, should avoid hostility and strife, cooperate with lumbermen, and manage the national forests in the best interests of both the industry and the public.[44]

William Greeley also gave assurances that the "Forest Service has no delusion that it is divinely commissioned to tell lumbermen how to run their business." Lumber operators, he stated unequivocally, should work out their own problems; the government could not provide solutions, although it could help lumbermen develop a workable forest policy and resolve such issues as timberland taxes. But it was vital to maintain cooperative relationships between government agencies and private industry.[45]

When the Forest Service finally released its study in early 1917, the *West Coast Lumberman* called it the "most important ever issued by [the] government," because no one had ever conducted "an investigation of the lumber industry in the same sympathetic manner as it has been handled in a report of W. B. Greeley." It was the first inquiry into industrial operations, the trade paper reported, that did not turn into an attack. The Greeley report, said E. T. Allen, was "easily the most important and significant document dealing with the American lumber industry" and would force lumbermen to confront issues too long avoided. George S. Long, who had advance knowledge of the study, praised Greeley for his thoughtful and unbiased analysis and for his even-handed and sympathetic treatment of the lumber industry. It "will make more friends for the lumber industry," he argued, "than can any effort of our own. To us it is a wet blanket. He has

tees of the Third Annual Meeting of the West Coast Lumbermen's Association," 1913, folder 23, box 1, West Coast Lumbermen's Association Records, Oregon Historical Society, Portland, Oregon; *West Coast Lumberman* 28 (August, 1915): 25; *Timberman* 16 (August, 1915): 30.

[44] *West Coast Lumberman* 29 (November, 1915): 39.

[45] *Timberman* 18 (November, 1916): 36, 38–39.

told us better than we knew ourselves how bad off we are. And he has told the truth." [46]

In a letter to Royal S. Kellogg, one trade official praised the study for showing that at certain points lumbermen lost money. Kellogg, who left the Forest Service to serve as secretary to the NLMA, agreed that vital information could be found in Greeley's report. The *Southern Lumberman* was less enthusiastic, because it believed the study merely emphasized the obvious. The trade paper urged lumbermen to read the report "if for no other reason than for the pleasure to be derived from stumbling up on such grave conclusion as that 'Overproduction has resulted from ineffective adjustment of the output of the industry to the changes in volume of consumption.'" However, it praised the study for putting "a quietus on the old 'Lumber Trust' delusion." [47]

When the United States entered the European war in 1917, trade leaders and Forest Service officials had firmly established the association between conservation policy and economic conditions. In this accomplishment, lumbermen had co-opted the crusading, people-oriented rhetoric of the conservation movement and made it over to suit their material needs. The industry defined the issues that contributed to a depressed market—exorbitant taxes, inequitable freight rates, the threat of cheaply marketed Forest Service timber, and the equally fearsome threat of duty-free lumber —and then associated those with the conservation of the timber resource. Economic conditions also shaped lumbermen's perceptions of the federal forest system. They reasoned that withdrawing timberlands from public entry would help stabilize the market, increase the price of lumber, and eventually enhance the practice of forestry on private lands. Trade association officials proved themselves skilled propagandists and lobbyists in their efforts to resolve their economic difficulties and to answer the public appeal to conserve resources. But the old problems persisted in the coming years, and trade spokesmen and their friends had to devise new schemes and revise old arguments.

[46] *West Coast Lumberman* 31 (February, 1917): 26–27; *Timberman* 18 (November, 1916): 39.

[47] J. R. Morehead, secretary, Southwestern Lumbermen's Association, to R. S. Kellogg, January 29, 1917, and Kellogg to Morehead, January 31, 1917, both in box 110, NFPA Records; *Southern Lumberman* 83 (January 27, 1917): 24, and (February 3, 1917): 19.

4

Lumber in Depression and War

"The important thing is to get the *big thing* done."
—Wilson Compton, 1918

WILLIAM B. GREELEY'S Forest Service study was published in the midst of demoralized conditions in the lumber industry that had persisted unremittingly since 1907. These convulsive periods of overproduction continued to plague operators who persisted in cutting timber irrespective of price or demand. Stumpage values declined even further and gloom spread throughout the trade. Lumbermen, well aware of the bleak and dreary circumstances sketched in the Forest Service study, recommended that producers improve their cooperative efforts through the network of trade organizations and urged Congress to relax the antitrust laws to permit industrial consolidation and merger. The modernists among them believed these steps would lessen excessive competition and increase the security of future investment decisions. They made it explicitly clear that the lumber industry's changing economic and institutional structure had produced destructive competition, which forced the move from small, marginal, and inefficient units to larger and more productive ones. Thus, the modernizers claimed, there was a need to adjust legislative and regulatory policy to accord with economic reality.

When the lumber market began to drop off after 1907, trade leaders devised schemes to improve cooperation between associations and to lessen internecine strife between different producing regions. Interregional competition, one trade journal editor noted, "was as genuine in its fierceness as it was consequently demoralizing to the . . . competitor." The logical solution, therefore, was close coordination between lumber interests. E. T. Allen thought the most vexing issue was the public's belief that a "lumber trust" existed, when, in fact, competition was relentlessly keen. Allen urged the public to recognize "that abstract ethics do not influence human action."[1]

Everett G. Griggs, president of the newly formed West Coast Lumbermen's Association, underscored the value of cooperation: "Collectively, we do amount to something in the lumber producing world and with our Association . . . we will receive new benefits." Another association leader said others should be deterred from investing in an industry saturated with speculation. George Cornwall of the *Timberman* remarked in 1914 that lumber prices were among the lowest ever recorded and required a quick and thorough cutback in production. Lumbermen "have the remedy in their own hands," he observed. "Curtailment is not only an economic necessity but is in a larger sense a moral responsibility which the business owes itself." More of the same problems plagued the South, where an excessive productive capacity brought increased yield whenever the market offered even a glimmer of optimism. These circumstances prompted progressive trade leaders to seek more efficient and effective means to control production and stabilize the market.[2]

In the Pacific Northwest, a group of trade leaders and bankers met to discuss solutions to problems plaguing the lumber industry. E. B. Hazen, a Portland lumberman, urged operators to reorganize the business "all the way through from the stump to the consumer," to improve cooperation at the regional level, and to increase support for the National Lumber Manufacturers Association (NLMA). To improve efficiency, he recommended larger operating units and a similar reorganization of the scattered, small-scale distributors and merchandisers of lumber products. Hazen encouraged bankers to assist lumbermen "to amalgamate their properties, [to] get the majority of the fir production into a dozen or two competent producing units."[3]

A series of Federal Trade Commission (FTC) hearings in 1915 and 1916 indicated that some lumbermen wanted to circumvent the Sherman

[1] *Timberman* 10 (June, 1909): 19; *West Coast Lumberman* 25 (December, 1913): 30, 42.

[2] Reports of officers and committees at the Second Annual Meeting of the West Coast Lumbermen's Association (1913), folder 23, box 1, West Coast Lumbermen's Association Records (hereafter cited as WCLA Records), Oregon Historical Society, Portland, Oregon; *Timberman* 15 (June, 1914): 25; James E. Fickle, *The New South and the "New Competition" : Trade Association Development in the Southern Pine Industry*, pp. 35–36.

[3] *Timberman* 16 (February, 1915): 36–37; E. B. Hazen, "The Fir Outlook," reprint from *Timberman* 17 (March, 1916): 14, in folder 23, box 1, WCLA Records.

Antitrust Act. John H. Kirby, a major southern producer, told the FTC in Chicago that the Sherman antitrust law handicapped the industry's ability to form combinations and made it more difficult to alleviate the depressed conditions in the lumber market. J. B. White, a Kansas City operator, told the commission that the investor's right to control and regulate the organization of business would help ease the crisis. E. B. Hazen, likewise, urged the government to allow manufacturers to curtail production and suggested that the government make cooperation compulsory and fix prices that "would force the consolidation of now small, independent producers" into larger ownerships. Hazen sketched a bleak future for the industry in the absence of retroactive legislation.[4]

When the FTC moved its hearings to Spokane, John R. Toole, president of the Western Pine Manufacturers Association, told the commissioners that lumbermen needed to curtail production and organize selling agencies supervised by the government. In Seattle, trade leaders urged the commission to allow manufacturers to cut back on production whenever they agreed on a minimum price. A prominent western Washington operator argued that lumbermen must be allowed to organize a corporation "to control production which will remedy the low prices which are prevailing." A Portland banker thought the industry should be permitted to organize combinations to improve its marketing situation. One northwestern Democrat recommended that the FTC act be amended to grant the agency broad jurisdiction over the interstate shipment of forest products. Under the plan, the commission could authorize mergers and combinations and guarantee lumber manufacturers "a fair net profit."[5]

West Coast trade leaders finally sought foreign sales as one means to ease the strains of a saturated domestic market. This posed difficulties for the smaller-scale operators who lacked an agency to carry on foreign sales work. The *Timberman* urged Congress to grant manufacturers freedom to combine in order to pursue overseas markets, without fear of antitrust prosecution; for "the Sherman anti-trust law was never intended to apply to the export trade." The *West Coast Lumberman* said bluntly that relaxing the Sherman act in the export trade was "essential in the rejuvenation of lumbering." Congress endorsed these suggestions in 1918 when it passed the

[4] Reported in *Timberman* 16 (August, 1915): 27–28.
[5] Ibid., pp. 30–34; *West Coast Lumberman* 28 (August, 1915): 21, 24–25, and 29 (January, 1916): 30.

Webb-Pomerene Act, which permitted cooperation on prices in the export trade. Although Congress proved unwilling to tamper with the Sherman act in other ways, it did set aside the antitrust laws in order to encourage foreign trade. When passage of the Webb bill was certain, lumber operators in the Pacific Northwest organized the Douglas Fir Exploitation and Export Company to push foreign sales, especially in Japan.[6]

Trade association leaders also favored industrial consolidation, because it would conserve the timber resource. The president of the Southern Pine Association, Charles S. Keith, convinced the U.S. Chamber of Commerce to pass a resolution permitting cooperative agreements in the natural resource industries. The chamber's resolution stipulated only that combinations should promote the conservation of resources and be in the public interest. The *Southern Lumberman* called the plan constructive, because it would eliminate destructive competition and utilize forest waste. The FTC noted in its later *Report on Lumber Manufacturers Trade Associations* that trade groups wanted to combine in order to regulate lumber production and to conserve national resources. The Forest Service, according to the report, had recommended withdrawing federal timber from the market and allowing combinations to control production. Cooperative sales agencies and price agreements, the service said, would aid the industry in controlling production.[7]

Chief Forester Henry Graves also pointed to the relation between economic conditions and forest conservation in his 1915 annual report. These resources, Graves reported, were "linked inseparably with the economic conditions controlling the exploitation and marketing of forest products." Two factors contributed to the ever-increasing waste of timber: (1) "the carrying of enormous quantities of raw material . . . with its far reaching financial burdens," and (2) "the financial necessities of the owners of stumpage."[8]

Sentiments expressed at the 1915 meeting of the NLMA portrayed a similar situation. One speaker called for an end to jealousy and for greater cooperative effort; another saw combination and merger as an attempt to

[6] *Timberman* 15 (June, 1914): 24; *West Coast Lumberman* 28 (August, 1915): 19; M. Browning Carrott, "The Supreme Court and American Trade Associations, 1921–1925," *Business History Review* 44: 321; *West Coast Lumberman* 31 (October, 1916): 19; Robert E. Ficken, *Lumber and Politics*: 134–37.

[7] *Southern Lumberman* 83 (January 27, 1917): 53; U.S. Federal Trade Commission, *Report on Lumber Manufacturers Trade Associations* (1922), p. 2.

[8] U.S. Forest Service, *Annual Report* (1915): 3–4, 27.

rationalize and bring order to the industry (large holdings and large-scale operations avoided waste and were more efficient economic units); and still another criticized the outdated philosophy that competition was vital to the lumber business. Royal S. Kellogg, secretary to the association, told the gathering that uncontrolled competition had never resulted in anything but the squandering of natural resources. Laws were needed, he said, to curtail output and allow full cooperation within the industry, because reckless competition had precluded conservation. A southern trade official later wrote Kellogg that lumbermen needed "a few Billy Sundays" to inform the consuming public of "the facts and truth . . . that relate to the lumber industry."[9]

Wilson Compton, who served as an economist with the FTC between 1916 and 1918, contributed an influential essay to the *American Economic Review* in 1917 on the problems of overcapitalization in the lumber industry. Compton pointed to the investment of borrowed capital in speculative holdings and the decentralization of the industry as factors contributing to its malaise. Unhealthy competitive conditions had forced lumbermen to seek relief through trade agreements, a quest that was "comparatively fruitless and was discouraged from within and repressed from without." Because of declining profits and the continued waste of timber, Compton said, trade leaders had asked the government for production controls. The success of forest conservation in the United States, Compton observed, depended primarily on lumber prices and could be accomplished only through a systematic national forest policy.[10]

On the eve of American entry into the European war, a small group of lumber leaders began to move more aggressively to resolve the industry's chronic economic problems. A growing body of public and private literature spurred this quest to rationalize and bring order to a volatile and chaotic business environment. Individuals like Compton, Royal Kellogg, William Greeley, and a few progressive lumbermen believed that the ruthless

[9] NLMA, *Annual Report* (1915): 21, 43, 63–64, 183 (Kellogg's address is printed in full in the *West Coast Lumberman* 27 [February, 1915]: 36–37); J. R. Morehead to R. S. Kellogg, November 13, 1916, box 110, National Forest Products Association Records (hereafter cited as NFPA Records), Forest History Society, Santa Cruz, California.

[10] "Chronology of Wilson Martindale Compton," Wilson Compton Papers (hereafter cited as Compton Papers), Forest History Society, Santa Cruz, California; Wilson Compton, "The Price Problem in the Lumber Industry," *American Economic Review* 7 (1917): 582–83, 590–93, 597.

frontier spirit of the nineteenth century was an outmoded and irrational way to conduct business in the twentieth century. The destructive tendencies inherent in excessive competition, they argued, called for a more stable and rational economic order where future business prospects could be predicted with a greater degree of certainty.

Because the war in Europe created new market demands, the lumber industry directed much of its production toward supplying the needs of U.S. and European military forces. However, trade officials also saw other opportunities created by the war. Just before American participation, a Commerce Department spokesman urged the systematic cultivation of foreign markets as one solution to the lumberman's dilemma. Because forest products were being used exhaustively to pursue war in Europe, lumber would be in great demand for construction and rebuilding. But there was uncertainty as well. L. C. Boyle, counsel for the NLMA, warned, "The drift of war conditions may precipitate legislation that might definitely involve natural resources, hence . . . we should . . . be on guard in the event of such an emergency." Boyle urged the association to prepare for every contingency but to avoid using propaganda "inimical to the public welfare, and thereby prejudice the popular mind against the industry."[11]

Government war orders did not reach the volume that some trade officials had expected. There were severe transportation problems and manpower shortages, and in the early stages of the war organized labor pushed vigorously for wage increases and an eight-hour day. In their struggle to control and channel labor agitation in acceptable directions, lumbermen enjoyed the full cooperation of the federal government. The industry also made dramatic progress in forestry research during the war, and the tangible benefits were readily apparent. The Forest Products Laboratory in Madison, Wisconsin, assisted military and civilian agencies in selecting, purchasing, and using wood products for many purposes. Raphael Zon, who headed the Forest Service research department in Washington, D.C., observed that the war had proved the worth of science and that, because of the application of research to industrial problems, the value of science would be more fully appreciated in later years.[12]

[11] *West Coast Lumberman* 31 (November, 1916): 29–30; Ficken, *Lumber and Politics*, p. 31; L. C. Boyle to Charles Keith, November 14, 1917, box 110, NFPA Records.

[12] Ralph W. Hidy, Frank Ernest Hill, and Allan Nevins, *Timber and Men: The Weyerhaeuser Story*, pp. 333, 350; Melvyn Dubofsky, *We Shall Be All: A History of the Industrial Workers of the World*, pp. 349–75; Samuel Trask Dana, *Forest and Range Policy: Its Development in the United States*, pp. 204–205; Raphael Zon to Barrington Moore, March 22,

Raphael Zon, a Russian emigré who had studied forestry under Bernard Fernow at Cornell University, originally entered federal work as an enthusiastic disciple of Gifford Pinchot. His long tenure with the Forest Service paralleled the careers of E. T. Allen, William Greeley, and Wilson Compton. Zon, a social progressive, was often at odds with lumber leaders and even Forest Service workers who seemed overly cooperative and friendly with trade association officials. But, like his contemporaries, he tried to envision the future direction of forestry practices and the institutional needs of the lumber trade in the postwar world. Zon suggested a planning agency to coordinate production allocations with the FTC. He also advised foresters to make greater efforts to limit output, institute compulsory fire protection measures, and place private and national forests on a sustained-yield basis.[13]

While Zon dreamed of a future in which foresters and technicians would manage forestlands through sustained yield, lumber trade leaders had something quite different in mind. Much of the industry's future lay in the restless mind and ambitions of Wilson Compton, a young economist with the FTC. Compton's ideas and strategies have powerfully influenced the policies of organized lumbermen in the twentieth century. His professional career included work as an economist, lawyer, and association executive; when he left the NLMA in 1944, he served as a college president and government administrator. When Compton joined the FTC in 1916, he had just completed a doctoral degree at Princeton University.[14]

The extremely bitter rivalries between producing regions in the prewar period and the generally positive relationship with the federal government during the war led directly to the reorganization of the NLMA in 1918. The revamped structure placed greater authority in a newly created position, the secretary-manager. The association standardized procedures for collecting dues and used its publicity department to promote a more positive image of the industry. Wilson Compton formally assumed the new position of secretary-manager in September, 1918.[15]

1918, box 2, Raphael Zon Papers (hereafter cited as Zon Papers), Minnesota Historical Society, St. Paul, Minnesota.

[13] Harold K. Steen, *The U.S. Forest Service: A History*, pp. 137, 178, 186; Dana, *Forest and Range Policy*, p. 203; Raphael Zon to Burt Kirkland, October 1, 1918, box 2, Zon Papers. For Zon's career, see Norman J. Schmaltz, "Forest Researcher," *Journal of Forest History* 24 (1980): 24–39, 86–97.

[14] "Chronology of Wilson Martindale Compton," Compton Papers; *Who's Who in America* 27 (1952–53): 496.

[15] *Highlights of a Decade of Achievement*, pp. 8–12, 30, 41.

Compton outlined his ideas in an important letter to L. C. Boyle early in 1918. The great task for lumbermen, he said, was to secure a lasting industrial organization that would promote reasonable and balanced competition. Then he hinted at the reason for his service with the FTC.

There you have, in a word, the programme of free and fair business, conservation of natural resources, and industrial prosperity which should be the flesh and blood of the association effort. *To help steer to that accomplishment was the purpose of joining me to the staff of this Commission.* It is still my purpose. Such an achievement is possible in the lumber industry [emphasis added].

Compton told Boyle that lumbermen could achieve rational and efficient operating conditions, but the national association would need " [c]oncentration, coordination and solidarity." Compton stressed that he would not defer to anyone in his knowledge of the methods of trade associations. "The important thing is to get the *big thing* done. Just how is not so vital [italics in original]."[16]

As part of its expanded activities the NLMA appointed a Committee on Governmental Relations, whose purpose was to wield political influence in Congress to promote the passage of beneficial and workable laws. Its chairman, Charles Keith of the Southern Pine Association, recommended the education of lumbermen in the basic economics of the industry, to enable them to intelligently inform congressmen about their difficulties. Wilson Compton suggested that lumbermen use their cooperative experiences with government agencies during the war as a model for building legislative and regulatory policy in the future. Compton promised to use his influence to gain leverage with the government agencies affecting the lumber industry. He also pleaded for "industrial solidarity . . . and reciprocal confidence" to confront "the spread of semi-Bolshevism, and the assertion by organized labor of a position in industry which it is not now either economically or morally capable of occupying."[17]

In the summer of 1918, the Treasury Department charged the Southern Pine Association with profiteering in wartime production. The accusations involved the efforts of the War Industries Board to fix the maximum price for southern pine lumber. The appointment of John H. Kirby, a southern lumberman, to the Materials Committee of the Council of National Defense complicated the government's predicament. Kirby, who was serving

[16] Wilson Compton to L. C. Boyle, February 6, 1918, box 110, NFPA Records.

[17] *Lumber World Review* 35 (August 10, 1918): 34–35; Wilson Compton to John H. Kirby, November 18, 1918, box 110, NFPA Records.

as president of the NLMA, was assigned the task of increasing lumber production in the South and restoring order. Because of the war-related need for southern pine, the government wanted to establish a price level acceptable both to itself and to southern lumber producers. In these complex negotiations, John Kirby occupied an anomalous personal position both as the chairman of the southern pine negotiating team and as an administrator with the Emergency Fleet Corporation. When the government handed down its maximum price list in June, 1918, Kirby warned the government that he could not guarantee compliance in the South because the government had dictated the decision.[18]

Charles Keith, another Southern Pine negotiator, lashed out at rumors accusing lumbermen of excessive profit taking. Comparative price figures for 1916 and 1917 were unreasonable, he said, because the industry was moving out of depression during that period. Furthermore, he charged, the blanket indictment against the entire industry was unfair, designed to mislead and perhaps even injure the public. Wilson Compton insisted that government prices satisfied only a small proportion of the more efficient mills that could afford to sell to the government on close margin.[19]

But the war was an exhilarating experience for most American industries. The mobilization of the war economy after April, 1917, vastly accelerated the formation of trade associations, and the government allowed industrialists to circumvent the Sherman Antitrust Act for the rest of the war. War-related demands for lumber required the federal government to deal through regional bureaus with the many thousands of mills scattered across the country. These agencies, in fact, spoke for regional and specialty trade associations.[20]

After the armistice in Europe, trade leaders from a wide variety of industries sought to relax the antitrust laws as a way to promote business cooperation. The president of the National Association of Manufacturers informed its members that the "march of progress" made revision of the Sherman act necessary. And the Industrial Board in the Department of

[18] Fickle, *The New South*, pp. 87–89.

[19] *Southern Lumberman* 89 (August 31, 1918): 22; "Confidential Memorial and Statement of Facts," prepared by Wilson Compton and filed with the Industrial Board of the Department of Commerce, March 22, 1919, box 110, NFPA Records.

[20] Robert Himmelberg, *The Origins of the National Recovery Administration: Business, Government, and the Trade Association Issue, 1921–1933*, pp. 5–6; "Government Regulation of the Lumber Industry During the War," excerpts from the *War Industries Board Price Bulletin*, no. 43 (1919), box 155, NFPA Records.

Commerce offered to aid industry in circumventing the Sherman act. William Ritter, a former War Industries Board member with large investments in lumber manufacturing, first convinced President Wilson to establish the board. However, when the effort to emasculate antitrust policy collapsed in mid-1919, Wilson abolished the Industrial Board.[21]

At the same time the U.S. Bureau of Internal Revenue backed a legislative effort to establish a policy for valuating timberlands. Once again Wilson Compton, legal counsel L. C. Boyle, and E. T. Allen took the initiative to influence the adoption of a tax policy favorable to the lumber industry. Boyle urged lumbermen to educate themselves about the effect the revenue bill would have on their operations and then to inform their congressmen about the bill. After Congress passed the measure, the Bureau of Internal Revenue asked the industry for help in collecting and digesting information necessary to implement the new law. E. T. Allen told Compton that this "affords the opportunity the National Association has long needed to give a real service and establish itself as recognized expert counsel in forest affairs." This, he said, was "the big chance you have always been looking for." All the association needed was the right person to carry on the investigation for the revenue office. Allen suggested David Mason, an ex–Forest Service employee then teaching in California.[22]

Mason accepted the appointment with the bureau, and, in cooperation with the NLMA, he conducted a series of hearings with regional trade associations. Wilson Compton was pleased that the national association would have an important part in gathering "the basic economic information which is necessary for the fair and intelligent administration of the Revenue laws." Effective cooperation with the government, Compton believed, would secure more support for the annual meeting; a large attendance, in turn, would provide the opportunity to present the matter to those industry leaders who could potentially set policy for the various regional groups.[23] Compton sought the support of the regional associations in an effort to show industrial solidarity at the revenue hearings. This was not the last occasion when the national association tried to forge a collective front at federal hearings.

[21] Himmelberg, *Origins of the National Recovery Administration*, pp. 5–7.

[22] L. C. Boyle to Wilson Compton, October 21, 1918, and E. T. Allen to Compton, March 6, 1919, both in box 110, NFPA Records.

[23] Wilson Compton to E. T. Allen, March 11, 1919, box 110, NFPA Records. The David Mason papers contain two large folders of material collected from the hearings Mason conducted around the country in 1919 (see box 2, David T. Mason papers [hereafter cited as Mason Papers], Oregon Historical Society, Portland, Oregon).

Wilson Compton quickly established himself as an aggressive spokes-man in national lumber affairs, and he continued to build that reputation in helping to resolve demobilization problems. When government agencies tried to dispose of their surplus lumber through ordinary marketing chan-nels, one trade association officer encouraged Compton to contact the proper authorities and "get them to refrain from forcing the lumber on the market." Compton reached a preliminary agreement with one federal agency, which promised to consult lumbermen in determining its disposal policy. Privately, Compton told a correspondent, "The lumber should be disposed of in Europe if possible." [24]

Compton also was praised for his efforts to lessen sectional rivalries, and government agencies continued to ply his office with offers and re-quests for cooperative public and private programs. Compton's open coop-eration and collaboration with government agencies undoubtedly enhanced the influence of the NLMA among most lumbermen. One regional trade manager commended Compton on his broad handling of the national asso-ciation, which meant money to the regional groups. [25]

The restructured NLMA consciously tried to rationalize and synthe-size the industry's operations and, equally important, to integrate real and potential opposition within the broader framework of its political economy. The association's effectiveness in achieving its peculiar brand of legislative and regulatory policy in the 1920s is testimony to a successful public rela-tions program that identified lumber industry needs with the public inter-est. Lumber trade leaders advocated a regulatory policy based on volun-tary initiative and collective action; in this effort they had the support of two vital government agencies, the U.S. Forest Service and the Depart-ment of Commerce.

The more aggressive trade association practices after the First World War revived the old charges of a lumber "trust." In the last months of the Wilson administration, the Department of Justice began an investigation of lumber business activities and requested the FTC to do the same. These investigations perplexed trade association officials, who wanted to achieve the cooperation and agreement necessary to curb the ravages of an unpre-dictable market. Wilson Compton pointed to confusion in the two inves-tigations. The Justice Department, he observed, would not consider itself

[24] W. B. Roper to Wilson Compton, December 21, 1918, and Compton to Roper, De-cember 24, 1918, both in box 110, NFPA Records.

[25] Earle Clapp to Wilson Compton, January 9, 1919, and T. A. McCann to Compton, January 22, 1919, both in box 110, NFPA Records.

"bound or limited" by statements of the FTC; the commission, on the other hand, feared the Justice Department's antitrust probes and would not recommend offering advice to industrial organizations despite their praise-worthy purpose.[26]

Compton was a vigorous proponent of more efficient business and industrial organization. There were no sacred canons in the conduct of capitalist enterprise as long as the hegemony of the dominant groups prevailed. Therefore, to cope with excess competition and unstable markets, he suggested abolishing "the now obsolescent theory that in the enforcement of unhampered and unrestrained competition lies the only sure security of the public against exploitation." Wilson Compton—lawyer, trade association executive, and exponent of progressive capitalism—observed that material conditions would determine the future course of events. "In the end the right always triumphs. Public understandings of the facts and needs of the industry can not be permanently withheld. Economic laws in the long run will overwhelm legislation set up in defiance of them."[27] But the lumber industry's inability to resolve its persistent bout with over-production sorely tested Compton's optimism for effective trade association accomplishment.

When rumors of the FTC investigation began to circulate, John Kirby, president of the NLMA, urged all lumber trade groups to keep clear of "entangling alliances" with retail organizations, because their practices were not well known. Wilson Compton was equally confident that the national association had nothing to fear from the investigation, except for the inconvenience of interfering with regular procedure. The antitrust investigation would provide an opportunity for the commission to state openly that NLMA activities were well within the law."[28]

When the Department of Justice formally requested the FTC to investigate the lumber industry, the move stirred up a hornets' nest of legal action, innuendo, accusation, and counteraccusation. The commission's report, delivered to Congress in January, 1921, covered the actions of the NLMA and several of its regional affiliates.[29]

[26] Himmelberg, *Origins of the National Recovery Administration*, pp. 7–16; Wilson Compton to E. W. McCullough, September 5, 1919, box 110, NFPA Records.

[27] Wilson Compton, "Trade Association Activities in Relation to the Law," box 155, NFPA Records.

[28] John Kirby to Charles Keith, May 22, 1919, and Wilson Compton to Kirby, December 5, 1919, both in box 110, NFPA Records.

[29] Ralph C. Bryant, *Lumber: Its Manufacture and Distribution*, p. 335; *Southern Lumberman* 83 (February 3, 1917): 20.

The Justice Department used the report to initiate cases against suspected illegal trade—the most important of these was a suit against the American Hardwood Manufacturers Association for its "Open Competition Plan." The hardwood scheme, begun in 1917, was designed to "disseminate among the members of the association accurate knowledge of production and market conditions so that each member may gauge the market intelligently instead of guessing at it." According to the *Southern Lumberman*, the plan was strictly legal and required only cooperation to make it work. The Justice Department also began action against the Southern Pine Association in 1921 for acting illegally in restraint of trade. The hardwood case eventually wound up in the Supreme Court, but the southern pine issue dragged on for a few years and finally was dropped.[30]

The antitrust prosecutions caused ripples of distrust and suspicion among lumber industry leaders. But the national association remained clear of legal snarls and extended litigation, largely through Wilson Compton's genius and diplomacy. At one point, Robert Allen, the manager of the West Coast Lumbermen's Association, asked Compton for a legal opinion concerning basic prices: "Is it legal to publish such a list?" Compton's reply was a classic of reason, diplomacy, and guile. The essential question, he insisted, was not the publication of such a price list, but rather how it was used. To avoid potential legal difficulties and public questioning, Compton recommended that the price lists be published by someone outside the association. In this way the association could circumvent "the more or less unsettled state of the public mind."[31]

Although the Wilson administration began the lumber industry investigation, the Justice Department did not prosecute the Hardwood Association until the presidency of Warren Harding. And even then a Supreme Court decision merely confused the legal situation for most trade associations. During this period the FTC published its report on lumber trade associations, which found the industry working in collusion and cooperation with the Forest Service to regulate and control production. The Forest Service, the report charged, had recommended congressional approval to withdraw national forest timber from the market, permission to limit lumber production, the right of the industry to establish cooperative sales agencies, and the freedom to make price agreements. The investigation

[30] *Southern Lumberman* 83 (February 3, 1917): 20; Bryant, *Lumber: Its Manufacture and Distribution*, pp. 342–43.

[31] Robert B. Allen to Wilson Compton, September 18, 1919, and Compton to Allen, September 23, 1919, both in box 110, NFPA Records.

revealed that lumbermen had sought advice from the FTC in 1915 concerning legally acceptable procedures to limit supply, prevent overproduction, and maintain prices.[32]

The FTC report singled out the Southern Pine Association and the West Coast Lumbermen's Association for acting in collusion to avoid competition in common market areas. The commission also censured the Southern Pine Association for using a trade barometer to inform members when to restrict production and increase prices. Southern trade journals, the study charged, had published editorials urging members to regulate production according to the predictions of the trade barometer. The commission concluded that lumber manufacturers joined trade associations to "restrict the supply and at the same time to enlarge the demand." The organizational genius behind this grand design was the NLMA, which coordinated the activities of the entire industry.[33]

The *West Coast Lumberman* angrily charged the FTC with using the same old tactics to attack business. Trade associations did circulate statistical information, the journal noted, but the information had very little influence on the market. "The only thing which made the price of lumber was the demand, and the thing which has caused the decline is the lack of demand." The trade paper concluded that members of the FTC "are not business men. They do not understand natural economic laws."[34]

In his annual report to the NLMA, Wilson Compton referred to the commission's antitrust attack as a charade. "The lumber industry," he said, "has a long way to go before it reaches that . . . perfection of sawmill efficiency . . . which even its fondest critics and censors assert it has already gained." A year later Compton complained that unfettered competition was the lumber manufacturer's greatest weakness and was chiefly responsible for his inability to maintain a balance between supply and demand.[35] The annual reports of the NLMA regularly expressed this dissatisfaction.

[32] Himmelberg, *Origins of the National Recovery Administration*, pp. 7–8; *Report on Lumber Manufacturers Trade Associations*, pp. 2, 44. The NLMA began publishing its weekly *Lumber Trade Barometer* in September, 1916. The *Barometer* incorporated statistics from the large regional associations—the Southern Pine Association, the West Coast Lumbermen's Association, and the Western Pine Association (see *Highlights of a Decade of Achievement*, p. 16).

[33] *Report on Lumber Manufacturers Trade Associations*, pp. 45, 57–59, 65, 71, 73.

[34] *West Coast Lumberman* 39 (March, 1921): 19.

[35] Wilson Compton, "National Lumber Problems and Prospects," in NLMA, *Annual Report* (1923): 4; Compton, "Will the Lumber Manufacturers Stand Up and Be Counted," NLMA, *Annual Report* (1924): 7.

Thus, at the outset of the Republican era, a decade historians characterize as an age of business hegemony in government, the trade association world was in turmoil. Federal policy seemed to equivocate between efforts to restore a Jeffersonian world of a freely competing market economy and the modernist argument that competition was disruptive to a stable economic order. Lumber association executives who favored rational and efficient operating procedures believed that a willful and sometimes malicious government was its greatest enemy. Some trade officials—Compton among them—blamed the federal government's enforcement of the antitrust laws for many of their difficulties. This conviction persisted through the 1920s, reached a fever pitch during the early years of the Great Depression, and remained a controversial issue after the death of the National Recovery Administration. According to Ralph C. Bryant, an early student of the lumber trust dispute, ideas about ethical business conduct were changing, but practice still lagged behind theory. Wilson Compton and other trade leaders used that argument when they asked Congress to adjust its policy toward industrial cooperation in accord with modern business conditions. But other forces were more important in the failure to control market activity—mutual suspicion, fear of losing control through corporate merger, and the lumber manufacturers' persisting desire to undercut and destroy the competition.[36]

[36] Bryant, *Lumber: Its Manufacture and Distribution*, p. 345. The Mason Papers contain an impressive collection of correspondence on attempted mergers and consolidations in the late 1920s and the early 1930s in the Douglas fir region.

5

Hegemony over National Forest Policy

"There are few problems before the country today that so sharply
concern the welfare of the whole people, as does that of a definite,
practicable and comprehensive forestry policy that will provide
replacement, year by year, of timber cut or otherwise
removed." —*Lumber* 64 (1919)

THE presence of the national government loomed large in the lumber industry's postwar plans. Trade representatives sought legislative support for
fire protection, reforestation, forest improvement, tax reform, accelerated
federal purchase of cutover lands, and increased financial aid for research.
Washington, D.C., seemed the place to turn for those who wanted to effect
a more stable, orderly, and rational economic environment. This effort,
which aimed to promote a national forestry policy and yet avoid government control of private timberlands, was broad ranging. The initiatives of
organized lumbermen are evident in congressional testimony, in professional publications like the *Journal of Forestry*, in the activities of trade
associations, and in an industry-oriented political action group, the National Forestry Program Committee (NFPC).

Both William Greeley and Wilson Compton played significant roles in
the legislative debates on forestry policy of the 1920s. Their "expert"
opinions stimulated thinking about the need and direction of a national forest policy, and their numerous publications forced trade leaders to consider
a variety of regulatory and legislative solutions to the industry's chronic
economic problems. Finally, the war experience itself convinced a small
group of sophisticated trade leaders and professional foresters to seek federal help.

Wilson Compton recognized the need for a "systematic national forest policy" well before his appointment with the National Lumber Manufacturers Association (NLMA). Others soon joined the cause. Austin
Cary, a professional forestry consultant with close ties to the industry, set

the tone for the discussion in a 1917 article in the *Journal of Forestry*. Cary concluded that "economic forces" had served the country well and that the productive energy of the lumber industry had been beneficial. Moreover, he observed, economic conditions in the United States would determine future forestry practices, and these techniques would be implemented through cooperation and not by government regulation.[1]

Cary believed that lumber operators would cooperate to promote better forestry practices, and he noted in a letter to Raphael Zon that Chief Forester Henry Graves supported the industry's effort. Zon disagreed and warned Cary that "private owners . . . must subordinate more and more individual interests to the general public good." Since Cary had the confidence of lumbermen, Zon advised that he urge them to mend their ways before increasing public pressures forced some form of strict public control. The critical issue to Zon was industrial stability and the need to create "permanent community settlements." To accomplish these ends, "sustained yield" practices must be implemented.[2]

But Raphael Zon's views did not represent those who were in positions to influence forestry policy. Burt Kirkland, in the forestry school at the University of Washington, encouraged an expanded government role in research, federal support to aid lumbermen in meeting exorbitant interest charges, and a similar subsidy to states and corporations to promote forest management. But any program to promote the practice of forestry, he cautioned, must avoid extending government activities in the manner most often suggested. He likened most government programs to "a new imperialism."[3] Kirkland's notion of beneficent government support for research and fire protection gained increasing credibility in the next few years. His proposals included financial assistance for forest management, but avoided what lumbermen termed "grinding federal restrictions."

The variety of national forestry policy proposals promised relief from the menace of fire, from heavy timberland taxes, and assistance for carry-

[1] Wilson Compton, "The Price Problem in the Lumber Industry," *American Economic Review* 7: 597; Austin Cary, "How Lumbermen in Following Their Own Interest Have Served the Public," *Journal of Forestry* 15 (March, 1917): 279–85. For an account of federal regulation of private timberland, see Lawrence Hamilton, "The Federal Forest Regulation Issue," *Journal of Forest History* 9 (April, 1965): 2–11.

[2] Austin Cary to Raphael Zon (August 29, 1917), Zon to Cary (September 1, 1917), and Zon to Roy Headley (December 7, 1917), all from box 2, Raphael Zon Papers (hereafter cited as Zon Papers), Minnesota Historical Society, St. Paul, Minnesota.

[3] Burt Kirkland to Raphael Zon, November 12, 1918, box 2, Zon Papers.

ing cutover lands. The rapid liquidation of forested stands in the South had left huge areas of wasted land; therefore, southern operators who owned these acreages formed land associations to advertise the denuded timberlands for use as farmland. Although the cutover land groups did not encourage federal acquisition of these acreages, they did recommend reforesting lands not suitable for farming.[4]

But by the end of the First World War, southerners promoted federal purchase of cutover lands and the creation of new national forests. John Kirby, president of the NLMA, advised a group of lumbermen that the appalling rate of timber cutting in the South required a national forest policy based on federal purchase and reforestation. Charles Keith, head of the Southern Pine Association, urged operators to formulate a national program of action to ensure reforestation. And in 1920 A. L. Clark, another president of the Southern Pine Association, recommended that nonresident owners of cutover land be granted federal assistance to reforest their lands. The "real comprehensive reforesting must be undertaken by the government, [which] . . . should acquire the large areas of cutover lands suitable for this purpose." These pleas for a national policy of reforestation show the irony of the states rights' doctrine in the face of compelling economic argument.[5]

Trade journals soon joined the chorus. *Lumber* called for the adoption of "a practical program of reforestation of areas, denuded either by the saw or by fire." Because it took time to grow new forests, the journal reasoned, the federal government must assume much of the responsibility of reforestation. A national forestry program was necessary, it argued, because America's prosperity depended on implementing this policy. Since lumbermen had a large stake in the matter and were closest to the problem, they were in the best position to effectively help solve it. The *Lumber* editor insisted that public and private interests were similar. "Owners of timber are custodians of the public interest—they should have an active interest in its wise solution."[6]

While lumber trade spokesmen articulated the prerequisites for a national forest policy, professional foresters carried on a hotly contested de-

[4] *Southern Lumberman* 84 (June 30, 1917): 20; "Editorial: Cut-Over Lands a National Problem," *American Forests* 23 (May, 1917): 304–305.

[5] *Timberman* 19 (August, 1918): 27–28; *Southern Lumberman* 95 (March 20, 1920): 33; *Timberman* 21 (April, 1920): 29.

[6] *Lumber* 64 (October 27, 1919): 43.

bate through the Society of American Foresters and its publication, the *Journal of Forestry*. Chief Forester Henry Graves served notice in 1919 that the public interest in forestry matters went far beyond the policies of the U.S. Forest Service. He warned that "the most difficult problem, that of the protection and the right handling of forests privately owned, is still before us." Graves noted that private timberlands produced 97 percent of the lumber manufactured in the United States; therefore, the nation should be aware that its sources of timber are greatly diminished, with grave financial consequences.[7]

Graves, whom Burt Kirkland described as "a weak and timid executive," did not believe that the situation would be corrected without widespread implementation of new and upgraded forestry and radical changes in the attitudes and methods of most timberland owners. Graves encouraged the public, "in a liberal spirit," to provide financial support for the practice of forestry and called for a change in the outlook and methods of timber owners.[8] Graves's argument appealed to progressive trade association leaders who sought programs and policies to resolve the industry's economic plight. Despite price increases, people close to the lumber business knew that the old problems had not disappeared—the speculative character of ownership, pressures to liquidate, excess mill capacity, and the lack of business cooperation. The big question concerned the appropriate resolution of these difficulties.

Royal S. Kellogg initiated a dialogue in *American Forests* on the Graves plan. Kellogg, the principal organizer of the NFPC, thought it was impractical and inexpedient to require the practice of forestry on private lands; it would prove unconstitutional and, because it was coercive, would "alienate and render hostile a large proportion of the timberland owners." He proposed that the state or federal government should assume responsibilities for reforestation, because such responsibilities were not attractive to private capital. Kellogg then outlined a four-point program that anticipated federal legislative policy for the 1920s: a timber census to determine present and future supplies, enlargement of cutover land purchases, increased federal cooperation in fire protection, and government purchase of more western timberland.[9]

---

[7] Henry Graves, "Private Forestry," *Journal of Forestry* 17 (February, 1919): 113.

[8] Kirkland to Zon, Zon Papers; Graves, "Private Forestry," pp. 118–19.

[9] Royal S. Kellogg, "A Discussion of Methods," *American Forests* 25 (August, 1919): 1282–83.

Wilson Compton, who worked closely with Kellogg and the NFPC, also favored a national plan for forest use and a program to adequately restock timberlands. However, this approach reflected the problem, not its solution. He ridiculed the faddist proposals of those whose attachment to the industry was transitory and "whose concepts of forest economics are apparently quite unsoiled by contact with the facts of industry." Describing himself as "a plain citizen," Compton argued that the need to provide for a permanent timber supply was "a problem of economics," in which the experience of business leadership must prevail. Compton then outlined in "Fourteen Points" a militant defense of industry practice. The lumberman's sole obligation to the public was to make and sell boards; therefore, any scheme to assure future timber supplies should be the responsibility of those who would benefit the most. The march of industrial progress, Compton observed, must be recognized. "Economic forces which rule all productive activities will overwhelm a forest policy set up in defiance of them."[10]

The lumber industry's national forest policy hinged upon several prerequisites. These included a survey of existing timber stands in the United States, federal and state purchase programs, reforestation of cutover lands, reasonable tax legislation, and federal support for states in fire protection. Lumbermen also recommended the purchase of more standing timber and its addition to the national forests. But the most notable refrain in the lumbermen's argument was the staunch opposition to federal control of forest practices on private timberland. There were no concessions on this point until the demoralized and desperate conditions of the 1930s, and even then the industry was divided on the issue.

But the debate in 1919 and 1920 aroused a storm of controversy. The Society of American Foresters conducted an open discussion of the issues, and individuals with traditional interests in conservation clashed both with lumbermen and with congressional spokesmen. The controversy embraced federal versus state regulation of forestry practices, the accelerated public acquisition of private forestland, greater state and federal cooperation in fire protection, a more equitable timber tax policy, and an increase in federal appropriations for research.[11] The most heated arguments concerned

[10]Wilson Compton, "Forest Economics: Some Thoughts on an Old Subject," *American Forests* 25 (September, 1919): 1337–39.

[11]Lawrence Hamilton, "The Federal Forest Regulation Issue," *Journal of Forest History* 9 (April, 1965): 4–6.

the role of the federal government and the states as regulatory agencies and whether regulation should be mandatory or voluntary and cooperative.

The *Journal of Forestry* published the arguments of the two leaders who emerged as rallying points for the different proposals—the ex-chief forester and aspiring politician, Gifford Pinchot, and the man who became chief forester in 1920, William B. Greeley. Pinchot was convinced that lumbermen had not taken the steps necessary "to ensure their own perpetuation, have made no effort to put an end to forest devastation, and have persistently avoided all responsibility for maintaining a dependable supply of forest products." At the same time, however, he recognized that forestry issues required basic changes in the economic makeup of the lumber business. Pinchot's plan included the mandatory regulation of cutting practices on private timberland. The issue was clear—timber operators could not be expected to change; therefore, "the field is cleared for action and the lines are plainly drawn. He who is not for forestry is against it. The choice lies between the convenience of the lumbermen and the public good." Henry Graves, who suspected Raphael Zon's influence behind Pinchot's statement, said the plan had overtones of socialism. And Zon, editor of the *Journal of Forestry*, predicted that with the publication of the Pinchot article, "the feathers will begin to fly."[12]

Because of his sympathy for the difficulties of the lumber industry, William Greeley emerged as its principal spokesman. The industry's problems, he repeated, could be resolved only through cooperative and collective action between the federal government and the private sector. In later years Greeley recalled that he came to like and understand "these plain-speaking, direct-acting lumbermen. It was not all beer and skittles," he noted. "The mills seemed to be shouldering far too heavy a load of timber investment and carrying costs. Both the forests and the industry appeared to be caught in the gears of highly competitive, ruthless economics."[13]

Greeley juxtaposed the two opposing views on forest policy: growing trees by regimentation and by free enterprise. Pinchot's plan for mandatory federal control, he said, was wrong-headed. Moreover, it was unconstitu-

[12] Pinchot's arguments are outlined in a committee report of the Society of American Foresters, "Forest Devastation: A National Danger and a Plan to Meet It," *Journal of Forestry* 17 (December, 1919): 900, 911–12, 936–39. Graves is quoted in Harold K. Steen, *U.S. Forest Service: A History*, p. 178. Zon's quote is from a letter, Raphael Zon to Earle Clapp, November 4, 1919, box 2, Zon Papers.

[13] William B. Greeley, *Some Public and Economic Aspects of the Lumber Industry*, pp. 99–100; Greeley, *Forests and Men*, p. 76.

tional, because it imposed federal control over jurisdictions belonging to the states. "In principle," Greeley declared, "I am opposed to public control of forest industries beyond the minimum requirements essential to stop devastation." In his first report as chief forester, Greeley argued that a national forest policy should use the police powers of the state in cooperation with federal leadership. But he advised timberland owners to cooperate with government agencies to prevent forest devastation.[14]

So the industry moved into action. Fearful that advocates of public regulation would gain the upper hand, the NLMA went on record in October, 1919, in favor of a comprehensive forest policy. The association declared its full support for the perpetuation of timber supplies and practical forestry and recognized the need for an American forest policy that was an intelligent, practical, equitable, and concerted effort to perpetuate forest supplies. John H. Kirby recommended that a national program should be channeled through the states as an exercise of their police powers and that federal control should be resisted. "I am not in favor of extending Washington's authority over anything that belongs to the states."[15]

The NLMA later appointed a "forestry committee," which made it clear that the industry would support any reasonable program of federal assistance and that it would vigorously oppose any form of government control. The committee's proposals included more liberal congressional appropriations for fire protection, accelerated federal purchase of cutover areas, timber tax reform, and increased appropriations for Forest Service research. The national association's board of directors resolved that an effective national program "means confidence and security in every legal and commercial phase, to industry and public alike."[16]

Trade officials worked on many fronts to lay the groundwork for a national forest policy acceptable to organized lumbermen. A delegation from the NLMA visited President-elect Harding to impress on the new chief executive the merits of the industry's legislative program. According to E. T. Allen, Pinchot "had been pestering him [Harding] with crank theories but he would take his dope from people who really dealt with forests." Allen, who worked as an adviser to the national association, considered the congressional campaign the most important, because the industry must insist

[14] Greeley, *Forests and Men*, p. 101; Greeley, "Self-Government in Forestry," *Journal of Forestry* 18 (February, 1920): 103–105; U.S. Forest Service, *Annual Report* (1920): 1.

[15] *Lumber* 64 (November 3, 1919): 33, 53.

[16] *American Lumberman* (July 17, 1920): 69.

that national legislation should not include regulatory features that would introduce fatal complications. Allen disapproved of the "extreme Pinchot doctrines" and called for harmony and cooperation as the proper approach to any federal program.[17]

The forest policy recommendations of the NLMA enjoyed broad support in the industry. A. L. Osborne, a Wisconsin operator and a member of the national association's forestry committee, told a southern trade meeting that lumbermen supported reforestation carried out in a sane, practical, and helpful manner. Moreover, federal measures must be in the public interest. After this generous bow to public relations, Osborne identified the kind of policy he had in mind. "Whoever may engage in the propagation or preservation of forest growth should have reasonable assurance that the time, labor and invested capital may not be used to better advantage." The only touchstone for public or private forest conservation was its profitability.[18]

Because of the tempest brewing in forestry and lumber circles and the concern of conservationists for the diminishing stands of timber, Senator Arthur Capper of Kansas introduced a resolution directing the Department of Agriculture to conduct a study of all forestry-related issues. The resulting Capper Report, a Forest Service undertaking, indicated that timber depletion contributed heavily to current high lumber prices, along with heavy demand and transportation costs. But the substance of the report was optimistic. The sad picture of excess mill capacity, large bonded indebtedness, and weak financial structure sketched in the 1917 investigation had given way to a lumber economy "more closely knit through the development of regional associations and other cooperative measures." Moreover, over the past four years many conditions that had earlier promoted excessive competition had been eliminated. Lumber trade associations appeared to be moving beyond the time when extreme competition was forced upon many as an inescapable financial reality.[19]

The Capper Report recommended that federal and state agencies and

---

[17] E. T. Allen to R. S. Kellogg, January 10, 1921, Allen to William B. Greeley, September 16, 1920, and Allen to Harris Reynolds, September 25 and 28, 1920, all from box 1, National Forestry Program Committee Records (hereafter cited as NFPC Records), Cornell University Libraries, Ithaca, New York.

[18] *Southern Lumberman* 97 (July 31, 1920): 39–40.

[19] U.S. Forest Service, *Timber Depletion, Lumber Prices, Lumber Exports, and Concentration of Timber Ownership*, Report on Senate Resolution 311 (1920): 56, 64–65.

private institutions cooperate to resolve the problem of timber depletion (Greeley's influence was apparent in the emphasis on cooperation). The study noted that change "cannot be attained if timber production is left to the initiative of the private owner . . . or is sought solely through the compulsory regulation of private lands." The public, it stated, should share part of the burden. The report listed six legislative proposals: (1) cooperation with the states in fire protection, (2) the extension of federal forest holdings, (3) the reforestation of denuded land, (4) a study of forest taxation, (5) a survey of forest resources, and (6) larger appropriations for forest research.[20]

The recommendations in the Capper Report proved attractive to lumbermen, especially when the industry returned to its prewar pattern of glutted markets and overcompetition in late 1920. The *West Coast Lumberman* reported in December, 1920, that the lumber and shingle market was "just about as dull as it could be."[21] Under these circumstances, some lumbermen believed the implementation of the Capper Report might offer relief. Tax reform, federal aid for fire control, a survey of timber resources, and an expanded forestry research program would rationalize and make more predictable the conduct of the lumber business. Furthermore, an expanded federal forest system would limit competitors and make it easier to withhold timber from the market during periods of overproduction (the latter was a long-standing policy of the Forest Service).

Lumber trade leaders made a concerted effort to translate these proposals into law, but there were challenges. Senator Arthur Capper introduced a bill drafted by Gifford Pinchot calling for mandatory federal regulaton of private timberland. The bill ignored the recommendations of the report that bore Capper's name. The industry's counterpose was Congressman Bertrand Snell's measure, which called for state regulation of private timberland and the implementation of the Capper Report.[22]

In nearly three years of congressional hearings concerning the various

[20] Ibid., pp. 69–70.

[21] *West Coast Lumberman* 39 (December, 1920): 19. David Mason observed in 1920 that when the industry was in deep depression in 1915, timber owners showed little interest in conservation. But due to improved market conditions early in 1920, there was an inclination to view the growing of timber as a permanent business (Mason, *Timber Ownership and Lumber Production in the Inland Empire*, pp. 7–8).

[22] Hamilton, "The Federal Forest Regulation Issue," pp. 5, 7; E. T. Allen, *The Leading Forest Policy Proposals* (Chicago: NLMA, 1920), copy in box 153, National Forest Products Association Records, Forest History Society, Santa Cruz, California.

Snell legislative proposals, the lumber industry effectively flexed its power and influence—testimony to the growing hegemony of the trade association movement in public policy. The story is one of coordination between the lumber industry and the Forest Service, cooperation with the Harding and Coolidge administrations, and a political atmosphere conducive to the predominance of business in government. Lumbermen and their friends in the Forest Service and elsewhere pushed their cause with great vigor, but in every instance trade leaders provided the initiative and effective force guiding the success or failure of congressional legislation.

To push their program association officials organized a political action group, the NFPC, in December, 1920. The committee, which originated in the American Paper and Pulp Association's Committee on Forest Conservation, acted as the legislative lobby for the lumber industry. Royal S. Kellogg, now with the American Paper and Pulp Association, served as chairman of the NFPC during the critical period leading up to the passage of the Clarke-McNary Act in 1924. Those active in the committee's work included representatives from major lumber groups, members of professional organizations, and government employees. The committee lobbied for federal fire protection support and opposed national regulation. Important contributors to its work included the NLMA, the National Wholesale Lumber Dealers Association, the American Forestry Association, the U.S. Chamber of Commerce, and the Forest Service. Through the committee's effort, the industry's viewpoint prevailed in congressional hearings, dominated discussions at professional meetings, and monopolized the subject matter in trade journals.[23]

Royal Kellogg kept the lobby together. When Congress took up discussion of a national forestry program, Kellogg, E. T. Allen, Wilson Compton, and William Greeley coordinated strategy to assure that the legislative program would be acceptable to lumbermen. Although four years passed between the introduction of the first congressional bills and the passage of Clarke-McNary, trade leaders worked hard to discredit public regulation. Kellogg and Allen courted Greeley's support with great skill, arranged speaking schedules, directed discussion at congressional hearings, and kept up a stream of propaganda emphasizing the lumberman's viewpoint. Allen insisted early in the campaign that Greeley "must be given much consideration in all the planning, for more and more it is becoming a

---

[23] Ralph S. Hosmer, "The National Forestry Program Committee," *Journal of Forestry* 45 (September, 1947): 629–30. This is the best account of the committee's work.

battle between him and G. P., which is correct strategy but entitles him to strong voice in the generalship." Although Greeley occasionally wavered on technicalities, he remained the industry's most important expert witness.[24]

The NFPC assumed direct responsibility for the various forestry bills before Congress. Through trade associations and friendly trade journals and professional groups, the national committee conducted a persuasive and ultimately successful campaign. Lumber spokesmen, who had insisted for nearly twenty years that economic difficulties inhibited forestry practices, used this argument as a propaganda tool in front of congressional committees and in their public statements. The NLMA insisted that the practice of forestry would be possible only if the federal government pursued "constructive economic principles." And Forest Service officials stressed the close ties between conservation and the stability of the lumber market. The substance of these discussions had changed little between 1910 and 1920, a tribute both to the lumbermen's perception of their world and to the effective public relations work of the NFPC.[25]

Trade journals kept lumbermen informed about the forestry proposals and castigated the Pinchot program because it required federal regulation. "The country is moving toward a constructive, conservative, well-considered forest policy," claimed the *American Lumberman*. "That policy will be shaped by practical men, not by visionary theorists." The Capper plan was believed to represent radical and extreme ideas. The *Timberman* predicted that the Capper bill would bring together the forces backing the Snell bill and ensure its passage. The "untiring efforts of the agitators of forestry reform" were behind the Capper bill, according to the *Southern Lumberman*. The *West Coast Lumberman* added that it opposed federal programs that required "cutting regulations and other more or less theoretical forestry matters."[26]

E. T. Allen called the Pinchot program the work of a "lunatic fringe" of agitators out to reap political capital and charged that Senator Capper

---

[24] E. T. Allen to R. S. Kellogg, June 1, 1921, box 1, NFPC Records. For Greeley's sometimes equivocal attitude, see Allen to William B. Greeley, November 14, 1921 (two letters), and Kellogg to Allen, November 21, 1921, all in box 1, NFPC Records. See also Steen, *U.S. Forest Service*, p. 186.

[25] NLMA, *Annual Report* (1912): 116, and (1913): 123–24.

[26] *American Lumberman* (October 23, 1920): 45, and (May 29, 1920): 47; *Timberman* 22 (May, 1921): 29; *Southern Lumberman* 99 (May 21, 1921): 40; *West Coast Lumberman* 39 (December, 1920): 19.

practically repudiated the report that carried his name when Capper forwarded the Pinchot proposal. Allen believed the alternative proposals before Congress were "distinct and crystallized": either federal regulation or federal support for local solutions, without a third option. He urged Congress to implement the Forest Service recommendations in the Capper Report.[27]

The persuasive comments of four individuals, E. T. Allen, David T. Mason, Wilson Compton, and William Greeley, dominated the federal forest policy debate. They testified at congressional hearings, addressed trade association meetings, and wrote articles for professional and trade journals. Allen represented the Western Forestry and Conservation Association and the NLMA and was a member of the NFPC. David Mason, increasingly recognized as an expert witness on national forestry matters, emphasized (like Allen and Greeley) federal cooperation and industrial self-regulation. These three men and Wilson Compton argued that lumbermen would adopt conservation practices when it proved economically feasible to do so.

Fortunately for organized lumbermen, Chief Forester William Greeley spoke at each of the congressional hearings in support of the industry's legislative program. He served as a special consultant to the respective congressional committees and was the author of the first Snell bill. The *Timberman* said of the chief forester, "The real soul of the industry is with him." Greeley advised a program that placed a premium on federal, state, and private cooperation; his first priority was a system of fire protection whose costs would be shared between the public and the private owner and implemented through the police powers of the state. On occasion, however, Greeley was capable of misstatement. When he testified in favor of the Snell bill early in 1922, he told a House committee that the Forest Service had drawn up a program for forestry, "not knowing who would support it or who would oppose it."[28] Greeley's previous career with the Forest Service shows that he consistently supported the viewpoint of progressive lumbermen.

---

[27] Allen, *Leading Forest Policy Proposals*, p. 3; E. T. Allen to Editors of Lumber Trade Journals, June 12, 1920, and Allen, "The Federal Forest Legislation," undated manuscript, both in box 5, Western Forestry and Conservation Association Records (hereafter cited as WFCA Records), Oregon Historical Society, Portland, Oregon.

[28] *Timberman* 24 (December, 1922): 26; U.S. Congress, House, *Forestry: Hearings Before the Committee on Agriculture*, 66th Cong., 3rd sess., January 26, 1921, pp. 32–33, 34.

Greeley also supported a plan of reforestation, expansion of national forests, and an equitable method of timberland taxation. The latter, he believed, was a prerequisite to reforestation. "The growing of timber is an economic process and timber can not be produced unless it is practicable and reasonable . . . for the owners of the land." But the prevention of forest fires outweighed all other considerations.[29]

E. T. Allen told the same House committee that private lumbermen wholeheartedly supported the Snell bill. A successful forest policy, he said, "must be based . . . upon the requirements of production." Allen opposed compulsory reforestation and argued that the Snell bill would inaugurate intelligent forest policy through the agencies of state governments. Like Greeley, he insisted that "the fire problem—keeping the stuff growing that is there now—is more urgent" than any other issue. Moreover, fire protection was in the public interest.[30]

While Congress dallied on the Snell legislation, friends of the bill urged support for cooperation and state control and condemned the Pinchot program of mandatory federal controls. Royal Kellogg remarked that Congress should reject all "purely theoretical courses without consideration of practical conditions." No forest plan would be successful, he claimed, that alienated the owners of the land designated for forestry practices. The American Forestry Association discredited the Pinchot plan in favor of a program of federal, state, and private cooperation. The public, it contended, needed to provide more equitable taxation, because a reduced tax burden would make it economically feasible to grow young timber. The organization also recommended public support for fire protection, federal purchase of denuded land, and improved forest research programs.[31]

David Mason published a study at the onset of the debate on national forestry policy, which found that instability was due to the pressure to liquidate stumpage investment to cover taxes, debts, fire protection, and timber administration. These economic tendencies increased competition and destroyed efforts to cooperate. "Stability in the lumber industry must be the starting point for clean use and systematic renewal of its forests."

[29] House, *Forestry: Hearings Before the Committee on Agriculture*, 67th Cong., 2d sess., January 9, 1922, pp. 9–21.

[30] House, *Forestry*, 66th Cong., 3rd sess., January 27, 1921, pp. 14–21, and 67th Cong., 2d sess., January 12, 1922, pp. 247–51.

[31] See Kellogg's comment on the Pinchot plan in the *Journal of Forestry* 18 (February, 1920): 113. The forestry association's statement is found in *American Forests* 26 (February, 1920): 67.

Mason suggested an accelerated public acquisition of timberland to lessen the need for private owners to cut regardless of market conditions. In a separate article, Mason warned that individual integrity and initiative should not be sacrificed for a bureaucracy. Cooperation, he advised, was the proper way to good forestry practice.[32]

To gain support for the Snell legislation, the NFPC published a series of pamphlets beginning in 1921. In addition, E. T. Allen busied himself coordinating strategy with regional trade associations, Greeley continued to advise the committee on appropriate tactics, and Kellogg sent out memos from his office in New York. By late 1921 the members and supporters of the Program Committee had carried on an extensive correspondence on national forestry matters. The confidential exchange reveals a general agreement on tactics and legislative policy. One of the chief obstacles at this point was the friendship between Secretary of Agriculture Henry C. Wallace and Gifford Pinchot and the reluctance of the former to support legislation that Pinchot opposed. Wilson Compton also reported to Kellogg that several "Southern Pine" lumbermen wanted greater assurance that an owner's use of his timberland would not be tampered with.[33]

But Gifford Pinchot was the most important opponent of the Snell legislative program. He wrote articles for professional forestry magazines and progressive journals and led the opposition to the Snell bill during its first congressional hearings. Finally, even Pinchot's considerable influence was diminished when he became increasingly involved in Pennsylvania's gubernatorial politics. However, his testimony in 1921 and his influence in conservation circles helped to block passage of the initial Snell bill.[34]

[32] Mason, *Timber Ownership and Lumber Production* pp. 12–14. See Mason's comment on the Pinchot proposal in *Journal of Forestry* 18 (February, 1920): 234.

[33] Hosmer, "The National Forestry Program Committee," p. 632; R. S. Kellogg to Mrs. Joseph R. Long, April 26, 1921, Allen to Kellogg, June 1, 1921, William E. Greeley to Kellogg, June 1, 1921, Kellogg to Allen, November 21, 1921, and Wilson Compton to Kellogg, November 16, 1921, all in box 1, NFPC Records.

[34] M. Nelson McGeary, *Gifford Pinchot: Forester*, pp. 273–85; Steen, *U.S. Forest Service*, p. 185. Steen indicates that lumbermen were divided widely over the issue of regulation, even the mild form of state regulation hinted in the Snell proposal. However, the industry was in general agreement on other fundamentals of the federal program: the subsidy for fire protection, tax reform, increased appropriations for research, and an accelerated program of federal acquisition. One recent scholar suggests that "legislators realized fully that the patient was sick, but when the 'doctors' could not agree over a remedy, the lawmakers refused to issue a prescription" (Hamilton, "The Federal Forest Regulation Issue," p. 8).

Pinchot provoked controversy when he told a House committee that the forestry issue was a matter of greater concern to the importing than to the exporting states. Congress, he said, should consider forest devastation a more important issue than the fire problem, and he accused lumbermen of being interested in fire protection only "to protect merchantable timber on their own land until it can be cut." Pinchot warned Congress that the Snell legislation would place control with state legislatures where lumbermen reigned supreme. This was the "nub of the matter." The regulation of forestry practices by the states, he said, left matters in the hands of the legislatures of Oregon, Washington, and California.[35]

George S. Long, who testified to the House committee on behalf of the NLMA, praised the work of the Forest Service, which, he said, had greatly benefited the lumber industry. Long repeated the lumbermen's admonition that it was not economically feasible to reforest cutover land; this task should be the responsibility of the states and the federal government. The Weyerhaeuser manager did not believe that timber owners had a public responsibility to reforest their lands. In later public statements, Long contended that reforestation was an unlikely possibility as long as doubt existed about future tax costs. "Until that knowledge is at hand," he observed, "private owners will be slow to grow timber."[36]

Because congressional progress on a forestry bill was at a stalemate, E. T. Allen suggested deleting the controversial state regulatory measures in the Snell proposal in favor of a broadly inclusive program to prevent fires. The elaborate details on patrol requirements and the disposal of logging debris in the original bill, Allen told William Greeley, "sounds like calculated appeal to prejudice against lumbermen only." In a note to Royal Kellogg, Allen expressed concern about Greeley's position and added, "It is bad medicine to develop a quarrel with the Forest Service." Shortly thereafter Greeley assured Allen that he had not changed his opinion about the need for forestry legislation or about the cooperative approach to the problem, but he was anxious to get the committee involved and active. Greeley, of course, had long been convinced that forest fire prevention outweighed all other considerations, and by the early spring of 1922 he was willing to drop cutting regulations in the Snell bill if they were too controversial.[37]

[35] House, *Forestry*, 66th Cong., 3rd sess., January 27, 1921, pp. 25–30.

[36] House, *Forestry*, 67th Cong., 2d sess., January 9, 1922, pp. 31–40; *Timberman* 25 (December, 1923): 78.

[37] Allen to Greeley, February 20, 1922, Allen to Kellogg, February 21, 1922, and Wil-

Through the influence of Secretary of Agriculture Henry C. Wallace, Greeley adopted a strategy that emphasized cooperative fire protection work as the critical feature of the Snell legislation. Because a few particulars remained to be worked out, Wilson Compton urged a recess in the legislative effort until after the fall elections. However, he assured Royal Kellogg, "We are all working . . . well in harmony." Meanwhile, the NFPC agreed to drop the provisions in the Snell bill that required states to adopt certain forestry standards. The earlier hearings had revealed considerable opposition even to these mild state regulations. Most of the opposition came from the South, while western operators who had been cooperating with the Forest Service for many years considered their fears groundless.[38]

Events now moved to implement the three-year-old Capper Report. Early in January, 1923, the U.S. Senate passed a resolution establishing the Select Committee on Reforestation, with Oregon's Senator Charles McNary as chairman. The group was commissioned to investigate reforestation issues and to develop a national plan to resolve the problem. While Royal Kellogg assisted the committee with scheduling arrangements, Wilson Compton clarified the national association's position in the reforestation controversy. He disputed the "recently expressed" view that the owner of private timberland had a public responsibility to reforest his cutover lands. Compton argued that "beneficiaries should pay costs in proportion to their benefits," and that these costs were therefore chargeable to the public. John W. Blodgett, president of the NLMA, expressed similar sentiments, noting that reforestation was a community problem, and any financial burden should be equally distributed. The Michigan lumberman said it was absurd to reproduce trees that would be realized only by a man's grandchildren.[39]

Just before the hearings began, Royal Kellogg established a close working relationship between NFPC and the Senate investigators. The Senate group invited Chief Forester Greeley to serve as the committee's expert counsel in its travels about the country. Kellogg told a colleague that "Greeley is having a good deal to do with the arrangements for the

liam B. Greeley to E. T. Allen, March 4, 1922, all from box 2, NFPC Records; House, *Forestry*, 67th Cong., 2d sess., January 9, 1922, pp. 20–21.

[38] Steen, *U.S. Forest Service*, p. 185; Compton to Kellogg, September 15, 1922, box 2, NFPC Records; Hosmer, "The National Forestry Program Committee," p. 635; *West Coast Lumberman* 41 (March, 1922): 36.

[39] U.S. Congress, Senate, Select Committee on Reforestation, *Hearings*, 67th Cong., 4th sess., March 26, 1923, p. 1; Steen, *U.S. Forest Service*, p. 185; Compton to Kellogg, January 15, 1923, box 2, NFPC Records; *American Lumberman* (February 10, 1923): 49.

Committee Hearings and between you and me I think the final report will be largely his work."[40]

Secretary of Agriculture Wallace, who offered the initial testimony at the hearings, attributed rising lumber prices to depleted supplies in some regions and to transportation costs of shipping western lumber to eastern markets. The latter tendency, he said, foreshadowed a more distant and concentrated lumber supply. Wallace attributed timber shortages to over-consumption and waste, noting that state regulation of cutting practices was virtually nonexistent and that the "intentional" growing of timber was negligible. The secretary advised a "gradual solution" that involved fed-eral, state, and private cooperation, especially in developing fire protection programs. Finally, he recommended using federal funds to support the pro-posal, without any reference to regulation.[41]

Wilson Compton provided the ideological framework for the lumber industry's testimony to the McNary committee. He reviewed the efforts of the federal government and lumbermen to cooperate to prevent waste in the use of forest products; he also reminded the committee that conserva-tion and the "forestry problem" were related issues and praised the Snell bill as a cooperative measure. Compton listed a five-step legislative ap-proach: (1) the adoption of a fire protection program through the coopera-tion of the federal government, the states, and private individuals; (2) the extension of state and federal ownership of forestlands; (3) adjustments in taxation; (4) public support for the reforestation of cutover and burned-over areas; and (5) a thorough survey of national forest holdings and land suitable for growing timber. Compton praised the U.S. Forest Service for "educational leadership and the promotion of practical forest conserva-tion." The agency, he said, was "an honor to the public service."[42]

As the hearings drew to a close in the fall of 1923, John W. Blodgett reiterated the position of the national association, outlined in Wilson Compton's testimony nine months earlier. Because taxation was a vital ele-ment in private forest management, Blodgett urged the government to "as-sist by study and recommendation, in furthering the reform of prohibitive

[40]Hosmer, "The National Forestry Program Committee," p. 637; R. S. Kellogg to A. B. Recknagel, April 26, 1923, box 1, Ralph S. Hosmer Papers, Cornell University Librar-ies, Ithaca, New York.

[41]Senate Committee on Reforestation, *Hearings*, 67th Cong., 4th sess., March 26, 1923, pp. 3–22.

[42]Ibid., pp. 34, 55–56, 59.

tax laws." But, he cautioned, federal cooperation in fire protection should not be withheld from a state because the state had not adjusted its tax policies to the general guidelines of the federal government. In addition, he believed reforestation was "a national question because its results will inure to the benefit of the people."[43]

To facilitate public reforestation programs, Blodgett recommended federal purchase of "great acreages" in the Lake states, Appalachia, and the South; these would be in the public interest and would primarily benefit posterity. The Forest Service would carry out the expanded program of reforestation, supported by necessary appropriations from Congress. Finally, Blodgett warned against government supervision of private cutting practices. "The Federal Government should have the right to withhold, but not the right to prescribe."[44]

E. T. Allen offered the summary argument for both the NLMA and the Western Forestry and Conservation Association. Allen, who had attended every hearing, told the committee that individuals, the state, and the federal government should operate on an equal basis rather than any one of them acting as "the prescriber of rules and regulations." He favored vastly increased federal expenditures for fire protection and recommended government support for reforestation and protection costs, because the public had a long-range vested interest in assuring timber crops. "It is not the lumberman," Allen concluded, who "is asking for protection of no-man's land. It is the public that is asking for it, because the public wants trees in 40 or 50 years."[45]

Frederick Rogers Fairchild, the acknowledged authority on forest taxation, made the closing remarks to the McNary committee. Fairchild argued, contrary to the claims of many lumbermen, that taxation of most forest property was not unfair. He also noted that unpredictable taxes made forest investment and reforestation a very precarious business. But like every witness before him, he said the fire hazard ranked ahead of the taxation problem. The federal government, he advised, should undertake a

---

[43] Ibid., November 22, 1923, pp. 1363–68.

[44] Ibid., pp. 1368–73. The Weeks Act provided federal matching funds to states having a protection agency in order to provide fire protection on nonfederal lands in the watersheds of navigable streams (Steen, *U.S. Forest Service*, p. 129; Samuel Trask Dana, *Forest and Range Policy: Its Development in the United States*, pp. 183–84).

[45] Senate, Committee on Reforestation, *Hearings*, 67th Cong., 4th sess., November 22, 1923, pp. 1384–89. For a commentary on Allen's activities with the Senate committee, see *Lumber World Review* 45 (October 10, 1923): 27.

state-by-state inquiry of forest tax policy, a critical issue for most progressive lumbermen.[46]

As the McNary hearings were grinding on during 1923, Wilson Compton noted improved economic conditions in nearly all lumber regions of the United States. The progress of federal forestry legislative proposals in accepting "the conservative wisdom . . . that this is an economic and not a political problem," Compton reported, were signs that "the law of supply and demand has not yet been declared unconstitutional." And he observed a "more . . . considerate attitude on the part of American newspapers toward the lumber industry."[47]

The rapport and good feeling established with the McNary committee pleased most lumbermen and trade journal editors. A writer in the *Lumber World Review* commented: "The people like the committee. Unlike some investigating bodies, it betrayed no bias." E. T. Allen assured an audience of Michigan lumbermen that the Senate committee "is not an inquisitorial body but is seeking information." The *American Lumberman* referred to the Seattle hearings as "informative . . . an event of the first importance," and commended the committee for its "breadth of information and . . . scope of knowledge."[48]

The political climate, which was conducive to the congressional success of the industry-sponsored proposals, must be attributed to the business leaders whose initiatives created those favorable conditions. Gifford Pinchot was preoccupied with the Pennsylvania governor's office, and the NFPC and William Greeley had carefully orchestrated testimony before the McNary committee to forge what they viewed as a consensus on forestry policy. Senator Charles McNary introduced a companion version of the Clarke bill in the Senate in January, 1924; the bill easily passed both houses of Congress and the president signed the legislation on June 7, 1924.[49]

The Clarke-McNary Act did not restrict silvicultural practices on

[46] Senate, Committee on Reforestation, *Hearings*, 67th Cong., 4th sess., November 23, 1923, pp. 1404–1405, 1412–13.

[47] Wilson Compton, "National Lumber Problems and Prospects," in NLMA, *Annual Report* (1923): 1, 6, 9.

[48] *Lumber World Review* 45 (October 10, 1923): 27; *American Lumberman* (May 12, 1923): 40, and (September 22, 1923): 40.

[49] Hamilton, "The Federal Forest Regulation Issue," p. 8. On the business leadership, see E. T. Allen's commentary in the *American Lumberman* (December 1, 1923): 55.

private timberland, nor did it proscribe lumber business activity. It did, however, offer greater federal assistance to states for fire protection, an objective lumbermen had sought for at least twenty years. The measure authorized federal matching funds to states to establish nurseries, provided for an expanded national forest system, and sanctioned the expenditure of federal money to study state tax policies. The act also called for a survey of all timberlands in the United States.[50]

The *American Lumberman* called Clarke-McNary a commitment of the American people to a sound and comprehensive forestry program and to practical reforestation. Wilson Compton saw it as a "wise legislative approach to permanent forestry settlements." Edward Hines, a prominent southern lumberman, thought Clarke-McNary would enhance cooperation between the federal government, the states, and private owners in fighting fire and provide valuable support for the extension of public land ownership. David Mason, from McNary's home state of Oregon, told the senator the bill "will be considered in future years a turning point in the history of American forests."[51]

Clarke-McNary was William Greeley's "greatest personal monument," according to his biographer; Greeley himself acknowledged that Clarke-McNary "cleared the air of controversy and launched an era of good will and joint effort." In his annual report for 1924, the chief forester referred to Clarke-McNary as the "outstanding event of the year in national forestry" and an indicator of progress. Secretary-Manager Wilson Compton of the NLMA reported general satisfaction with the 1924 legislative program and with the fall election of Calvin Coolidge. Compton praised the lumber industry for cooperating to promote constructive government and for its ability to govern itself.[52]

Clarke-McNary represents much more than the praise its supporters heaped upon it. The actual designers of the 1924 law were the lumber industry's well-financed and aggressive spokesmen, whose subjective economic arguments prevailed at every point in the long debate over national

[50] Dana, *Forest and Range Policy*, pp. 221–24; Steen, *U.S. Forest Service*, pp. 189–93.

[51] *American Lumberman* (June 14, 1924): 36, and (April 19, 1924): 39, 56; David Mason to Charles McNary, June 16, 1924, McNary folder, file 310, David Mason Papers, Oregon Historical Society, Portland, Oregon.

[52] George T. Morgan, *William B. Greeley, A Practical Forester*, p. 65; Greeley, *Forests and Men*, p. 110; U.S. Forest Service, *Annual Report* (1924): 1; Wilson Compton, "Will the Lumber Manufacturers Stand up and Be Counted," in NLMA, *Annual Report* (1924): 4.

forest policy. Association officials defined forest policy in relation to the social and economic conditions in the lumber trade and argued that a policy acceptable to lumbermen would be in the "public interest." This sentiment, however, was more window-dressing than objective fact and cloaked the actual design of a legislative policy that avoided federal regulation and promised more rational and stabler modes of business. The measure signaled industrial hegemony over the legislative and regulatory process and an attempt to rationalize and integrate forest resource policy in the United States. Lumbermen had achieved their objective—the act warded off, for the time being, the threat of federal regulation and provided a partial subsidy for fire protection.

In the end the McNary committee had approved a forestry program whose essentials had been worked out through trade associations, the NFPC, and, finally, in cooperation with Chief Forester William Greeley. Long after the passage of the Clarke-McNary Act, E. T. Allen discussed his affiliation with the NLMA and the "working arrangement with key men" in the Senate. These "key men," he said, valued the testimony of foresters connected with the national association because of "our neutral expert reputation." When problems arose, government agencies "came to us for expert neutral facilities. When the 1923 Senate forestry committee travelled the country," he related, "we did the courier work and picked the witnesses. . . . Throughout this period we had and kept federal confidence and good will because we had the machinery and money to do the essential work." Royal Kellogg, in retirement, was equally blunt, remarking that Clarke-McNary originated in "the National Forestry Program Committee in cooperation with Bill Greely [sic]." The act, Kellogg said, established "the principle of federal cooperation," and afterwards "the proponents of federal control of private operations—led by Pinchot—had no chance of success." [53]

Lumber spokesmen believed that Clarke-McNary offered something for every ailment. The purchase of cutover lands and the expansion of the national forests would assure future timber supplies. Enlarging the national forests would help stabilize the market and limit the number of competi-

---

[53] Senate, Committee on Reforestation, *Hearings*, 67th Cong., 4th sess., November 22, 1923, p. 1384; *American Lumberman* (April 19, 1924): 56; memo to George F. Jewett, December 10, 1939, box 4, WFCA Records; R. S. Kellogg to Elwood Maunder, October 31, 1962, Royal S. Kellogg—Letter File, Forest History Society, Manuscripts Collection, Santa Cruz, California.

tors. All of this, they thought, would rationalize the system so that lumber investors could make decisions with reasonable expectations. Also, the subsidy for fire protection would protect the valuable capital assets in the existing stands of timber. Although tax reform was still in the future, there were other provisions to enhance the industry's prospects. This legislative initiative represented only one field of operations for an aggressive trade leadership determined to bring order to the lumber market.

6

Voluntary Cooperation and the Search for Stability

"You are Exhibit A of government by cooperation. We have never sought to impose anything upon this industry. . . . The work has been cooperative action in the highest sense."—Herbert Hoover, 1927

THE 1920s was an auspicious and optimistic decade for American capitalism; the business community aggressively and confidently asserted its influence and authority and, with equal conviction, insisted that it acted in the public interest. Industrial and financial leaders promoted the idea that self-regulation and cooperative, voluntary action were the keys to prosperity and happiness. This influence was manifested in the domination of the Republican party in all three branches of the federal government and in the majority of state houses. Of the established political groups, only a few western progressives (who advocated agrarian reform and public power) protested the self-assertive influence of business in government. Presidents Harding, Coolidge, and Hoover established a variety of self-regulatory agencies and organizations to control the competitive order and to curb instability. Federal officials and industry modernists believed the government could help achieve economic stability and maintain the hegemony of dominant groups. The 1920s, therefore, was not a period without reform, as many writers have claimed. Leaders of the political economy preached change and the pursuit of voluntary and associative action as the wave of the future.[1]

[1] For the traditional interpretation of the 1920s, see Harold U. Faulkner, *From Versailles to the New Deal*; Arthur M. Schlesinger, Jr., *The Crisis of the Old Order, 1919–1933*; and John D. Hicks, *Republican Ascendancy, 1921–1933*. The best recent synthesis of the decade that emphasizes its significant ideological and institutional innovations is Ellis W. Hawley, *The Great War and the Search for a Modern Order, 1917–1933*.

Progressive capitalists argued that cooperative industrialism was the way to a rationalized and systematized political economy. The trade association movement was to be the institutional expression of collective business actions designed to avoid the tyranny of excessive competition. Corporate leaders and government workers had nurtured the association idea, which eventually flowered in the 1920s. David T. Mason, a man with close ties to the lumber industry, observed that the most noticeable features of the prewar system were sharp competition and lack of cooperation. "What is needed in the lumber industry," he argued, "is the modern spirit of cooperation rather than the extreme spirit of individualism which now exists." Like other trade association supporters, Mason proposed a relaxation of the antitrust laws.[2]

The Department of Commerce best expressed the philosophy of government-industry cooperation in the 1920s. And lumber trade associations, in addition to their amicable relationship with the Forest Service, also established reciprocal and positive ties with the Department of Commerce and its dynamic head, Herbert Clark Hoover. No other individual articulated the idea of government-industry cooperation more forcefully than Herbert Hoover, who believed that cooperation between government and industry served both the interests of industry and the public. Hoover's policies struck responsive chords, and his expansion of Commerce Department activities excited the imaginations of industrial spokesmen who wanted to achieve a more stable economic order. Hoover's version of New Era industrialism emphasized the standardization and simplification of production, the elimination of waste, and the exchange of statistical information.[3] The lumber industry, with its endemic problems of overproduction, waste, excessive competition, and demoralized markets, found the commerce secretary's appeals attractive.

Shortly after Hoover's appointment, enthusiastic reports began flooding the commerce office in response to his call for a close working relationship between the Department of Commerce and trade groups. Lumber

[2] David Mason, *Timber Ownership and Lumber Production in the Inland Empire*, pp. 13, 76, 79. For an account of the postwar effort to repeal antitrust legislation, see Robert Himmelberg, *The Origins of the National Recovery Administration: Business, Government, and the Trade Association Issue, 1921–1933*, pp. 5–25.

[3] The expanded activities of the Department of Commerce under Herbert Hoover are treated in Ellis W. Hawley's essay, "Herbert Hoover, the Commerce Secretariat, and the Vision of an 'Associative State,' 1921–1928," *Journal of American History* 61 (June, 1974): 116–40.

trade people assured Hoover that they would cooperate in all possible ways. George Sisson, president of the influential American Paper and Pulp Association, thought Hoover's plan for trade association cooperation would aid "the revival of business." Sisson called for "more business in government" and suggested that government continue to encourage industrial associations as it did during the Great War, because costly competition did not improve the general welfare. Hoover, he said, had struck "a refreshing note" and "has a high conception of the duties and relations of his department toward industry." [4]

Secretary Hoover moved quickly to promote lumber trade associations as an aid in stabilizing the industry. Two months after his confirmation as secretary of commerce, Hoover convinced regional trade leaders to turn monthly reports on production statistics over to the Department of Commerce, as part of a plan of cooperation with the government agency. Commerce, in return, would make this information available to lumbermen, thereby providing them with the knowledge necessary to make intelligent production decisions. If this statistical service had been available during the previous year, Hoover believed, it would have "minimized the depth of [the] present slump." [5]

The trade journal *Lumber* called the Hoover proposals "revolutionary —even sensational—when compared with other emanations from Government sources . . . concerning the lumber industry." Hoover's suggestions for compiling statistics on production and consumption were well in advance of the Forest Service, which had compiled yearly statistics of production. Hoover, *Lumber* observed, has put forth the most constructive suggestion ever to flow to the industry from government. The Hoover initiatives, said the *Southern Lumberman*, provided an alternative to the lawsuits and rumors directed at the lumber industry over the previous eighteen months "for doing the very things which Mr. Hoover now proposes to do with the co-operation of the lumbermen." [6]

Although the legal relationship between trade associations and antitrust laws was not clear, Hoover viewed the work of most trade groups as a

[4] W. W. Schupner to Herbert Hoover, March 24, 1921, "National Wholesale Lumber Dealers Association, 1921–1922," Commerce Papers, Hoover Papers (hereafter cited as CPHP), Herbert Hoover Presidential Library, West Branch, Iowa; George Sisson to Hoover, April 5, 1921, "Paper and Pulpwood, 1920–1925," CPHP; annual address of the president, American Paper and Pulp Association, *The Paper and Pulp Industry*, Bulletin no. 11 (April, 1921), filed in "Paper and Pulpwood, 1920–1925," CPHP.

[5] *Lumber* 67 (May 27, 1921): 23.

[6] Ibid. (June 3, 1921): 11; *Southern Lumberman* 99 (May 28, 1921): 29.

constructive contribution toward the public welfare. He praised the high percentage of manufacturers actively cooperating, "all of which . . . contribute to stability and the increasing efficiency of industry and to the protection both of the smaller manufacturers and the consumer." But the association movement had its greatest potential in promoting voluntary cooperation and in avoiding regulatory legislation.[7]

Cooperation between trade associations and the Department of Commerce received a legal setback in December, 1921, when the Supreme Court in the Hardwood case declared certain kinds of association actions illegal. The *Southern Lumberman* called the Hardwood decision a stunning blow, and said the "chaos and demoralization" that would accompany its enforcement staggered the imagination. The trade paper concluded, "Clearly the Sherman Act has outlived its usefulness." Other trade journals were less critical; *Lumber* thought the publication of prices for the use of buyers and sellers alike did not restrict competition and therefore was not proscribed by the court.[8]

The Hardwood decision confused trade association leaders and commerce officials, and Herbert Hoover had to defend his department from accusations that it acted in collusion with private businesses. He argued that making statistical information public "acts alike to protect legitimate business enterprise and the public interest." He believed the Hardwood case, in the long run, would affect only a small number of trade associations.[9]

Actually, the Supreme Court did not make a clear-cut decision against trade associations, because the Hardwood Manufacturers Association was somewhat unusual. It had limited the circulation of price listings to its own members and then added interpretations and predictions of the future activity of the hardwood industry. Even before the court handed down its findings, one trade journal warned that the Hardwood Manufacturers Association was in violation of the law. The circulation of price information to members only, it charged, was illegal, because this policy meant withholding information from the general population.[10]

The Harding administration's first response to the Hardwood decision

[7] U.S. Department of Commerce, memo, June 2, 1921, and Nathan B. Williams, president, National Association of Manufacturers, memo of conversation with Hoover, July 7, 1921, "Trade Associations—1921," CPHP.

[8] *Southern Lumberman* 104 (December 24, 1921): 36; *Lumber* 68 (December 30, 1921): 13.

[9] *Lumber* 69 (January 6, 1922): 21.

[10] Ibid. 65 (February 23, 1920): 17.

was equivocal. Secretary of Commerce Hoover exerted his considerable influence to gain a more moderate interpretation of the case, while Attorney General Harry Daugherty apparently wanted stricter enforcement. Hoover and Daugherty partly resolved the issue early in 1922; in an exchange of correspondence, Daugherty agreed with Hoover that it was legal for associations to collect statistics on prices, to average them, and to circulate the results through the Commerce Department. The *American Lumberman* observed that the compromise offered a little encouragement for trade associations and that Daugherty had recognized the legality of "most ordinary activity." [11]

Other supporters of organized trade were optimistic. Gilbert Montague, a prominent New York corporation lawyer with close ties to trade associations, told Hoover that his compromise with Daugherty "was the most important step forward in Governmental assistance to business that has been taken in our time." Montague also praised the commerce secretary's willingness to use the department's facilities to collect, digest, and distribute trade information. The trade movement, he predicted, could look forward to "a new era of voluntary cooperation with the Government, which will open up possibilities of almost limitless benefit to industry and to the public." And the president of the American Trade Association Executives, George D. McIlvaine, expressed great satisfaction that in Hoover, "a Cabinet officer and representative of all that is best in American business, they have a friend and advocate." [12]

The Hardwood decision did not deter most lumber trade groups from cooperating with the Department of Commerce, which continued to publish, on an expanded scale, its *Survey of Current Business*. Trade organizations praised the Commerce Department for providing information about the legality of statistical data, and the *American Lumberman* called Hoover a champion of industry and a supporter of trade activity. Assistant Forester Earle H. Clapp added the Forest Service's support when he offered the services of the agency to compile and circulate lumber price information.

[11]Himmelberg, *Origins of the National Recovery Administration*, pp. 16–21; correspondence between Department of Commerce and Department of Justice upon activities of trade associations, February 3, 1922, "Trade Associations," CPHP; *American Lumberman* (February 18, 1922): 36, 40.

[12]Gilbert Montague to Herbert Hoover, February 15, 1922, in "Trade Associations, Correspondence on Press Releases and Proceedings, Daugherty-Hoover Correspondence, Feb. 1922," Montague News-Release, February 16, 1922, and George McIlvaine to Hoover, February 27, 1922, in "Trade Associations—1922," all in CPHP.

Clapp argued that the Forest Service could provide a public service by collecting and disseminating lumber prices, which, in turn, would be in the public interest, including lumber manufacturers and distributors along with consumers.[13]

In 1925 the National Industrial Conference Board, a cooperative industrial research agency, published a lengthy study. The report found the facts in the Hardwood case relatively simple and undisputed: the Hardwood people had used a scheme of cooperation called the Open Competition Plan, which required each member to submit daily reports of sales and shipping, monthly production reports, stocks on hand, and monthly price lists. The association compiled and interpreted this information and then relayed it to members in weekly summaries, which included editorial comment about the evils of overproduction and urged members to restrict supply to maintain prices. The Open Competition Plan, the Conference Board suggested, provided intimate and detailed disclosures on a confidential basis. The Supreme Court had declared the secretive nature of the shared information in restraint of trade, spreading doubt and indecision throughout the trade association world.[14]

The absence of a clear and definitive legal statement about appropriate trade activity continued to bother proponents of association work. Federal Trade Commission investigations, Justice Department threats, and the occasional prosecution of antitrust violations kept lumber trade officials on the alert.[15] In May, 1923, the Justice Department filed suit against the Western Pine Manufacturers Association for acting in restraint of interstate trade and commerce.

The *American Lumberman* called the charges absurd and said the government was accusing the association of conspiracy to control prices "and asking the courts to restrain them from doing some of the things that another department of Government is urging the lumbermen to do." It was also spending the people's money to harass the lumber industry for carrying on activities that would remove the incentive to cooperate in the "splendid work" of the Department of Commerce. One western pine lumberman responded to the Justice Department charges, "There is no com-

[13] Himmelberg, *Origins of the National Recovery Administration*, pp. 17, 21, 26; *American Lumberman* (March 3, 1923): 31. Clapp is quoted in the *National Lumber Bulletin* 2 (March 5, 1922): 5.

[14] National Industrial Conference Board, *Trade Associations: Their Economic Significance and Legal Status*, pp. 89, 115.

[15] *American Lumberman* (March 31, 1923): 52.

modity . . . that is subject to such violent competition at the present moment as lumber." And a West Coast Lumbermen's Association (WCLA) official protested that the Justice Department had constituted "itself complaining witness, prosecuting attorney, jury and judge."[16]

During this time of uncertainty, Wilson Compton continued to speak and write enthusiastically about the benefits of cooperation for trade associations. He urged regional association executives to cooperate with the Department of Commerce and to keep their statistical work in accord with Supreme Court decisions. Western Pine's secretary-manager wondered to what decisions Compton referred, and skeptically doubted that any such decisions shed light on the subject of statistical activities.[17]

Most trade leaders did not share Compton's view that court decisions were clear enough to act as a guide to the practice of trade associations. In the midst of doubt and charges of recrimination, Compton counseled lumbermen to be conciliatory and cooperative, especially with the Department of Commerce. Early in 1924 he advised the WCLA to work with the Department of Commerce in its statistical gathering, because the secretary of commerce considered it constructive and "helpful both to the industry in question and to the general public."[18]

Under Compton's guidance, the National Lumber Manufacturers Association (NLMA) cooperated fully with the Department of Commerce. Compton told Hoover early in 1924 that the national association was forming "statistic exchanges in accord with your recommendations." Compton then advised the North Carolina Pine Association to maintain a "constructive" relationship with the Department of Commerce, even though the department was not extending its cooperative plan because of certain recent events.[19]

The most puzzling problem for trade officials was the equivocal character of the Justice Department. Compton accused the attorney general's

[16] Ibid. (May 5, 1923): 38, 42–43; Robert B. Allen to National Association of Cost Accountants, February 8, 1924, box 94, National Forest Products Association Records (hereafter cited as NFPA Records), Forest History Society, Santa Cruz, California.

[17] Wilson Compton to Stephen B. Davis, solicitor, Department of Commerce, January 21, 1924, "National Lumber Manufacturers Association, 1921–1927," CPHP; Compton to A. W. Cooper, July 11, 1923, box 94, NFPA Records.

[18] Wilson Compton to Earl Constantine, January 24, 1924, and Compton to J. N. Teal, January 16, 1924, both in box 94, NFPA Records.

[19] Wilson Compton to Herbert Hoover, January 19, 1924, and Compton to North Carolina Pine Association, January 19, 1924, both in box 94, NFPA Records.

office of merely tossing the issue back to the Department of Commerce when Hoover requested an opinion regarding statistical compilations. Such action reminded Compton of an Omar Khayyam piece:

> Myself when young did early frequent,
> Doctor and Saint, and heard great argument,
> About it and about; but evermore went out
> By the same door wherein I went.[20]

Herbert Hoover expressed his frustrations in his annual report for 1924, when he complained that the antitrust issue "is not today clearly defined whether by law or by court decision and in consequence we are losing the value of much admirable activity." His report called for clarification of the antitrust debate so that legality and proper conduct could be assured. The WCLA expressed similar sentiments in its report for 1924; "Prospective members," it said, were lost because "of the present administration's seeming inclination to regard all associations as illegal combinations."[21]

Lumber executives vigorously denied the allegations that trade groups acted monopolistically. Herbert Hoover argued in their defense that trade associations provided a means to resolve national problems "without creating dominations of groups that would stifle equality of opportunity." Moreover, they benefited smaller businesses lacking capital resources. Wilson Compton was equally blunt: trade associations promoted competition.[22]

Robert B. Allen, the veteran secretary-manager of the WCLA, contended that trade associations fostered rather than retarded competition; they enabled men with limited capital to conduct intelligent business transactions. Without this information, he noted, "the little fellow, operating without definite trade facts would be lucky to survive," while the larger-scale operators had the facilities "to secure this service without association aid." Allen thought the antitrust laws were being used against trade groups that provided services to small-scale operators (which, in turn, preserved competition). The Commerce Department's report for 1924, likewise,

---

[20] Compton to Davis, CPHP.

[21] U.S. Department of Commerce, *Annual Report* (1924): 16–18; WCLA, *Annual Report* (1924): 2, filed in folder 23, box 1, West Coast Lumbermen's Association Records (hereafter cited as WCLA Records), Oregon Historical Society, Portland, Oregon.

[22] Statement by Herbert Hoover to Chamber of Commerce of the United States, April 12, 1922, box 94, NFPA Records; Wilson Compton, "How Competition Can Be Improved Through Association," *Proceedings of the Academy of Political Science* 11 (January, 1926): 32.

praised "legitimate" trade associations for providing small businesses with facilities equivalent to those that big business could afford independently. This system, the report indicated, would prove a strong force for maintaining a competitive system if properly directed.

There is a vast difference between the whole social conception of capital combinations against public interest and cooperative organization profoundly in the public interest. The former extinguishes individualism, legitimizes and fosters monopoly, dams up our channels—all of which penalizes the consumer and make for less efficiency in production. The latter encourages individualism, fosters competition and initiative resulting in efficient service and reasonable prices to the consumer.[23]

Much of the anxiety among trade groups reflected the Justice Department's equivocation on the antitrust issue through 1923. Although lumber associations feared a renewed antitrust campaign, that danger never materialized. Attorney General Daugherty, one of the chief proponents of restricted trade cooperation, was coming under congressional criticism for corruption and mismanagement. One senses an element of glee in Wilson Compton's letter to Robert Allen in February, 1924, when he remarked that the Department of Justice was "absorbed somewhat in other directions right now." Finally, with Daugherty's exit from the attorney general's office in March, 1924, and the Supreme Court's less restrictive decision in the Maple Flooring case in June, 1925, Herbert Hoover's more liberal version of associative activity emerged triumphant.[24]

The Maple Flooring opinion cleared the way for most forms of lumber trade cooperation. The court, which defined a more liberal interpretation of the antitrust laws, declared legal the gathering and dissemination of statistics on costs, sales prices, production, and stocks on hand. The *American Lumberman* called the decision "a victory of very real importance to trade associations . . . a new magna charta of legitimate organized business." More important, the opinion delineated the precise conduct associations might pursue and cleared the confusion surrounding the statistical work of the Department of Commerce.[25]

[23] WCLA, *Annual Report* (1924), filed in folder 23, box 1, WCLA Records; Allen to National Association of Cost Accountants, box 94, NFPA Records; Department of Commerce, *Annual Report* (1924): 18.

[24] Himmelberg, *Origins of the National Recovery Administration*, pp. 33–34, 43–47; Wilson Compton to Robert Allen, February 28, 1924, box 94, NFPA Records.

[25] *United States Supreme Court Sanctions Collection and Dissemination of Lumber Statistics* (reprinted from *American Lumberman*, June 6, 1925), pp. 2–3, filed in box 94, NFPA Records; *American Lumberman* (June 6, 1925): 37–38.

Joseph N. Teal, legal counsel for the WCLA, contended that the Maple Flooring decision permitted "intelligent cooperation in the compilation of business information," recognized economic law, and adjusted the Sherman Act in accord with changing circumstances. The court had put its "stamp of approval" on the work of the Department of Commerce. Charles S. Keith of the Southern Pine Association thought the Maple Flooring opinion vindicated his association and provided for the "rational control of production and distribution." But O. T. Swan of the Northern Hemlock and Hardwood Manufacturers Association put it more positively, "The logical thing happens if you wait long enough." [26]

Most lumber trade groups applauded Herbert Hoover's wide-ranging commitment to voluntary industrial cooperation. Wilson Compton told an annual meeting of the NLMA that lumbermen should fully exploit the opportunity to demonstrate their ability to conduct their "own business economically and without waste." Self-discipline and honesty, he observed, would effectively end "wasteful experiments of Government control and regulation." [27]

Secretary Hoover reciprocated these shared expressions of good will. Hoover congratulated the membership of the NLMA in 1924 for its leadership in "the great national values of trade association work." The heart of association work, he noted, was the efficient production and distribution of goods and the elimination of waste. [28] The participation of the private sector with the government to promote the standardization and simplification of lumber products enhanced this sense of mutual respect and good will.

The adoption of uniform and standardized grades and cuts of lumber was an early objective of lumber trade groups. The industry's leaders associated standardization with conservation and the more efficient use of lumber and argued that its adoption would bring greater marketing efficiency and stability to the business. Trade spokesmen argued that standardization promised increased profits, stability, and more efficient and economic service to the public and would further rationalize the system of production and distribution. The Forest Service had been recommending the adoption

[26] *Lumber World Review* 48 (June 10, 1925): 33–34; National Industrial Conference Board, *Trade Associations*, p. 115.

[27] Wilson Compton, "National Lumber Problems and Prospects," in NLMA, *Annual Report* (1923): 12.

[28] Hoover is quoted in NLMA, *Annual Report* (1924): 46–47.

of national standards for many years, and by the early 1920s the larger lumber trade groups had joined the campaign.[29] They found a champion in the person of the dynamic commerce secretary.

At the request of the NLMA, representatives from all phases of the trade met in May, 1922, to formulate common lumber standards and to decide on methods to enforce their recommendations. Secretary Hoover advised the industry to "develop these things from the internal machinery of the trade" and argued that government should not need to police business ethics. The national trade group later appointed a Central Committee on Lumber Standards to serve as a clearinghouse for establishing regularized grades and cuts of lumber. The committee completed its work late in 1923.[30]

To allay the fears of some association members, Wilson Compton defended cooperation between the lumber trade organizations and the Department of Commerce. Hoover indicated his high purpose, Compton insisted, with his desire "to keep the wasteful hand of the Government out of the affairs of ordinary business enterprise." Then Compton complimented lumbermen who were aware of the public's interest in the "efficient, stable and honest conduct of the lumber industry," but who wanted to do their own regulating. He noted that government grading recommendations had been offered for at least twenty-five years and lumber trade groups had sponsored some of the proposals. But the industry's present need was to "develop these things through the internal machinery of the trade itself," a task the associations could accomplish more efficiently and effectively than government. Then the final assurance: the commerce secretary "has the wisdom and the courage . . . to confine his cooperation to helping the lumber industry help itself."[31]

---

[29] Circular distributed to organized consumers, technical experts, distributors, and manufacturers interested in lumber, December 13, 1923, "Conferences—Lumber," CPHP. For an example of arguments for adoption of standardization, see the testimony of Everett Griggs in National Conservation Congress, *Proceedings of the Fourth National Conservation Congress*, p. 187.

[30] Circular distributed to organized consumers, "Conferences—Lumber," CPHP; Hoover's address to the NLMA, May 22, 1922, in "National Lumber Manufacturers Association, 1921, 1927," and memo on the Central Committee on Lumber Standards, July 22, 1922, in "Lumber, 1921–1924," all in CPHP.

[31] Press release, "Keeping the Government out of the Lumber Business," July 12, 1922, box 144, NFPA Records.

Except for a recalcitrant hardwood group, most lumber trade associations cooperated with the Commerce Department to establish uniform lumber standards. Secretary Hoover praised the industry's committee for its efforts to "eliminate fraud from the trade and waste of our forests" and for taking a "definite step toward the continued stability and sound ethical practice of the lumber industry." He was particularly pleased that standardization was achieved through the initiative of the associations.[32]

At its concluding session in December, 1923, the Central Committee on Lumber Standards indicated that a standardized lumber product would bring a roseate future for the lumber industry. It meant "large direct savings" and "a direct contribution to the sound, honest and efficient conduct of the lumber trade. . . . It has been characterized as a vital aid to the orderliness, stability and profitability of the lumber business." Secretary of Commerce Hoover praised the committee for its effort to forestall government regulation through voluntary action, because the industry itself originally demanded the service. William Greeley, speaking for the Forest Service, also commended the adoption of uniform standards that would stabilize the industry, bring order, efficiency, and economy to the use of forest products, and assist "the growing of timber as part of a general conservation program."[33]

The following year Hoover directed a subordinate, William Durgin, chief of the Division of Simplified Practice, to address the annual meeting of the NLMA and to praise its leadership for undertaking the enormous problem of standardization. Hoover commended the association's accomplishment and its ability to overcome its inherent complexity and competitiveness. The lumber industry, he remarked, should be praised for bringing "greater stability to business, great economies to production and distri-

---

[32]*American Lumberman* (June 16, 1923): 52–54 (For information on dissension within the hardwood industry, see John McClure, president, National Hardwood Lumber Association, to Membership, September 13, 1922, "National Lumber Manufacturers Association, 1921, 1927," CPHP); Herbert Hoover to the Associated Press, June 16, 1923, in "National Hardwood Lumber Association, 1921–1927," and Hoover to Central Committee on Lumber Standards, December 12, 1923, in "Conferences—Lumber, 1923–1928," both in CPHP. It is never made clear in any of Hoover's statements precisely how consumers fit into this scenario. Hoover's vague reference to consumers is mentioned in his brief 1922 treatise, *American Individualism* (reprint, Washington, D.C.: Herbert Hoover Library Association), pp. 15–21.

[33]Minutes of the General Standardization Conference on Lumber, December 12–13, 1923, "Conferences—Lumber, 1923–1928," CPHP.

bution, greater conservation of our natural resources and improved skill and business ethics." [34]

The task of implementing lumber standards on a voluntary basis proved difficult, especially during periods of overproduction and in depressed regions like the South and the Far West. Trade officials complained to the Commerce Department that adoption was moving slowly, and occasionally Hoover was requested to use his influence to bring recalcitrants into line. The worst problems were in the South, where the larger-scale lumbermen viewed the implementation of grading standards as an opportunity to eliminate the smaller, "peckerwood" mills. And the large operators dominated the Southern Pine Association, which determined standardization policy. The secretary-manager of the Southern Pine Association noted that "the competition of these small mills must be met," and the best way to accomplish this was by grade marking. John W. Blodgett, who headed the Central Committee, told a correspondent that standardization offered protection for large, efficient mills "now competing directly with the portable mills cutting only second growth stumpage." [35]

More important, however, were the shared ideals between association spokesmen and the secretary of commerce, who contended that common standards would contribute to a stabler and more orderly economy. Lumbermen found the proposals of the Commerce Department attractive, because they avoided the hoary specter of federal regulation but promised to help achieve a rationally ordered industry. On the eve of Hoover's resignation as commerce secretary in order to take up presidential politics, Frederick K. Weyerhaeuser thanked him for "the splendid contribution you have . . . made in the interest of standardization in the lumber industry." [36]

Weyerhaeuser and the southern trade leaders expressed the view of the larger-scale operators on the issue of standardization. But the numerous

[34] Herbert Hoover to William Durgin, April 15, 1924, "Conferences—Lumber, 1923–1928," CPHP.

[35] J. F. Martin, secretary, Pennsylvania Lumbermen's Association, to Herbert Hoover, September 8, 1924, in "Lumber, 1921–1924," and John W. Blodgett, chairman, Central Committee on Lumber Standards, to Hoover, April 13, 1925, in "Lumber, 1925," both in CPHP; Herbert C. Berckes, "Association Activities," in the report of the Ninth Annual Meeting of the Subscribers to the Southern Pine Association, March 11–12, 1924, pp. 25–26, quoted in James E. Fickle, *The New South and the "New Competition": Trade Association Development in the Southern Pine Industry*, p. 189; John Blodgett to A. C. Goodyear, December 1, 1924, box 74, NFPA Records.

[36] Frederick Weyerhaeuser to Herbert Hoover, May 25, 1928, "Lumber, 1926–1928," CPHP.

complaints from lumber officials about small millmen who refused to comply made it clear that there was no community of interest when it came to implementing standardization. It was evident that the attempt to institute efficient and rationalized marketing practices would not benefit the smaller business units. This same type of resistance ultimately undermined the work of the Lumber Code Authority under the National Recovery Administration in the 1930s.

As part of a move to improve the efficient use of timber resources, Secretary of Agriculture Henry C. Wallace called for a conference in the fall of 1924 on the use of forest products. Its objective was to urge the lumber and wood manufacturing industries to "adopt improved methods of manufacturing and using wood and thus to greatly cut down our enormous drain and lessen the severity of the timber shortage." Wallace requested the cooperation of Commerce Secretary Hoover, who had done a great deal to stimulate interest in industrial waste problems and in conserving natural resources. When Wallace died in October, 1924, Herbert Hoover became the moving force behind the officially designated National Conference on the Utilization of Forest Products. President Coolidge set the tone at the November conference when he told the forest industry representatives that their survival depended on "economic fitness," which could be achieved through "good management and good technical processes." [37]

Coolidge and Hoover made brief speeches to the first wood utilization conference. Chief Forester William B. Greeley followed with an ideological synthesis that tied the conservation of resources and the elimination of waste to the industry's need for order, stability, and improved profits. Changing economic circumstances and new commercial incentives, he said, were inducing lumbermen to use waste materials. Greeley added that an industry free of government controls would be the best means to eliminate waste and achieve the conservation of timber resources. "In the last analysis the commercial incentive . . . will be the driving power behind the whole movement." [38] Profit making, he intimated, was both compatible and necessary to effective conservation.

The chairman of the Central Committee on Lumber Standards, John

[37] Henry Wallace to Herbert Hoover, October 8, 1924, in "Conferences—Wood Utilization, 1924–1925," CPHP; Donald L. Winters, *Henry Cantwell Wallace as Secretary of Agriculture*, p. 291; Coolidge's address to the National Conference on Utilization of Forest Products, November 19, 1924, in "Conferences—Wood Utilization, 1924–1925," CPHP.

[38] *American Lumberman* (November 22, 1924): 45–47.

W. Blodgett, told the conference that the chief cause of waste in logging was the handicap of economic conditions. Since it was profitable to take only the best logs out of the woods, he recommended restrictions on the sale of public timber as long as private stands could supply the nation's lumber needs. Other conference speakers also emphasized the relation between waste and economic conditions. A Weyerhaeuser executive recommended increased fire protection and wise timber taxation as the way to use "everything but the whispering in the tree tops." [39]

One trade leader drew a parallel between the wood utilization conference and the issue of standardization, saying neither would be successful unless consumers purchased the lesser grades of lumber. One hardwood association executive told William Greeley that his organization was completely in accord with the efforts to better use forest products. As one means to this end, he urged increased congressional appropriations for the Madison laboratory to encourage further scientific research. [40]

Frank G. Wisner, president of the NLMA, thought continuing overproduction had contributed to many of the wasteful practices. Economic conditions, he said, had forced owners to liquidate their standing timber and had brought "about a condition which is not conducive to conservation." The *American Lumberman* put it simply. There was one legitimate principle to the utilization issue—"Will it pay?" Asking the lumberman to save otherwise wasted timber was "equivalent to asking him to run a charitable institution." [41]

Secretary of Commerce Hoover appointed a quasi-permanent National Committee on Wood Utilization in May, 1925. Axel Oxholm, chief of the Lumber Division in the Department of Commerce, served as chairman and worked closely with the committee to find markets for otherwise wasted materials. Efficient wood utilization, he said, would raise timber values and stimulate commercial reforestation. [42] Like Chief Forester William Greeley, Oxholm believed the market system would eliminate waste and achieve resource conservation.

[39] Ibid., pp. 48–50.

[40] B. F. Dulweber to W. M. Ritter, November 15, 1924, and J. M. Pricehurd to William Greeley, December 1, 1924, both in box 74, NFPA Records.

[41] *Lumber World Review* 48 (January 10, 1925): 38; *American Lumberman* (January 31, 1925): 31.

[42] Herbert Hoover to John W. Blodgett, March 28, 1925, "Conferences—Wood Utilization, 1925," CPHP; U.S. Bureau of Foreign and Domestic Commerce, *Services Available to the Lumber Industry Through the Department of Commerce*, p. 14.

Secretary of Commerce Hoover saw efficient wood utilization as part of a broader strategy that would contribute to "an economic structure infinitely more stable than the world has ever known before and a standard of living infinitely higher." The role of the federal government, however, was to cooperate with the "voluntary agencies of industry" to pursue a program aiding both lumbermen and the public. The *American Lumberman* remarked that the industry was fortunate in having "an able and sympathetic collaborator in Herbert Hoover," and urged its readers to heed Hoover's warnings that "if industry does not want the government to interfere in its affairs, . . . businessmen must get together and themselves solve the problems that vitally affect the public interest.[43]

There was still more praise for the Commerce Secretary. E. C. Hole, manager of the *American Lumberman*, told Hoover that "the Department of Commerce . . . is one of the educational institutions . . . for business men." Moreover, Hoover was showing lumbermen how better to serve both their government and themselves. The *Southern Lumberman* called the wood utilization effort promising, and a southern lumber manufacturer told Axel Oxholm that traditionally suspicious lumbermen from his region were overcoming their prejudice and suspicions about the federal government.[44]

Through the remainder of his appointment as secretary of commerce, Hoover persisted in his unstinting praise for the wood utilization program. In April, 1927, Hoover told the NLMA that the industry's prosperity depended on efficient wood utilization, which would help stabilize the industry and reap more profits for lumbermen. One month later, Hoover told the National Wood Utilization Committee: "You are Exhibit A of government by cooperation. We have never sought to impose anything upon this industry. . . . The work has been cooperative action in the highest sense." The success of voluntarism, he observed, made congressional regulation a creature of the past.[45]

Just before his resignation as chief forester in 1928, William Greeley repeated to Axel Oxholm the important relation between timber growing,

[43] Hoover's address to the Second Annual Meeting of the National Committee on Wood Utilization, 1926," CPHP; *American Lumberman* (May 1, 1926): 42.

[44] E. C. Hole to Herbert Hoover, November 22, 1924, "Conferences—Wood Utilization, 1924–1925," CPHP; *Southern Lumberman* 122 (May 1, 1926): 20; William Nichols to Axel Oxholm, July 13, 1927, "Lumber, 1926–1928," CPHP.

[45] Herbert Hoover to Frank Wisner, April 6, 1927, in "Conferences—Wood Utilization, 1927," and NLMA, news release, May 7, 1927, in "Lumber, 1926–1928," both in CPHP.

the economic requirements of the lumber industry, and the efficient use of forest products. Forests "cannot be widely and generally produced," he noted, unless there was an adequate market and closer use of the forest crop to increase its value and enhance production. Although this was an industrial problem, the chief forester urged public agencies to help through research and by "such admirable work as that of the National Committee on Wood Utilization." [46]

Toward the close of the 1928 presidential campaign, candidate Hoover told a Saint Louis audience that the voluntary initiatives of lumbermen had eliminated abuses "without resorting to legislation and regulation." The candidate effusively recalled that in 1923 "we created a series of committees . . . [and] perfected a system for the grading of lumber," and because everyone cooperated, "there has been no . . . [call for] legislation from congress." One trade journal carrying Hoover's speech remarked that if "progressive element[s] in the lumber industry" had not pursued this objective, the federal government would have instituted "onerous regulations of its own." [47]

Although lumber trade association officials were optimistic about the benefits to be derived through the standardization and utilization programs, in the actual conduct of the lumber business this enthusiasm proved unwarranted and misleading. Herbert Hoover, and to a lesser degree William Greeley, based their optimism on the mistaken assumption that the open cooperation of the Commerce Department, the Forest Service, and the lumber trade associations would usher in a stable and orderly industrial world. By the end of the decade, the realities of contracting markets eroded the bright hope that New Era politics had ended the business cycle. The problems were partly the traditional ones of excessive mill capacity and rapid liquidation of timber stands, which contributed to overproduction and glutted markets. But the impressive increases in the manufacture of nonlumber building materials in the 1920s (cement, steel, and cellulose products) added to the industry's dilemma. These substitutes induced greater instability in the market and inspired lumbermen to action: trade

[46] William Greeley to Axel Oxholm, January 25, 1928, "Conferences—Wood Utilization, 1928," CPHP.

[47] After the election, Hoover's speech was published in *Lumber Manufacturer and Dealer* 81 (December, 1928): 39.

leaders resorted to better advertising and merchandising techniques and developed a program of public education in the uses of wood products.[48]

Beginning in 1926, the NLMA countered the threat of substitute building materials through a series of radio addresses in cooperation with the National Farm Radio Council. Trade journal editors and lumbermen active in trade association work addressed the symbiotic relation between conservation, reforestation, and the economic health of the lumber industry. To make reforestation pay, the radio scripts repeatedly insisted, people must use lumber, and "no man need worry about forest utilization as a forest menace." The broadcasts combated the notion of timber scarcity; the woods were full of aged and dying trees that should be used to prevent waste; a perpetual demand for forest products would bring effective reforestation, whereas the use of substitute materials would be ruinous to forest conservation. One broadcast argued that America had been afflicted with too much forested land and that until recently, the public applauded axmen for their efforts—the old forests simply "had to go." In the wake of the 1927 Mississippi flood, a trade journal editor told his listeners that deforested lands had not contributed to the flood. He titled his address "Forest 'Facts' That Aren't So."[49]

The national trade group also purchased advertising space in professional journals and magazines, which drummed home the industry's argument that conservation meant profits and that forests were renewable resources that would do better with man's help. One advertisement insisted that healthy forests depended on profitable markets; they "must pay for themselves or there will be none." To have perpetual forests and healthy industries, the ad concluded, "one element is yet required—a profit for the forest builder."[50]

The *American Lumberman*, the most widely read journal, called upon the states to match Clarke-McNary appropriations for fire protection and to

[48] Orion Howard Cheney, "The New Competition in the Lumber Industry," in NLMA, *Annual Report* (1927): 3.

[49] Platt B. Walker, "What is Forest Conservation," February 12, 1926, A. Fletcher Marsh, "A Perpetual Supply of Forest Products," October 19, 1926, C. W. Defebaugh, "Forests and Prosperity," December 31, 1926, M. W. Stark, "Origin of the American Forest Problem," March 10, 1927, and W. E. Crosby, "Forest 'Facts' That Aren't So," June 1, 1927, all in box 154, NFPA Records.

[50] *American Forests* 34 (July, 1928): 424, (October, 1928): 642, and (December, 1928): 770.

revise their tax laws to encourage reforestation. It also urged Congress to increase appropriations for reforesting cutover lands and entreated the public to become "forestry-minded." The Chicago paper argued that operators were not obligated to reforest cutover lands unless the public helped create an economic environment that would make such an undertaking profitable.[51]

Despite the aggressive propaganda efforts of the NLMA, the editorializing of the trade press, and the overweening optimism of the commerce secretary, economic conditions in the lumber trade worsened as the decade advanced. In the midst of what association officials heralded as great successes—the achievements in national lumber standards, the passage of the Clarke-McNary Act in 1924, and the wood utilization effort—the industry's troubles persisted. Even the Commerce Department's enterprising promotion of foreign trade did little to halt the continuing decline in lumber consumption after 1925.[52] Chronic overproduction plagued lumber operators in the Pacific Northwest, and smaller producers, especially in the South, grumbled about their unfavorable competitive situation. In addition, a few astute trade association executives and a handful of professional foresters were aware that the industry had not reached the promised land.

Wilson Compton was wary of the increasingly sensitive marketing problems of the trade as early as the mid-1920s. At the height of the enthusiasm over Clarke-McNary, he warned of the inability to keep supply in a reasonable balance with demand. "This inherent condition of ill-adjusted production in the lumber industry is notorious and visible," he cautioned, and required remedy before constructive work could begin in forest conservation. One year later, Compton complained that overproduction had led to "irretrievable and profitless waste of timber resources" and a chronic "condition of demoralization." To counter this tendency, he urged carefully planned financial consolidations, a move that would bring economy of operation, stability, increased profits, "the conservation of natural resources and the promotion of public interests."[53]

[51] See the following editorials in *American Lumberman*: (January 10, 1925): 33, (May 8, 1926): 36, (May 29, 1926): 32, (September 11, 1926): 46–47, (November 27, 1926): 35, (March 12, 1927): 41, (April 30, 1927): 26, (August 13, 1927): 34, (October 22, 1927): 28–29, (October 29, 1927): 36, (November 19, 1927): 36, (March 3, 1928): 29, (October 6, 1928): 32, (October 13, 1928): 36, (October 27, 1928): 26, (November 3, 1928): 36, (November 10, 1928): 28, (December 8, 1928): 32, and (December 15, 1928): 26.

[52] For the Commerce Department's promotion of foreign trade, see Bureau of Foreign and Domestic Commerce, *Services Available to the Lumber Industry*, pp. 7–12.

[53] Wilson Compton, "Will the Lumber Industry Stand Up and Be Counted?": 2, Comp-

While Compton was laying blame elsewhere, Ward Shepard, a professional forester, took lumber industry ideologists to task for promoting what he called Economic Fatalism. "Stated briefly, economic fatalism holds that destructive logging is the necessary outgrowth of natural economic laws and that it can be advanced only as these laws change. . . . It is a comfortable theory. It transfers the struggle . . . from the present to the vague future, and it furnishes an auto-matic, all-inclusive, and awe-inspiring alibi to the long tale of forest destruction and waste." The promise of a national forestry policy at the beginning of the decade, Shepard said, had narrowed to a program of voluntary cooperation between government and industry to stop forest fires. And because lumbermen were interested only in taking their profits from the volume of the cut, forest destruction continued. Moreover, the only incentive to fire protection was the operator's desire to protect his investment. "As the old timber is cut out," he warned, "this cooperation will be reduced."[54]

Robert Y. Stuart, who replaced William Greeley as chief forester in 1928, brooded over conditions in the forest products trade in his first annual report. Stuart concluded that lumbermen were not overly prosperous. Sharply competitive conditions "have resulted in chronic market instability, [and] low profits," he reported, and chronic overproduction "is the outstanding feature of the present situation as seen from within the lumber industry."[55]

Raphael Zon, who headed the Lakes States Experiment Station, believed that the activities of large corporations, which swayed "the thought and politics of the country," had created the forestry problem. Zon doubted that a "small bunch of foresters" could buck the march of events, especially since the NLMA was "riding on the top of the economic wave." He saw little hope that the industry could be regulated effectively, observing that "you can not meet a rapid-firing gun with wooden swords."[56]

Then, at decade's end, a plunging stock market precipitated a general contraction throughout the American economy. The optimistic and ener-

---

ton, "Will the Lumber Industry Settle Down or Settle Up," in NLMA, *Annual Report* (1925): 1–2, 4, 16–17.

[54] Ward Shepard, "The Necessity for Realism in Forestry Propaganda," *Journal of Forestry* 25 (January, 1927): 11, 14, 16, 19.

[55] U.S. Forest Service, *Annual Report* (1929): 2.

[56] Raphael Zon to George P. Ahern, September 19, 1929, box 6, Raphael Zon Papers, Minnesota Historical Society, St. Paul, Minnesota.

getic Herbert Hoover, now president, began a wide-ranging series of government-sponsored voluntary and cooperative programs to slow economic decline and to restore industrial growth.[57] All to no avail as conditions continued to worsen. But lumbermen, like farmers, already understood the problems of a contracting economy.

[57] For a discussion of Hoover's economic recovery initiatives, see David Burner, *Herbert Hoover: A Public Life*, pp. 245–83; Hawley, *The Great War*, pp. 192–205; Joan Hoff Wilson, *Herbert Hoover: Forgotten Progressive*, pp. 122–67; and Hicks, *Republican Ascendancy*, pp. 260–80.

7

The Early Depression

"You see, therefore, that Government control of industry is not the clamor of radicals but of the leaders themselves in the industries concerned with natural resources." —Raphael Zon, 1930

THE efforts of organized lumbermen to achieve economic stability and a rationally ordered market involved a myriad of cooperative arrangements between the industry and government agencies. Although lumber trade groups succeeded in influencing legislative and regulatory policy, the unpredictable force of the market continued to wreak its vengeance on the lumber trade. Like other association leaders in excessively competitive industries, lumber officials sought to control competition through cartellike arrangements. The emergence of these new structural mechanisms conflicted with the notion of a freely competitive market economy and provided a striking illustration of a progressive, maturing capitalist order at war with established tradition. These new modes of business organization represented efforts to adjust to changing economic conditions in the hopes that trade groups would rationalize market conduct.

Lumber trade associations sponsored numerous legislative and regulatory measures in the 1920s that emphasized voluntarism and cooperation, but avoided what lumbermen called grinding federal restrictions. Although these reforms did not achieve the stability and order that lumbermen sought, they did exert considerable influence in the political economy. As the broader outlines of the depression became more apparent, some trade leaders moved to adopt more coercive means to control production and compel market behavior.

Most statistical indicators show clearly that the Great Depression came early to the lumber industry. Wilson Compton put the case forcefully as early as 1924, when he predicted that "ill-adjusted production" could be eliminated only through "financial consolidations in the lumber industry."

One year later John W. Blodgett, a veteran association leader, supported a move toward larger "capital aggregations in lumber" to curtail production. Although he was a firm believer in competition, Blodgett recognized that it must be contained within reasonable limits.[1]

These views were widespread. A West Coast trade leader remarked in 1925 that the "erratic and mercurial" market would convince lumbermen to "consolidate their selling activities into well organized, competitive groups." Mark Reed, a prominent Puget South operator, wrote Herbert Hoover in 1926 that the industry was passing through a disastrous period; he recommended restraint and patience in order to gear production levels to the limited demand.[2]

The peripatetic Wilson Compton argued that a complete solution to the forestry problem merely required putting into practice "the principle embodied in existing policy." He believed the problem was essentially practical and economic and was outlined in the Clarke-McNary law, which recognized a federal and state responsibility to forestry. This "public" commitment included an increased subsidy for fire protection, more equitable timberland taxes, and the expansion of the federal forest system. Compton also urged a more flexible national policy "regarding the concentration in relatively large units of the ownership of forest lands." The implementation of such policies, he contended, would enable the industry to overcome its difficulties.[3]

Compton also was a master of the double entendre, especially when it came to splitting definitive hairs about the functioning of capitalism. "Competition," he told a meeting of the Academy of Political Science, "although it may have an exact meaning in the abstract, has in business practice no description which is . . . uniformly acceptable." Trade associations, he said, improved competition, because they provided all competitors with the same opportunity to make intelligent decisions about the marketplace. Compton advised competitors to merge to improve their "physical and financial ability" to cooperate and control the market. Wisely planned financial consolidation, he said, would enhance the indus-

---

[1] Wilson Compton, "Will the Lumber Industry Stand Up and Be Counted?" in National Lumber Manufacturers Association (NLMA), *Annual Report* (1925): 7; *Lumber World Review* 48 (June 10, 1925): 37.

[2] *Lumber World Review* 48 (February 10, 1925): 31. Reed is quoted in Robert E. Ficken, *Lumber and Politics: The Career of Mark Reed*, pp. 147–48.

[3] *Lumber World Review* 48 (January 25, 1925): 32, and (October 25, 1925): 23–24.

try's ability to adhere to standard grades and sizes and to eliminate the "burlesque in the lumber business . . . solemnly called competition."[4]

As the decade ended, trade leaders insisted that the deteriorating economic situation called for drastic action. The total volume of lumber produced in the United States reached a postwar peak of forty-one billion board feet in 1925, declined sharply to twenty-six billion board feet in 1930, and finally reached a low of just over ten billion board feet in 1932. This great contraction in production caused reverberations throughout the industry. John B. Woods, forester of the Long-Bell plant in Longview, Washington, remarked in 1930 that the forest products business had descended to the "slough of despond"; moreover, it lacked the organizational structure and legal authority to meet the crisis. Woods complained that Clarke-McNary funds were insufficient to meet the costs of adequate fire protection and that the funds allotted to implement a national timber survey were also inadequate.[5]

During the summer of 1928, J. D. Tennant, another Long-Bell executive, recommended a reorganization plan for the lumber industry that would establish an institute with power vested in an executive committee and an appointed head. Referred to as the "lumber czar" plan, the proposal also called for the appointment of a presidential commission to set mandatory production quotas. Tennant's suggestions, similar to plans circulating in the coal and oil industry, challenged the authority of the national association and its chief executive officer, Wilson Compton. The scheme was coercive in its insistence on production controls and might be described as a rigorous form of business syndicalism. Compton viewed the proposal as a personal affront to his leadership of the national association.[6]

Despite these fears, most lumbermen active in lumber trade affairs appear to have supported Compton and discredited the need for a "lumber czar." W. W. Stark, an Ohio lumberman, attributed the proposal to the

[4]Wilson Compton, "How Competition Can Be Improved Through Association," *Proceedings of the Academy of Political Science* 11 (January, 1926): 32–38.

[5]U.S. Forest Service, *Lumber Production, 1869–1934*, p. 74; John B. Woods, "The Forestry Situation in the U.S. Today and a Simple Workable Remedy," *Journal of Forestry* 28 (November, 1930): 930.

[6]For the sketchy correspondence regarding the background to the "lumber czar" proposal, see Wilson Compton telegram to NLMA, August 16, 1928, Frederick Haskin to Harry G. Uhl, August 21, 1928, W. W. Stark to Compton, September 10, 1928, John W. Blodgett to Compton, December 8, 1928, Blodgett to Edward Hines, December 8, 1928, and Compton to J. H. Eddy, January 3, 1929, all in box 75, National Forest Products Association Records (hereafter cited as NFPA Records), Forest History Society, Santa Cruz, California.

"imperfect development of the right spirit among the individual opera-tors." The failures of national and regional associations to resolve the lum-berman's problems, he said, "means nothing in favor of a new or different organization." The respected John W. Blodgett feared the extension of fed-eral authority suggested in the plan and doubted that the states would per-mit production controls. He cautioned Edward Hines, a Chicago lumber-man, to "wait and see what they do with the coal industry, or with the oil industry" before declaring in favor of such a drastic proposal. Blodgett urged Hines to consult President-elect Hoover regarding the plan because of Hoover's strong ties to the industry.[7]

The idea of a lumber institute originated with a group known as the Committee of Fifteen. According to Wilson Compton, the institute would replace the regional and national associations with one central agency, with authority vested in forty-eight directors and an appointed president. Comp-ton, who attributed the committee's effort to his refusal "to submit to indi-vidual or individual company domination," bitterly opposed the institute idea and its plan to organize separate departments for each species of lumber.

This plan, although described as progressive, is really fantastic, is predicated on a theory that somehow the individual lumber companies can be "forced" . . . to ac-cept the dictation of a centralized authority and that by the use of the word "Insti-tute" instead of the word "Association," and by calling a person who administers its activities "President" instead of "Secretary-Manager," the transformation will have been accomplished in the lumber business.

This was a "whispering campaign," carried out under cover, to provide lumbermen with "a short cut into the 'promised land.' " The adoption of such nostrums, Compton thought, would absolve lumbermen from any di-rect responsibility in the conduct of their affairs and only delay the inevita-ble day of reckoning.[8]

West Coast lumbermen were the chief proponents of the reorgan-ization plan. In addition to J. D. Tennant, others included the influential

[7] Stark to Compton, Blodgett to Compton, and Blodgett to Hines, all in box 75, NFPA Records.

[8] Compton to Eddy, and Wilson Compton to A. Trieschmann, December 8, 1928, both in box 75, NFPA Records. There is no extant copy of the timber institute plan in the files of the NLMA. See the file on the Committee of Fifteen in box 75, NFPA Records. For informa-tion on Compton's undocumented charges, see A. C. Dixon, "Efforts of the Lumber Industry at Production Controls Prior to NRA," in U.S. National Recovery Administration, Division of Review, *Work Materials No. 79*, Appendix 1, p. 243.

George S. Long, superintendent of Weyerhaeuser timber operations in the Northwest, and Frederick E. Weyerhaeuser, one of the founder's sons. The original program of the Committee of Fifteen got nowhere, according to Wilson Compton. The board of directors of the National Lumber Manufacturers Association (NLMA) adopted a considerably amended and watered-down version and then repudiated even this modest proposal. Although the institute plan lingered on, the idea was dropped as a practical plan early in 1929.[9]

In mid-January Frank Wisner, an officer in the national association, informed Compton that its board of directors had decided against any action, following Blodgett's recommendation to hold off on the matter. Wisner contended that marketing and overproduction problems depended on the individual lumbermen, because they were "very largely 'individualists' with fixed ideas of their own." Compton agreed. The proposal, he said, involved "chasing the end of the rainbow." In a letter to Tennant, Compton argued that the proposal would circumvent existing organizations, "most of them deeply entrenched in the confidence" of lumbermen. Progress in national cooperation, he observed, depended on the voluntary actions of individual businesses. He saw no need to adopt the name *Institute* for the national organization, and remarked, "I know too many 'Institutes' that are medieval, and too many 'Associations' that are up-to-the-minute."[10]

By May, 1929, Compton was confident that the threat to undermine his authority and reorganize the lumber industry had dissipated. The proposal, which originated with one lumberman who had a new solution to save the lumber business, was now less real than imaginary. The national association's board of directors gave Compton a unanimous vote of confidence, and the somewhat chastened secretary-manager reported that he passed up "an exceedingly desirable official appointment because of the attack on the Association, *which largely I had built up* [emphasis added]."[11]

Compton worked hard to protect his position and influence within the national association, and he enjoyed the support of important people in the

[9] See the list, "Committee of Fifteen," and Compton to Trieschmann, both in box 75, NFPA Records.

[10] Frank Wisner to Wilson Compton, January 12, 1929, Compton to Wisner, January 15, 1929, and Compton to J. D. Tennant, February 5, 1929, all in box 75, NFPA Records.

[11] Wilson Compton to Donald Conn, May 8, 1929, box 75, NFPA Records.

industry. At the height of the reorganization furor Compton wrote a strongly worded letter to John Kirby, insisting that this "greatest trade association in the country" was doing better work and "with a stronger public appeal than ever before." M. W. Stark, a member of the national association's board of directors, praised Compton as a "clear thinker" and a man of "unusual ability." Another director, John W. Watzek, applauded Compton's efforts to keep government out of the lumber industry. Watzek also disapproved of the plan to appoint a "lumber czar" as impractical and because it would "mean the loss of Wilson Compton." In the Puget Sound region Mark Reed discounted the practicality of the institute idea, because there were "too many cutting units of our industry to hope for anything like a unanimous sentiment" for the plan.[12]

Although the reorganization plan died aborning, it indicated a growing restiveness, even desperation, within the industry in response to the problems of contracting markets and overproduction. Lumber trade officials, who hoped to avoid government control, continued to support proposals to relax the antitrust laws and looked with increasing favor toward financial consolidation as a way to offset the industry's excessive decentralization.[13]

Herbert Hoover, like Wilson Compton, was no laissez-faire purist when it came to resolving business and industrial problems. As early as May, 1925, Hoover proposed business mergers and restrictions on production to help resolve lumber difficulties in the Pacific Northwest. A short while later, Calvin Fentress, representing a major Chicago banking firm with heavy investments in lumber, told the commerce secretary that his thoughts about business merger were heartening, because "we are working along that line in the hope that in some way order may be brought out of the present chaotic conditions." Hoover supported other mergers in the lumber industry, some of them involving large amounts of capital.[14]

[12] Wilson Compton to John Kirby, December 20, 1928, M. W. Stark to A. Trieschmann, January 14, 1929, and John W. Watzek to E. L. Carpenter, January 12, 1929, all in box 75, NFPA Records. Reed is quoted in Ficken, *Lumber and Politics*, p. 154.

[13] Compton to Kirby, box 75, NFPA Records; Dixon, "Efforts of the Lumber Industry at Production Controls," p. 243.

[14] Edgar Rickard Diaries, May 5, 1925, Herbert Hoover Presidential Library, West Branch, Iowa; Calvin Fentress to Hoover, May 15, 1925, in "Lumber, 1925," memo from J. C. Nellis to Hoover, February 5, 1927, and memo from Nellis to Hoover, July 1, 1927, in "Lumber, 1926–1928 and Undated," all in Commerce Papers, Hoover Papers, Hoover Presidential Library.

Because lumber production continued to run well ahead of demand, the merger issue was the most frequently discussed topic at regional and national meetings. Late in 1927, over two hundred lumbermen and paper and pulp and other wood-using industrialists attended a forestry conference sponsored by the U.S. Chamber of Commerce. Lumber spokesmen told the gathering that the industry needed greater public cooperation, including a relaxation of the antitrust laws. Everett Griggs, of the Saint Paul and Tacoma Lumber Company, recommended a program to educate the public about the economic conditions affecting forestry. And the conference speakers reiterated the lumberman's perennial argument that conservation and reforestation would be impossible unless burdensome taxes were removed and the industry was allowed to operate profitably.[15]

Some of the proposals to resolve the industry's problems were strikingly innovative. David Mason suggested in 1927 that sustained yield forest management would remedy overproduction. Sustained yield management, which later became the all-encompassing solution to overproduction and industrial stability, was still a relatively new idea in 1927. Mason believed that through federal and private cooperation and extensive pooling arrangements, lumbermen would be encouraged to "voluntarily adopt sustained yield to put effective brakes on production." Sustained yield would lessen the "recurrence of the industrial evil now experienced from the swarm of small mills" and would assure permanent and economically stable communities. But, Mason observed, the federal government must create the proper conditions.[16]

Organized lumbermen were taking more aggressive action to resolve their problems through both public and private channels as the depression crisis deepened. They convinced Herbert Hoover in May, 1930, to appoint the Timber Conservation Board, a public fact-finding body to investigate economic conditions in the lumber industry. Modernizers like William Greeley of the West Coast Lumbermen's Association (WCLA) thought the most pressing problem was to adjust productive capacity to the declining market. Greeley told the WCLA in 1929 that it must adjust to the "requirements and trends of its markets," because a sound market was vital to "stability and financial success."[17]

The *American Lumberman* proposed a two-pronged attack to meet the

[15] *American Lumberman* (November 19, 1927): 59–89; Samuel Trask Dana, *Forest and Range Policy: Its Development in the United States*, pp. 239–40.

[16] *West Coast Lumberman* 53 (October, 1927): 35–36.

[17] *American Lumberman* (August 17, 1929): 53. See also William Greeley, Secretary-

demoralized conditions—curtailed production and a campaign to increase consumption. The trade journal argued that the only way to control prices was to control production, a precedent already established and successful in the steel industry. W. E. Delaney advised a similar approach in his presidential address to the American Hardwood Institute in 1930: members should limit production to consumptive capacity and then use part of their increased profits for advertisements to expand the markets.[18]

But the depression deepened, and trade executives devised more drastic proposals to curtail production. William Greeley concluded early on that the difference between a firm and a weak market depended on a very small percentage of excess production. The WCLA, he said, had carried on successful curtailment programs until mid-1929, when it was unable to cope with a sharply declining market. He recommended a stabilization program based on production for current demand only. The key to effective industry cooperation and orderly competition, he claimed, was a firm price policy. If the WCLA was interested in such a program, Greeley promised to arrange a conference with the Federal Trade Commission to avoid unnecessary legal snarls.[19]

J. D. Tennant, the Long-Bell executive, thought industrial cooperation would become a natural trend, because "the day of individualism has almost . . . passed." He applauded the WCLA for its sense of cooperation and observed that "the industry that can bring about the closest unity" would make the best progress in the future.[20] Despite Tennant's praise for industrial unity and Greeley's call for greater cooperation, the situation continued to deteriorate. Effective curtailment was never a realistic possibility, because the market continued to contract and outstrip all efforts to control production.

Although lumber mills were operating at half their capacity by the end of 1930, demand was even further reduced. The veteran Mark Reed observed that lumber was "being offered that could not be sold at any price.

Manager, Annual Report to the West Coast Lumbermen's Association, 1929, folder 23, box 1, West Coast Lumbermen's Association Records (hereafter cited as WCLA Records), Oregon Historical Society, Portland, Oregon.

[18] *American Lumberman* (August 23, 1929): 30, (November 1, 1930): 22, and (February 8, 1930): 41.

[19] *West Coast Lumbermens Association, Newsletter* (January 31, 1930), folder 23, box 1, WCLA Records.

[20] Ibid.

It isn't a question of price," he worried, "it is just not being consumed."
The *American Lumberman* declared in the spring of 1931 that the depress-
ing conditions could have been prevented only "by a nearly unanimous determination" to stop cutting trees at a loss. It was the lumbermen's fault,
the journal charged, that the industry had become so demoralized.[21]

Most trade association executives advised production controls to cope
with increasingly glutted markets. To be sure, other elements were part of
the industry's strategy, but most agreed that the key to the immediate problem was the oversupply of lumber. Some trade leaders, like Wilson Compton, recommended full cooperation with smaller mills and wholesalers to
secure the orderly control and "intelligent forward-planning of lumber production." The effectiveness of production controls, he argued, could be
improved through more accurate statistical data and the dissemination of
these "facts" in each of the major timber-producing regions.[22]

A more controversial element in Compton's plan, and one that clearly
anticipated the policies of the National Recovery Administration, was the
establishment of production quotas for each manufacturing plant. Compton
cited the difficulties in fixing quotas as part of a stabilization program: it
would work, he believed, if all units cooperated; however, suspicion about
the operator in the next yard would ruin the plan. Compton pointed to the
work of the Federal Oil Conservation Board, which cooperated with the
federal government to establish production quotas, as one way to "discourage competition where there is too much."[23]

The attempt to obtain the cooperation of smaller mills in production
stabilization schemes proved difficult. This was especially true in the Southern Pine Association, where even the larger-scale producers were dropping
their membership because of financial problems. To counter this trend, the
association levied special assessments, cut its operating budget, formed
mergers with lesser subregional associations, and made an effort to recruit
smaller-scale operators. According to James Fickle's recent history of the
association, these efforts were not notably successful. But in typical Hoo-

---

[21] Forest Service, *Lumber Production, 1869–1934*, p. 74; and *American Lumberman*
(March 14, 1931): 20. Reed is quoted in Ficken, *Lumber and Politics*, p. 186.
[22] Wilson Compton, "A Course of Action for the Lumber Industry in the Orderly Control of Lumber Production and Distribution," report to the meeting of the board of directors,
NLMA, April 24, 1930, box 145, NFPA Records.
[23] Ibid.

verian fashion, one Department of Commerce official looked for a glimmer of optimism in a letter to lumber trade leaders:

> We are hoping to learn of . . . optimistic events happening in the industry, and it is our intention . . . to give such events publicity, thereby working toward a helpful change in the psychology of the public as a whole. We feel that now is the time to give publicity to all optimistic happenings.
>
> If you can send us such items as may come to your attention kindly drop me a line and let me know.[24]

Obviously, this bright hope for a revival in the lumber market never materialized, and the industry continued to explore various strategies to curtail production.

Because of the rapidly contracting markets, lumber trade leaders pressured the Hoover administration to prohibit federal timber sales and to modify the terms of long-term purchase contracts with the Forest Service. The *West Coast Lumberman* recommended that the Forest Service ease up on its cutting regulations. Because small logs could not profitably be cut and shipped, operators should be allowed to leave them in the woods. The Seattle journal thought the attitude of the Forest Service in these matters was "stiff-necked."[25]

Association leaders wanted to restrict federal timber sales, believing that the difference between a strong and a weak market involved only a narrow margin of production. Restricting sales of government timber, they believed, might provide the critical margin that would stabilize production. But other factors complicated the handling of federal timber. Although national forest timber represented only a small portion of the annual harvest, many mills and communities were totally dependent on it, and others depended on timber sales from Indian reservations. Hence, to satisfy these interests, President Hoover acceded to some requests and modified or delayed action on others. Restricting government timber sales during periods of depressed markets was not a new idea. Just before the market crash, the *West Coast Lumberman* suggested that government stumpage be withheld from sale until demand equaled production. Everett Griggs, a prominent

---

[24] James E. Fickle, *The New South and the "New Competition" : Trade Association Development in the Southern Pine Industry*, pp. 117–19. The chief of the Commerce Department's Lumber Division is quoted on p. 118.

[25] *West Coast Lumberman* 58 (February, 1931): 11.

Tacoma businessman, thought it was a crime to market large tracts of federal timber "when the industry is suffering from overproduction." And Charles Keith, the veteran leader of southern pine growers, said government timber should be kept off the market until it would bring a fair value. But Chief Forester Robert Stuart reminded the *West Coast Lumberman* that the Forest Service had considered the dangers of overproduction in formulating its sales-disposal policy; furthermore, its timber was "not a material factor in the conditions controlling the production and value of timber."[26]

Lumber's chronic difficulties finally convinced President Hoover to restrict the "leasing of the national forests for wood production" because of manifest overproduction. The Forest Service later prohibited sales of national forest timber "during the present economic situation where the value of the timber is in excess of $500." The order listed three exceptions: (1) to supply mills dependent upon the national forests, (2) to supply domestic paper mills, and (3) to salvage damaged timber. The *American Lumberman* thought the new policy would improve market conditions, but David T. Mason wanted a broader application of the president's order. He wired Oregon's Senator Charles McNary to urge Hoover to suspend sales on Indian reservations and the revested Oregon and California grant lands and to limit cutting to the sustained yield capacity of the forests.[27]

John H. Kirby, speaking for the Southern Pine Association, praised Hoover for avoiding paternalism and helping a "languishing industry." Frederick E. Weyerhaeuser, who thought government timber contributed to overproduction, applauded the president for his wisdom and courage and for proper and intelligent cooperation with business.[28]

Despite Hoover's decision, the complaints persisted. Contractors for national forest timber requested that stumpage prices be reduced in view of the depressed lumber market. Also, supporters of the move introduced a measure in the House to authorize the Department of Agriculture to reduce

[26] Ibid. 56 (June, 1929): 7, 19, 27, and (July, 1929): 34.

[27] Herbert Hoover to Secretary of Agriculture, May 14, 1931, and R. W. Dunlap to Hoover, May 18, 1931, both in "Agriculture—Forest Service Correspondence," Presidential Papers, Hoover Papers (hereafter cited as PPHP), Hoover Presidential Library; *American Lumberman* (June 6, 1931): 22; David Mason telegram to Charles McNary, May 20, 1931, file 310, David Mason Papers (hereafter cited as Mason Papers), Oregon Historical Society, Portland, Oregon.

[28] John Kirby to Herbert Hoover, June 23, 1931, "Forests—Fires, Reforestation," and Frederick E. Weyerhaeuser to Hoover, July 2, 1931, "Agriculture—Forest Service," both in PPHP.

stumpage prices on existing contracts. They urged its adoption because many of the prices were fixed "prior to the depression and when the market value of lumber . . . was much higher than at the present time." Lower stumpage prices, its proponents claimed, would permit mills to continue operating, aid local communities, and spare the government the embarrassment of broken contracts.[29]

Secretary of Agriculture Arthur Hyde opposed the measure, claiming it would grant contractors a cash subsidy and further glut "a lumber market already overstocked with the products of privately owned timberlands." Hyde pointed out that federal policy already allowed purchasers to be released from their contracts and to suspend operations; therefore, the resolution before Congress "would be a reverse of a policy of not stimulating production."[30]

William Greeley, speaking for the WCLA, objected to lowering contract prices for national forest timber. He saw no difference between the dilemma of government timber purchasers and that of operators who had invested in their own timber, because all forest industry values had suffered. By reducing the contract price for federal timber, he concluded, the government would be encouraging further production and altering "competitive relationships within the industry." Greeley advised the government to relieve purchasers from time requirements and to defer cutting until the market improved. A group of prominent Pacific Northwest lumbermen also opposed lowering stumpage prices, because it would "relieve parties . . . of their contractual obligations." These protests were effective because Congress took no action on the resolution.[31]

Contractors for timber on Indian reservations made similar requests to reduce stumpage prices. The commissioner of Indian affairs, Charles J. Rhoades, however, advised against passage of House Resolution 6684, which would have authorized such reductions. Again, the same northwestern lumbermen who opposed reductions in national forest contract prices balked at changes in the price of contracted Indian timber. The president subsequently approved a vastly amended version of House Resolution

---

[29] Arthur W. Hyde to Marvin Jones, February 19, 1932, and William Greeley to Ralph A. Horr, February 5, 1932, both in "Agriculture—Forest Service," PPHP.

[30] Hyde to Jones, "Agriculture—Forest Service," PPHP.

[31] Greeley to Horr, and J. P. Hennessy and A. W. Clapp to Marvin Jones and Edgar Howard, House of Representatives, February 19, 1932, both in "Agriculture—Forest Service," PPHP.

6684 in early March, 1933, which established a minimum sales price and required the consent of both the purchasers and the Indian tribal councils before prices could be altered. The act also granted the secretary of the interior the authority to act according to market conditions and the wishes of the Indian people.[32]

The precipitous drop in the demand for lumber after 1929 and the government's effort to curb timber sales had a dramatic effect on the annual cut of national forest timber. The harvest dropped from 1,421,188,000 board feet in 1929 to 1,254,963,000 in 1930, then plummeted to 793,816,000 board feet in 1931, 544,560,000 in 1932, and 473,910,000 for 1933.[33]

Lumber industry leaders concocted a number of ambitious proposals to counter the worsening economic crisis. These included marketing agreements, stabilization schemes, efforts to revise the antitrust laws, and repeated attempts to encourage the merger of small-scale operators into larger producing units. Most of the marketing agreements and stabilization plans were designed to keep mills operating on a limited basis. One regional trade group, the Northern Hemlock and Hardwood Lumber Manufacturers Association, recommended that the antitrust laws be suspended, especially as they applied to the natural resource industries. But the most ambitious of these proposals were stabilization plans that, their proponents argued, would serve the public interest. Uncontrolled production, they claimed, was detrimental to conservation and contributed to unstable, transient communities.[34]

When the NLMA asked the government for permission to enter into stabilization agreements similar to those in the oil industry, Chief Forester Robert Stuart supported the move. Both needed the aid of public authority to cope with their problems, he noted, and "in both cases overproduction is due to the fact that these irreplaceable natural resources are temporarily in too abundant supply" to establish rational systems of production.[35]

The Northern Hemlock and Hardwood Lumber Manufacturers Association drafted a stabilization plan in mid-1931, better known as the Wisconsin Stabilization Agreement. The proposal called for steady employ-

---

[32] Charles J. Rhoads, memo for the secretary, January 12, 1932, Ray L. Wilbur to Edgar Howard, chairman, House Committee on Indian Affairs, March 3, 1932, and Hennessy and Clapp to Jones and Howard, all in "Agriculture—Forest Service," PPHP.

[33] U.S. Forest Service, *Annual Report* (1931): 10, (1932): 17, and (1933): 21.

[34] Stabilization Plan of the Northern Hemlock and Hardwood Manufacturers Association, April, 1932, box 108, NFPA Records.

[35] Forest Service, *Annual Report* (1929): 3.

ment, rational use of natural resources, and reasonable profits for the industry. Such an agreement, the association contended, would contribute to social stability and to planned and more rational production, and it would preserve the lumber industry "from the chaos which would come from an unwise level of production." To dissuade its critics, the association directed its appeal to the public and disavowed private advantage. The proposal was not to go into effect until a certain percentage of lumber manufacturers had signed the agreement.[36]

The plan eventually was implemented and remained in operation until the adoption of the lumber code under the National Recovery Administration. And to protect the "public" interest, the state of Wisconsin exercised legal jurisdiction over the stabilization agreement through its Department of Agriculture and Markets. Finally, because industry leaders considered the Wisconsin plan a model for curtailing production, it was studied closely in other producing areas.[37]

Lumbermen in the Pacific Northwest, through Oregon's Senator Frederick Steiwer, promoted a system to rationalize production and prohibit the sale of lumber below a minimum price. The proposal involved the establishment of a corporation to control the manufacture and shipment of lumber from Oregon and Washington; each company subscribing to the agreement would purchase stock equal to its normal annual productive capacity. But the Steiwer plan raised serious questions. *Business Week* feared that it violated antitrust laws and noted that the NLMA was "holding aloof" and that the WCLA had not endorsed the idea.[38]

In addition to the Pacific Northwest stabilization plan, Senator Steiwer also tried to amend the Federal Trade Commission Act in order to permit natural resource industries to make agreements controlling production. He argued at a Senate hearing in March, 1932, in favor of liberalizing agreements to curtail production "so that industry may produce in accord with demand." The amendment, he said, would make it possible to control production in accord with Federal Trade Commission authority. The Oregon senator pointed out the obvious parallels between oil, coal, and lumber "in

[36] Wisconsin Stabilization Agreement, ca. 1931, box 108, NFPA Records.

[37] Dixon, "Efforts of the Lumber Industry at Production Controls," pp. 255–57.

[38] *Timberman* 33 (July, 1932): 14; "Plan for Corporation to be Organized for the Purpose of Preventing Unnecessary Cutting of Timber and Its Manufacture and Shipment Out of the States of Washington and Oregon and Failure to Bring Back into these States the Equivalent of the Value of the Raw Material Taken Out," undated, and *Business Week* (July 27, 1932), both in box 108, NFPA Records.

Weyerhaeuser Mill "B," Everett, Washington. At the time of its construction in 1915, this mill was the most technologically advanced operation in the country. Everett was also the scene of some of the most violent and callous lumber management procedures in the twentieth century. *Courtesy of Forest History Society.*

Left: E. T. Allen, ca. 1917. Like William B. Greeley, Allen began his career with the Forest Service. In 1909 he joined a newly formed cooperative fire protection agency in the Pacific Northwest. Allen, along with Greeley, Wilson Compton, and David T. Mason, must be considered one of the most important lumber industry spokesmen from 1900 to 1930. Allen also served as an expert witness on many national commissions. *Courtesy of U.S. Forest Service, Forest History Society collection. Right*: John Henry Kirby, a prominent southern lumberman and a leading figure in the Southern Pine Association, served as president of the National Lumber Manufacturers Association from 1918 to 1922, its critical period of reorganization. He also helped the federal government increase lumber production during World War I. *Courtesy of Forest History Society.*

Gifford Pinchot, "The Forester," greatly influenced both the practice of forestry and the Forest Service from 1900 to 1910. After he left office, Pinchot found himself on the radical wing of forestry causes because of his support for cutting regulations. *Courtesy of Forest History Society.*

Franklin Delano Roosevelt and his secretary of the interior, Harold Ickes, on a train to the Democratic State Convention at Syracuse, 1938. As governor of New York, Roosevelt established a reputation as a conservationist. As president, and as a self-styled "tree farmer," he pursued a variety of conservation programs. *Courtesy of Franklin Delano Roosevelt Library, Forest History Society collection.*

Spruce Production Division, World War I, Civilian Conservation Corps crew. To meet war production needs, the federal government and prominent northwestern lumbermen combined their efforts to crush labor unions through the use of conscripted troops, the Spruce Production Division, and the subsequent formation of a government-backed company union, the Loyal Legion of Loggers and Lumbermen. *Courtesy of U.S. Forest Service, Forest History Society collection.*

William B. Greeley, in his long career with the Forest Service (chief, 1920–28) and as an executive with the West Coast Lumbermen's Association, argued eloquently for the lumberman's cause. He formulated the earliest, and perhaps best, analysis of the industry's economic problems. Always cautious, Greeley was careful not to ruffle the feathers of industry leaders. *Courtesy of Forest History Society.*

Wilson Compton, trained in political economy at Princeton University, served a short stint with the Federal Trade Commission before becoming the chief executive officer of the National Lumber Manufacturers Association in 1918. He served in that capacity for over twenty-five years and was the industry's most important national figure. *Courtesy of Forest History Society.*

Raphael Zon, Russian immigrant, disciple of Gifford Pinchot, and leading progressive within the ranks of professional foresters. He served as head of the newly formed Lakes States Forest Experiment Station for two decades and edited the leading professional forestry publication, *Journal of Forestry*. *Courtesy of Forest History Society*.

David T. Mason, an iconoclastic and brilliant spokesman for progressive forestry. Modernists within the industry looked to Mason for leadership in times of crisis. A forestry consultant working out of Portland, Ore., Mason served as executive officer for trade associations and as the last head of the Lumber Code Authority under the National Recovery Administration. *Courtesy of Forest History Society.*

Ferdinand A. Silcox, chief, U.S. Forest Service, 1933–39. Referred to by his colleagues as a "forester's forester," Silcox had a broad social view of what he defined as responsible forest practices. He was feared by major lumber executives both for his persuasive oratory and for his "socialist" views. *Courtesy of U.S. Forest Service, Forest History Society collection.*

the sense that cutthroat, unrestrained and ruinous competition, brings disaster to the industry."[39]

Wilson Compton told the Senate subcommittee that the Steiwer amendment would aid natural resource industries that were "impoverished, stripped of working capital [and] depleted of credit." The alternative, he said, was merger or "continued chaos." He concluded that the causes of overproduction were "not casual and transitory, but fundamental and chronic"; the current depression had only made a bad situation worse. Compton disputed the notion that the Steiwer proposal would result in restraint of trade; lumbermen, he pointed out, already were operating "under conditions of jungle competition."[40]

Wilson Compton was skilled in the art of "stroking" committees. He told the Senate hearing that he sympathized with those who criticized business for running to government in times of need. "Business," he said, "should put its own house in order," and the lumber industry merely wanted the opportunity to do so. In February, 1933, he asked the House Judiciary Committee for a relaxation of antitrust laws "to establish the effective means of self-regulation." Although nothing came of these proposals, they indicated the steps some trades were willing to take in this hour of great crisis.[41]

William M. Ritter, a prominent lumber financier with extensive ties throughout the trade association world, also put forward a plan to revise the antitrust laws to aid the natural resource industries. In the lumber and coal industries, Ritter observed, consolidation and merger had not progressed very far, because antitrust laws prohibited such cooperation. These laws, originally designed to work in the public interest, now functioned in reverse and "have resulted in over-development, over-production, unstable employment and great physical waste." Because competition was wasteful and expensive, the Sherman law, which compelled excessive competition, should be repealed.[42]

[39] U.S. Congress, Senate, "Amendment of Federal Trade Commission Act and Establishment of a Federal Trade Court," *Hearings Before a Subcommittee of the Committee of the Judiciary*, 72nd Cong., 1st sess., March 31, 1932, pp. 219–20, 225–26.

[40] Ibid., pp. 228–30.

[41] Ibid., p. 231; statement of Wilson Compton, Washington, D.C., representing the NLMA (before the House Judiciary Committee, February 8, 1933), box 108, NFPA Records; Dixon, "Efforts of the Lumber Industry at Production Controls," p. 259.

[42] William M. Ritter, "A Plan to Assist Stabilizing Natural Resource Industries," ca. 1932, box 108, NFPA Records.

The Ritter plan, the Wisconsin Stabilization Agreement, and the Steiwer proposal clearly anticipated the ideas embodied in Franklin D. Roosevelt's National Recovery Administration. Lumber industrialists created these schemes to control production, and the depression prompted them to look to the federal government to achieve a rational and stable industrial order. Because of these desperately competitive conditions, progressive-minded lumber leaders were willing to move beyond voluntary cooperation to more coercive and rigorous efforts to control the industry's chaotic productive relations.

By 1931 lumber production was only half the 1929 output, but even this dramatic reduction did not stabilize prices. When it became obvious that voluntary curtailment could not cope with the steadily contracting market, some industrial leaders proposed a fundamental restructuring into larger operating units. Discussions about merger proposals and consolidations date from the mid-1920s and then became more frequent in the early 1930s. Most of the early efforts failed because of the reluctance of operators to surrender their independence and the fleeting hope that the business cycle might soon be on the upswing.[43]

The economy, however, did not right itself; instead, it contributed to a feeling that conventional remedies were inadequate. One of the more serious proposals to form larger operating units was a plan conceived by Minot Davis of Weyerhaeuser, who suggested a series of mergers in the Pacific Northwest as "the very best prescription" for putting a sick industry back on its feet. Because trade association cooperation could never supply all the needs of the industry, regional mergers provided one possibility of improving the economic situation. Davis suggested two mergers in the Pacific Northwest, one to include Puget Sound and Grays Harbor mills and the other to include mills along the lower Columbia River and in the Willamette Valley. He pledged the cooperation of the Weyerhaeuser group and listed the many benefits to be gained: economies in operation, more consistent grade marking, and improved cooperation with the Forest Service and the state forestry departments. "Problems of sustained yield," he remarked, could be worked out, which, in turn, would enhance the cause of conservation and stabilize the lumber industry.[44]

---

[43] For an account of merger talks in the Pacific Northwest between 1927 and 1929, see Ficken, *Lumber and Politics*, pp. 154–55.

[44] Minot Davis, memo regarding lumber industry, January 24, 1931, file 338, Mason Papers.

The Washington group contracted with consulting foresters David Mason and Carl Stevens to coordinate the merger talks, and the latter emphasized that the merged corporation would be in an infinitely better position to implement sustained yield management policies, "the only sound, adequate and permanent basis for merger proceedings."[45]

Early in the negotiations, however, it became apparent that dissension within the Weyerhaeuser group had brought matters to a stalemate. Some of the corporation's leaders objected to the Puget Sound proposals, and others doubted the abilities of Minot Davis. One junior official observed that "the Executive Committee [of the Weyerhaeuser group] has delegated a job to an individual too big for him." But Weyerhaeuser support was crucial. Mark Reed of the Simpson interests put it simply: "Nothing effective can be accomplished without the Weyerhaeuser Timber Company taking an active and concrete part in the organization." Their "influence and financial investment" were necessary, Reed insisted, before the negotiations went any further.[46]

Carl Stevens informed his partner, David Mason, in July, 1931, about the "moaning, wailing and gnashing of teeth" among the Weyerhaeuser executives "over the idea that the Washington merger negotiations sought to 'dismember' the Weyerhaeuser Timber Company." Moreover, he feared that the executive committee had only a "half-baked idea" of sustained yield and was unprepared to deal with it. Stevens suggested emphasizing the economic advantages of combining operations and implementing sustained yield management.[47]

Suspicion was rampant in the discussions over the proposed Washington merger. One operator remarked that cooperation must replace individualism or lumbermen would face ruin, and then in the same breath he decided to continue his "conservative individualistic policy." Some of the companies even balked at having their property evaluated. William C. Butler, a prominent Everett banker and investor in lumber operations, informed Carl Stevens that his companies would have their property valued only if the others did. Stevens later agreed that self-interest should be considered in the merger talks, because "corporations are justly motivated that

[45] Ficken, *Lumber and Politics*, p. 194; and C. L. Hamilton to Carl Stevens, January 8, 1931, file 338, Mason Papers.

[46] J. P. Weyerhaeuser to F. E. Weyerhaeuser, June 8, 1931, and Mark Reed to F. E. Weyerhaeuser, July 11,1931, both in file 338, Mason Papers.

[47] Carl Stevens to David Mason, July 31, 1931, file 338, Mason Papers. Stevens observed that the success of the Oregon merger was dependent on what happened in Washington.

way." However, when the Butler interests were unwilling to concede on certain technical issues, Stevens accused them of jeopardizing the merger talks and "attempting to bend the entire industry to its peculiar will." Moreover, he warned, the group's unwillingness to compromise might discourage the Weyerhaeuser group from further participation.[48]

The Everett banker argued that his companies should not be made the "heavy villain" in the merger talks that never "seem to get beyond the initial rehearsal stages." Butler told Carl Stevens that mergers were difficult to bring about, because "when it comes time to sign on the dotted line and turn over individual properties to alien control, the final act is usually a stumbling block impossible to avoid." Like the Weyerhaeuser executives who "wailed and gnashed their teeth," Butler fully understood the practical implications and the psychological factors involved in such an act. Carl Stevens was less pessimistic. While he agreed that mergers were impossible under normal circumstances, he was certain that compromise was possible then because of the decidedly abnormal conditions.[49]

The Washington merger talks clearly were on the rocks early in 1933. The Polson logging interests were reluctant to see their properties subsumed in a large corporate merger. Alex Polson had reportedly refused to join for technical reasons, but Mark Reed told Laird Bell, the negotiator for the Weyerhaeuser group, that Polson "had put his whole life in building up the organization" and did not want to see his operation lose its identity in a larger corporation.[50]

Carl Stevens, in a letter to Mark Reed, expressed dismay at the lack of progress in the negotiations. The plan, he believed, was "no grandiose ill-conceived and elaborate scheme," but rather a carefully planned proposal. He saw little indication that industrial conditions would otherwise improve, and, if the industry failed to take constructive action, he predicted "cut throat competition and strangulation, the like of which the Industry has never dreamed of." He told Reed that the Weyerhaeuser interests had gone a considerable distance to cooperate in the discussions, but if the effort failed, Stevens warned, "the Company can fully protect its own competitive position if it really continues as a knock down and drag out."[51]

---

[48] William C. Butler to Carl Stevens, December 5, 1931, and January 2, 1932, and Stevens to Butler, January 18, 1933, all in file 338, Mason Papers.

[49] Butler to Stevens, January 25, 1933, and Stevens to Butler, January 26, 1933, both in Mason Papers.

[50] Reed is quoted in Ficken, *Lumber and Politics*, p. 197.

[51] Carl Stevens to Mark Reed, February 4, 1933, file 338, Mason Papers. Robert Ficken

A few industry spokesmen advocated collective sales agencies as an alternative to merger and consolidation, but none of these plans went beyond the discussion stage. Chief Forester Robert Stuart opposed David Mason's sustained yield proposal because it required the merger of private timberlands into larger units, and because it interfered with the role of the national forests in providing "not only economic but also social welfare." Another Forest Service official, Raphael Zon, observed that lumbermen would merge and eliminate competition if they were left alone. But when they moved to establish larger units, "the American people immediately proceed against time on the ground that they create a monopoly." Thus, when the industry requested federal cooperation in relaxing antitrust laws, Zon urged the government to exact a quid pro quo to assure that any stabilization plan would serve the interests of the public as well.[52]

But the demoralized market for forest products continued to reap its toll in business failure and bankruptcy. Although the depression deeply influenced the way lumbermen perceived competition within the industry, their conventional economic values and their proprietary attitudes proved a substantial barrier to effective cooperation and business merger. Occasional combinations were arranged in the South and the Pacific Northwest, but the more ambitious plans had to await another time, when competitive conditions were more conducive to forming monopolies.

The deepening economic crisis accelerated the support that lumbermen, professional foresters, and privately funded conservation groups gave to the federal acquisition of cutover lands. The idea had gained credibility and practical application in the Weeks Act of 1911 and again in the Clarke-McNary Act of 1924. Federal acquisition became even more popular when economic conditions worsened in the late 1920s, and in 1929 the NLMA passed a resolution supporting a greatly expanded program to acquire forestlands. The depression broadened these ideas even further.[53]

Wilson Compton told a regional association gathering in 1931 that the historic process of converting the public domain to private timberland had left the owners with an excessive reserve stumpage whose carrying charges

contends that the Weyerhaeuser group destroyed the spirit of cooperation and ultimately was responsible for the failure of the merger discussions (see Ficken, *Lumber and Politics*, pp. 204–205).

[52] *Timberman* 31 (June, 1930): 35; Robert Stuart to Timber Conservation Board, October 31, 1931, in "Agriculture—Forest Service," PPHP; Raphael Zon to W. H. Kenety, March 3, 1930, box 6, Raphael Zon Papers, Minnesota Historical Society, St. Paul, Minnesota.

[53] Harold K. Steen, *The U.S. Forest Service: A History*, pp. 217–18.

were increasing faster than the value of the timber. To relieve these high
tax and interest charges, Compton recommended adoption of sustained
yield programs and expansion of both state and federal acquisition programs. He also urged that strategic acreages of mature timber be added to
the national forests "to aid in the control of production of forest products." [54]

The proposal puzzled Chief Forester Robert Stuart. The Forest Service, he said, did not pursue an aggressive acquisition program, because it
believed that timber owners "were not prepared to accept a large scale application of the principle." But if those circumstances changed, the Forest
Service would pursue acquisition in a constructive and liberal manner. Wilson Compton praised this willingness of the Forest Service to help in the
"economic rehabilitation of the forest industries"; as part of the public acquisition program, he proposed that timber owners be permitted to donate
their land to the federal government while reserving timber-cutting rights.
Under such a policy, the government would provide the protection and
administrative costs and relieve the timber owner from the carrying
charges. [55]

Compton's argument had some effect; in his annual report for 1931
Chief Forester Stuart recommended the "compulsory enlargement of public ownership." Two years later, Stuart saw acquisition as "a means of ob-
taining . . . greater . . . public benefits than would flow from private ownership." The controlling principle in Stuart's plea for public ownership was
planned development—a view that differed ideologically from Wilson
Compton's rationale—to lessen the costs inherent in private ownership of
timberland. This was a drastic remedy, to be sure, but its proponents argued that the desperate conditions required such measures. [56]

Although panaceas to cure the lumber industry's unsettled condition
abounded, not all trade leaders were as optimistic as the perpetually active
Wilson Compton. Western Forestry's E. T. Allen thought that modifying

[54] Wilson Compton, "Who Shall Absorb Lands Present Owners Cannot Carry?" address to the Annual Meeting of the Western Forestry and Conservation Association, March
19, 1931, box 146, NFPA Records.

[55] Ibid. Compton quoted Stuart in his address.

[56] Forest Service, *Annual Report* (1931): 5, and (1933): 1. The Forest Service report to
the Timber Conservation Board also recommended an expanded forest purchase program as a
measure of public security against destructive forest exploitation (see U.S. Forest Service,
The Forest Situation in the United States: A Special Report to the Timber Conservation Board
[January 30, 1932], copy in "Agriculture—Forest Service," PPHP).

the antitrust laws, implementing sustained yield policies, and a large-scale return to public ownership might have some effect in stabilizing production, but he could see no end to liquidation pressure and demoralized markets. Allen predicted "more wreckage before adjustments result in management strong enough" to stabilize the situation. He regretted that the industry's leadership had passed from the "wide-visioned men who got the properties together" to a group "familiar only with, and obsessed by, the more pressing problems of lumber manufacture and sale." [57]

By the summer of 1932, economic conditions in nearly every part of the American economy had reached a crisis. The ever-worsening markets in the lumber industry convinced its leadership that desperate action was necessary. And lumbermen, who otherwise were committed individualists, began increasingly to look to the federal government as a stabilizing agency. Some trade leaders suspicious of state intervention thought such action reckless and venturesome; others argued that these were desperate times and required bold and imaginative remedies. Traditionalists were disillusioned and in rout as their favored world crumbled about them.

[57] E. T. Allen to Hermann Von Schrenk, October 13, 1931, box 5, and Allen to A. W. Laird, April 9, 1931, box 4, Western Forestry and Conservation Association Records, Oregon Historical Society, Portland, Oregon.

8

Presidential Boards and Committees

"The present general depression has served in the lumber industry
only to accentuate an accumulated adverse condition."—Wilson
Compton, 1932

HERBERT HOOVER'S political ideology embraced a belief in voluntary and
cooperative enterprise between the government and the private sector and
the use of social science and engineering stratagems to resolve economic
and social problems. In this respect, Hoover fit the mold of the modernizers who believed that the application of businesslike and scientific methods would achieve a rational and broadly distributive economy. Hoover
was one of a community of progressive business people who believed that
collaborative councils, investigating boards, and other voluntary coordinating mechanisms would lead to a smoothly functioning political economy. Described by their proponents as apolitical and scientific, these investigating bodies were presumed to act objectively and in the public
interest. To underscore their legitimacy, they conducted extensive investigations and disseminated what they construed to be authoritative information.[1] These boards and committees, however, were more subjective
apologists for the status quo than they were objective social scientists.

By the 1920s, these quasi-corporate elites and their entourage of technical experts dominated the government's investigations. Their studies, reports, and findings invariably were addressed to the entrepreneur's perennial nemeses—disorder, destructive competition, and inefficiency. During
periods of economic and social distress these groups accelerated their
efforts to influence the world about them; they were intelligent and aggressive defenders of the modern industrial order who wanted to substitute
planned economics for the competitive market and who believed that state

[1]Ellis W. Hawley, *The Great War and the Search for a Modern Order, 1917–1933*,
pp. 54–55.

resources could accomplish this end. These innovative programs alarmed the more conventional business and industrial classes, but the Great Depression gave their proposals increasing credibility.

The lumber industry enjoyed a full complement of progressive leaders and technical experts like Wilson Compton, William Greeley, E. T. Allen, and David Mason, all of whom enjoyed legitimacy at the highest levels of government. In addition, these leaders worked through associates in the American Forestry Association (AFA) and the Society of American Foresters (SAF), groups which included memberships largely receptive to the industry's problems. And the Forest Service usually responded affirmatively to their proposals. Through industrial and professional organizations, these modernizers recommended innovations in industrial and business practice, tried to influence government policy, and sought more rational and stabler modes of operation. President Herbert Hoover's appointment of the Timber Conservation Board in May, 1930, was one of these attempts.

The restless Wilson Compton first recommended the appointment of a Timber Conservation Board to conduct a public investigation of the lumber industry's economic difficulties and to recommend practical ways to eliminate overproduction and the resulting waste of timber. A broadly representative board, he believed, would help secure the public confidence "without which, in the long run, no program of industrial stabilization may be expected to succeed." The leaders of the national association delayed action on Compton's recommendation until late December, 1929, when they approved the proposal.[2]

Compton's move was part of a broader effort to establish a feasible plan to stabilize the lumber industry on the Pacific Coast and "to remove the deadening influence" this situation imposed on forestry practices elsewhere. The critical issue was the rapid liquidation of northwestern timber and its corresponding effect on the national lumber market. To promote its "national forestry program," the National Lumber Manufacturers Association (NLMA) recommended increased Clarke-McNary appropriations, completion of the government's study of timberland taxes, and a nation-

---

[2] *American Lumberman* (August 17, 1929): 53. See also Compton to J. H. Eddy, January 3, 1929, box 75, National Forest Products Association Records (hereafter cited as NFPA Records), Forest History Society, Santa Cruz, California; *American Lumberman* (January 4, 1930): 36.

wide, all-inclusive program to acquire public forests. An impartial investigation, the association believed, would support these proposals. The
American Lumberman concurred, saying a public fact-finding commission
was "the best possible answer to the self-exploiting propaganda of discredited government-control enthusiasts of the Pinchot type."[3]

When Wilson Compton outlined his recommendations to the Hoover
administration, he stressed the need "to bring order out of threatened economic chaos in the lumber and wood-using industries." This vital matter,
he told the president, required the interest and cooperation of the public.
Hoover, who was concerned about funding the committee's work, nevertheless ordered Secretary of Commerce Robert P. Lamont to "get ahead
with the selection of the Board." Hoover's support for the lumber industry
inquiry was consistent with his backing of the Federal Oil Conservation
Board, in which his overriding concern was industrial stabilization.[4]

The formal organization of the National Timber Conservation Board
was delayed until late 1930. In the meantime the industry's leaders continued to seek resolutions to its economic plight. Rumors of operating mergers abounded, and there were attempts to emasculate the antitrust laws.
But through all this turmoil, Wilson Compton counseled self-reliance and
initiative. "The success of our industry will depend far less upon what others may do for us than upon what we do for ourselves." This sentiment was
best expressed in the work and policy recommendations of the Timber
Conservation Board.[5]

Chief Forester Robert Y. Stuart agreed with lumber trade leaders that
the economic situation warranted a public inquiry, but, he warned, its
promise "lies in its character and representation." His subordinate, Raphael Zon, was less optimistic. Given the current social and economic
forces, he feared, there would be "little chance of getting a commission

[3] *American Lumberman* (August 17, 1929): 53, 58, and (January 4, 1930): 36.

[4] Wilson Compton to Walter H. Newton, March 18, 1929, and April 1, 1930, Compton
to Herbert Hoover, April 2, 1930, Hoover to Compton, April 9, 1930, and Hoover to Robert P.
Lamont, May 15, 1930, all in "National Timber Conservation Board," Presidential Papers,
Hoover Papers (hereafter cited as PPHP), Herbert Hoover Presidential Library, West Branch,
Iowa. Robert Himmelberg contends that Hoover was concerned with stabilizing industries
and was willing to alter or abolish antitrust restrictions to achieve this end (Himmelberg, *The
Origins of the National Recovery Administration: Business, Government, and the Trade Asso-
ciation Issue, 1921–1933*, pp. 102–103).

[5] Preliminary copy of address by Wilson Compton to Board of Directors, NLMA, April
24, 1930, box 146, NFPA Records.

that would start us on a good line of approach to the problem of privately-owned forests." In an obvious slap at ex–Chief Forester Greeley, Zon told Stuart that the Forest Service should regain its independence and should "rely upon popular support instead of the support of Dr. Compton and similar pillars in the lumber industry." The service, he said, had lost its old crusading zeal and was too much under the influence of such apologists and defenders of the lumber industry as R. S. Kellogg and David Mason.[6]

The AFA approved of the conservation board's appointment, because economic chaos threatened the forest industries. The association noted that the "almost chronic overproduction [that] . . . has characterized the forest industries for the past decade and a half" was worsening steadily. A fact-finding commission, it believed, would help resolve the industry's economic problems, and, with public cooperation, "the disordered state of supply and demand . . . can be largely remedied."[7]

The SAF, although not without dissenting opinion, also endorsed the industry-sponsored Timber Conservation Board. It adopted a series of recommendations closely paralleling trade association proposals for increased public support and the accelerated acquisition of cutover lands. The public should meet its responsibility, the society argued, through increased public spending for fire protection. The potential for fire and the unfavorable economic conditions, it observed, induced overcutting, which resulted in a glutted market.[8]

While the president was making appointments to the Timber Conservation Board, Wilson Compton took steps to assure that the board focused its inquiry on the appropriate issues. He told E. T. Allen, who served on the NLMA's forestry committee, to submit recommendations to the board for its consideration. Compton could see no need to await a formal request from the board, noting, furthermore, that "there will be some advantage if the Forestry Committee were able to submit for consideration some con-

[6] Robert Y. Stuart to Raphael Zon, March 26, 1929, and Zon to Stuart, March 30 and September 19, 1929, box 6, Raphael Zon Papers (hereafter cited as Zon Papers), Minnesota Historical Society, St. Paul, Minnesota.

[7] AFA memo to the president, April 30, 1930, and Ovid Butler to George Akerson, September 23, 1930, both in "National Timber Conservation Board," PPHP; *American Lumberman* (May 3, 1930): 31.

[8] SAF report of Forest Policy Committee, December, 1930, box 69, Society of American Foresters Records (hereafter cited as SAF Records), Forest History Society, Santa Cruz, California.

structive suggestion at a reasonably early time." Allen's special knowledge, Compton indicated, would be critical in finding a practical way to
control production. He also urged Allen to stick to the "economic" side of
conservation and to keep the board from wandering "into wide and general
forestry fields" that would arouse conflict.[9]

Hoover appointed a twenty-one member advisory committee to gather
information and make recommendations to the Timber Conservation Board.
Both the advisory committee and the board were then organized into seven
subcommittees, six to report on specified subjects and a seventh to integrate all of the recommendations into a final report. The advisory committee, however, was the more important group, because it gathered information and advised the respective subcommittees. It included Chief Forester
Robert Stuart, William B. Greeley, E. T. Allen, David T. Mason, Wilson
Compton of the national association, and two lumbermen.[10] The make-up
of the committee assured organized lumbermen a controlling voice in the
"public" inquiry.

The trade leaders then coordinated the work of the Timber Conservation Board. Greeley urged the board to make preliminary reports, because
the "critical conditions" required action that "need not wait for the completion of the comprehensive investigation." The board, he advised, should
act with the least possible delay in proposing action to resolve the crisis.[11]

The Timber Conservation Board began to issue quarterly reports
through its Lumber Survey Committee in January, 1932. Lumbermen re-
acted favorably to the board's recommendations, which invariably called
for production cutbacks to "restore lumber supply and demand." But the
rapidly contracting market quickly made the quarterly reports obsolete.
The board reported in January, 1932, that the decline in lumber consumption and the failure to reduce production proportionately continued to
be the lumber industry's greatest problem. Four months later, the board
praised production cutbacks but recommended a further reduction if the
industry was to achieve a balance between supply and demand. "The immediate need of the lumber industry is to adjust its production . . . to the

    [9] Wilson Compton to E. T. Allen, November 22 and December 4, 1930, box 5, Western
Forestry and Conservation Association Records (hereafter cited as WFCA Records), Oregon
Historical Society, Portland, Oregon.
    [10] Samuel Trask Dana, *Forest and Range Policy: Its Development in the United States*,
p. 241; *American Lumberman* (March 28, 1931): 48–49.
    [11] William Greeley to Ripley Bowman, March 21, 1931, box 5, WFCA Records.

present demand." Subsequent quarterly reports warned against premature optimism when the market showed the slightest improvement.[12]

Lumber trade leaders presented their case to the Timber Conservation Board in June, 1931. Wilson Compton described the lumber business as perilous and ominous and said the industry had been in a depression during much of the previous decade without sharing in the industrial expansion between 1922 and 1929. "The present general depression," he argued, "has served in the lumber industry only to accentuate an accumulated adverse condition." To improve these conditions Compton suggested a series of temporary relief measures: (1) the withdrawal from sale of all government-owned timber, (2) a "moratorium" on requirements for harvesting government-owned timber, (3) the periodic publication of statistics to aid in setting production quotas, (4) the right to make reasonable trade agreements to control lumber production, and (5) protection against foreign competition.[13]

Compton also recommended long-range correctives to place the industry on a stable and lasting basis. He urged the timber-growing states to adopt a yield tax; he advised the federal government to allow private owners to donate their land to the government, but to reserve timber-cutting rights (to relieve the pressure for premature liquidation to pay taxes and maintenance costs); he urged operators to merge into larger units to promote economy and stability; he supported David Mason's sustained yield management program requiring the "blocking-up" of large federal units and the consolidation of private holdings; and finally, Compton recommended the establishment of federal grading requirements and reasonable protection from imported lumber.[14]

William Greeley, who presented the case for Pacific Coast lumbermen, did not believe that conditions had changed appreciably from those reported in his 1917 study. The chaotic circumstances could be attributed to the federal government's mistaken policy of disposing of public forestlands and the lumberman's assumption that large private acreages of timber could be carried profitably. To make matters worse, he told the board, lum-

[12] Report of the Lumber Survey Committee, January 27, April 22, and October 29, 1932, in "Commerce—Timber Conservation Board, 1932," PPHP.

[13] Wilson Compton to members of the U.S. Timber Conservation Board, June 11, 1931, box 71, NFPA Records. The industry's presentation was reported fully in *American Lumberman* (June 20, 1931): 26–28.

[14] Compton to Timber Conservation Board, box 71, NFPA Records.

bermen had overestimated consumer demand and the rate at which virgin forests would be depleted. Speculation, overcapitalization, taxation, and other carrying charges led to the "conversion of trees into dollars" and the building of logging and manufacturing facilities far exceeding market capacity.[15]

E. T. Allen shared Greeley's skepticism that conditions had changed much since the First World War. A few statistics and predictions, he thought, might be revised, but these were "scarcely more than details of the same old problem." To counter the industry's chronic problems—keen competition, overproduction, low stumpage values, and constant instability—Allen urged the board to adopt the proposals outlined in Wilson Compton's report.[16]

As part of its fact-finding effort, the Timber Conservation Board requested all forest products trade associations to submit reports on economic conditions and make suggestions to help formulate policy. The response of the Southern Pine Association was a classic in evasion, betraying an inability to take a hard look at its own problems but a willingness to blame the operator over the next hill. The report attributed depressed conditions in the South to the "premature opening of new timber sources in the West," the general contraction of the market, the need to maintain working capital, the continued liquidation of timber to meet excessive taxes, and the industry's inability to cooperate in curtailing production because of antitrust laws. Competition from Forest Service timber also provided an additional element of uncertainty "not conducive to the widespread practice of forestry."[17]

Frederick W. Fairchild, who headed the Timber Conservation Board's subcommittee on taxation, repeated his long-held conviction that the "real problem" for timberland owners was the threat of unreasonable taxation in the future. Investors wanted to calculate future taxes with some degree of certainty, and timber taxes in this respect were an "undoubted obstacle." But, he argued, taxation was not responsible for the rapid cutting of private

[15] William Greeley, "Problems and Needs of the West Coast Lumber Industry," presented to the Timber Conservation Board, June 11, 1931, box 71, NFPA Records.

[16] E. T. Allen, "Relation of Forest Ownership to Manufacturing Problems," June 11, 1931, box 71, NFPA Records.

[17] Southern Pine Association, *Economic Conditions in the Southern Pine Industry*, pp. iii, 11, 15, 121.

timberland, nor did it have "any substantial effect upon the management of mature forests." [18]

Wilson Compton called this statement astonishing. He charged that Fairchild's evidence was incomplete and that it did "violence to the common knowledge of the lumber industry." Fairchild then reminded the quick-tempered Compton that his judgment about timber tax policy was "a matter upon which I have been seeking evidence for more than 20 years." Moreover, he said, Compton would need figures to support his charges, and Fairchild was convinced that none existed. In a letter to Ripley Bowman, secretary to the board, Fairchild remarked that simple business and economic principles indicated that "taxation cannot, by and large, in the ordinary run of cases be the predominant cause of cutting." [19]

While the various subcommittees of the Timber Conservation Board presented their findings to the public, Raphael Zon circulated a private memorandum charging that the board represented powerful interests in the natural resource field who had maneuvered themselves into positions of influence. The NLMA, he said, had brought the board into being, and its members, "all safe (?) men, were carefully selected . . . and were told to formulate and advance a plan of forest conservation." Its members were interested only in consolidating timber ownership and production to the extent permitted by antitrust laws. Zon was pessimistic about the future and the ability of the Forest Service to control such onslaughts on the public interest. Because many of "the men we depend upon are sympathetic with the enemy," he feared that the public interest was being sacrificed, and powerful groups with intelligent, aggressive, and well-paid agents were in the ascendant. Zon told one board member that it would be unfortunate if its recommendations served "only as a cloak for the National Lumbermens Association to obtain the modification or the entire abandonment of the Sherman Anti-trust Law." [20]

[18] "Taxation of Timberlands: Report of the Subcommittee on Taxation of the Advisory Committee of the Timber Conservation Board," undated, pp. 36–37, box 77, NFPA Records.

[19] Wilson Compton to Frederick Fairchild, November 4, 1931, and Fairchild to Compton, November 12, 1931, box 77, NFPA Records; Fairchild to Ripley Bowman, February 27, 1932, box 27, SAF Records.

[20] Franklin Reed, executive secretary of SAF, urged the earliest possible publication of the board's findings, because many of the recommendations involved future legislation. Reed thought early publication would prepare the public for the recommendations in the final report

Raphael Zon stood alone in his criticisms, which had little effect, since civic, industry, and conservation groups friendly to lumbermen funded the board and its activities.[21] Differences of opinion usually concerned technical matters such as those between Fairchild and Compton on timberland taxes. Except for Zon, no one questioned the lumber industry's domination of the board's actions; even when disagreements arose, they were muted, and the final reports represented the full force of the industry's viewpoint.

The report of the Subcommittee on Publicly Owned Timber provides a good example of the influence of lumbermen in policy recommendations. Henry S. Graves, the former chief forester who drafted its final report, argued that publicly owned timber contributed an element of stability to the present crisis and that the sale of Forest Service timber greatly increased the economic problems of overproduction. He also repeated the industry's long-standing view that the sale of publicly owned timber during a period of glutted markets worsened its problems.[22]

One of the more controversial matters the Timber Conservation Board considered was David T. Mason's sustained yield management proposal. The plan, designed to stabilize the industry and conserve forest resources, required owners to form cooperative agreements to limit the annual harvest to the rate of reproduction. The proposal, Mason argued, would reduce production to the amount the market could absorb, usher in fair prices, and stabilize the industry. One part of the market-centered plan involved agreements between the Forest Service and private owners "to provide . . . management for both privately and publicly-owned land in logical operative units or working circles."[23] It was a grand design but with broad implications for public policy, affecting the management of public lands and raising serious questions about the application of antitrust laws.

Chief Forester Robert Stuart opposed the sustained yield proposal,

---

and make it easier to achieve stability in the industry (see Reed to Wilson Compton, ca. June, 1931, box 27, SAF Records). Raphael Zon, "A Warning (Not for publication): Conservation of Natural Resources Threatened," May 21, 1931, box 6, Zon Papers.

[21] For information regarding the funding of the board, see the conclusions and recommendations of the Timber Conservation Board, August 1, 1932, in "National Timber Conservation Board," PPHP.

[22] Report of the Subcommittee on Publicly Owned Timber, November 14, 1931, box 71, NFPA Records. E. T. Allen, David Mason, William Greeley, Ovid Butler of the AFA, and George Sisson, a pulp and paper industrialist, were members of the subcommittee.

[23] The Mason sustained yield proposal is summarized briefly in Robert Y. Stuart to Timber Conservation Board, October 31, 1931, "Agriculture—Forest Service, Forest Management," PPHP.

and Fred Morrell, who conducted a Forest Service inquiry into the potential for cooperatively managed public and private forestlands, was equally unenthusiastic. Federal cooperation with private timber owners under the Clarke-McNary legislation, Morrell indicated, had not "improved cutting practices" on private lands, nor had any of the other bright hopes been realized. He believed that private owners would be interested in timberland only if it supported commercial timber.[24]

Stuart was even more critical. He thought Mason had exaggerated the effect of sustained yield on controlling production and had overestimated the federal timber suitable for sustained yield management. But the provision to merge private units into larger ones as a preliminary to cooperative management agreements with the federal government bothered him more. This violated the principle that public property should be distributed by open competition. Sustained yield would negate competition in Forest Service sales, because the law required competitive bidding on all federal timber sales above $500. The proposal, Stuart said, was inconsistent; it restricted the ability of the Forest Service to manage federal timberlands in the public interest, and it would bring the federal government into the "conduct of private enterprise for purely private ends."[25]

When he learned that the final report of the Timber Conservation Board included support for sustained yield management, Stuart refused to endorse it, because it gave an overly optimistic picture of the nation's forests and their prospects for being maintained in "continuous productivity." He found parts of the report outright objectionable, because they glossed over the private sector's failures in reforestation and forest management. Moreover, the report dealt with forestry only as a commodity, whereas the chief forester insisted that "consideration of the forest situation from the standpoint of public concern must go beyond commodity needs."[26]

The Timber Conservation Board published its final report in August, 1932. It recommended consolidation of all public properties under one ad-

[24] Fred Morrell, "Report on Possibilities of Cooperative Management of National Forest and Private Lands," October 31, 1931, "Agriculture—Forest Service, Forest Management," PPHP.

[25] Harold K. Steen, *The U.S. Forest Service: A History*, p. 225; U.S. Forest Service, *Annual Report* (1931): 60; Stuart to Timber Conservation Board, PPHP; Stuart to Timber Conservation Board, November 23, 1931, box 77, NFPA Records.

[26] Robert Stuart to Paul Redington, June 28, 1932, box 71, NFPA Records. Stuart also requested that the report should make it clear that the Forest Service furnished the statistics but that the conclusions were those of the board.

ministrative head, expansion of programs to acquire public timberland, "extreme conservatism" in disposing of public timber, increased federal outlay for fire protection, more equitable systems of taxation, implementation of sustained yield management, relaxation of antitrust laws, greater effort in forest products research, and the merger of timber holdings into larger operating units.[27]

The report was thoroughly economic, directed toward political means to stabilize the lumber industry. Some of its proposals repeated the recommendations of previous federal investigations, while others clearly grew out of the economic crisis of the early 1930s. The provisions for sustained yield management, controlled production, and the merger into larger operating units reflected changing competitive conditions. Economic circumstances had convinced progressive trade leaders in the natural resource industries to move away from competition toward cooperative action in order to stabilize the market. The board predicted that allowing greater cooperation to control production would stabilize the industry and "conserve natural resources and provide continuity and security of employment."[28]

The final recommendations of the Timber Conservation Board also ignored the counsel of some of its expert advisors. It ignored Frederick Fairchild's claim that taxation was not a significant cause of overproduction and reported just the opposite. "The . . . annual burden of taxation on mature standing timber is the most important . . . factor forcing the sale or cutting of timber." Chief Forester Robert Stuart's opposition to sustained yield management received no mention. The final report differed only in length and minor detail from Wilson Compton's first proposals. And it did not dissipate its energies as E. T. Allen feared in one of his homilies, "When a hen hovers [over] too many eggs, none hatch but all rot." Finally, when the National Recovery Administration established the Lumber Code Authority, it tried to implement many of the recommendations of the Timber Conservation Board. The recovery administration, in fact, based its production quotas on the quarterly reports of the Hoover board.[29]

Lumber industry leaders, who applauded the recommendations of the Timber Conservation Board, were less enamored with another Hoover in-

[27]Conclusions and Recommendations of Timber Conservation Board, in "National Timber Conservation Board," PPHP.

[28]Ibid.

[29]Ibid.; Compton to Timber Conservation Board, NFPA Records; Steen, *U.S. Forst Service*, pp. 225–26. Allen is quoted in *American Lumberman* (March 28, 1931): 49.

vestigating body, the Committee on the Conservation and Administration of the Public Domain. Because of the steadily deteriorating condition of western rangelands and because of Hoover's commitment to reduce the federal bureaucracy, the president recommended a public inquiry to examine the feasibility of returning all federal lands to the states. Hoover proposed in August, 1929, to achieve "more constructive policies" for conserving grazing lands, mineral resources, and water storage systems and to pursue his political ideology of reducing federal interference in local affairs.[30]

Secretary of the Interior Wilbur, mindful of the sensitive nature of the undertaking, urged the president to "emphasize that this is primarily a conservation measure" to protect grazing lands on the public domain. Most easterners and westerners initially praised Hoover's appointment of the Committee on the Conservation and Administration of the Public Domain, but some had reservations. The *Oregon Statesman*, speaking for the timber-rich Pacific Northwest, feared the plan would revive "one of the bitter political controversies of twenty years ago" when "Pinchotism" was attacked from "Point Barrow to Nogales." The newspaper reminded its readers that circumstances were different now, and even the West Coast Lumbermen's Association (WCLA) wanted the Forest Service to continue its administration of the national forests. The *Statesman* opposed turning the federal forests over to the states because of the uncertainty that would accompany such a radical shift in administering natural resource lands. Raphael Zon, from his vantage point as director of the Lakes States Experiment Station, feared that if the committee adopted the principle of returning public lands to the states, there would be little hope of maintaining the national forests under federal supervision.[31]

The Portland-based *Timberman* let the Public Domain Committee know that it stood "squarely on the platform that there be no juggling of ownership of the national forests which could jeopardize their perpetuation." The journal informed its readers that the alienation of the national forests would be contrary to the public interest and that state management of forest resources betrayed "a disheartening record of profligacy." Moreover, the "big-minded" lumbermen opposed the transfer of federal timber-

---

[30] Herbert Hoover to Joseph M. Dixon, August 21, 1929, in "Public Lands Commission," PPHP.

[31] Ray Wilbur to Herbert Hoover, October 2, 1929, and F. W. Mondell to James Garfield, November 4, 1929, in "Public Lands Commission," PPHP; *Oregon Statesman*, August 21, 1929; Raphael Zon to George P. Ahern, September 19, 1929, box 6, Zon Papers.

land to the states because federal control was "fairer and . . . more stable." The experiences of the past few years, the *Timberman* pointed out, proved that the federal government should have kept the title to all of its timberland. The transfer of the federal forests to private ownership "would witness a consistent and aggravated repetition of the present unsatisfactory situation."[32]

Herman H. Chapman, a professor of forestry at Yale, conducted a survey of state forestry officials for the SAF and found only two foresters who favored state acquisition of the national forests. Western conservationists, he contended, favored administration of public lands at the local level but by a federal agency. William Greeley, first an ex–chief forester and then an executive with the WCLA, also impressed upon the committee the necessity of maintaining the national forest system. He defended the work of the Forest Service and was adamant in his insistence that the size of the national forests should not be reduced.[33]

Greeley's defense of the federal forests was effective because the draft report of James R. Garfield, chairman of the Public Domain Committee, praised the management of the national forests and even recommended that they be enlarged in some cases. But there were dissenters—ex-Governor James P. Goodrich of Indiana favored surrendering to the states "the absolute, fee simple title to all the Public Domain." He was convinced that the states could handle reclamation, forestry, and grazing matters better than the federal government. Indeed, Goodrich puzzled at his appointment to the committee, because his ideas were "so diametrically opposite to that of the rest of the Commission."[34]

But when the time came to approve the final report, William Greeley was the only committee member who refused to sign. Even Garfield's last-minute effort to modify its objectionable language failed to change his mind. Greeley concurred with the committee's major recommendations, but he balked at a vaguely worded proposal advising that lands containing "cer-

[32] *Timberman* 30 (October, 1929): 35, and (September, 1929): 35.

[33] Herman Chapman to James Garfield, January 3, 1930, in "President's Committee on the Conservation and Administration of the Public Domain—Correspondence, Articles, Pamphlets, Speeches," and William Greeley to Garfield, January 3, 1931, in "Public Domain—Committee Correspondence," both in PPHP.

[34] James Garfield to Herbert Hoover, December 11, 1930, draft report of the Committee on the Conservation and Administration of the Public Domain, in "Public Lands Commission," and J. P. Goodrich to Garfield, January 25, 1931, in "Public Domain—Reports," both in PPHP.

tain mineral resources" be turned over to those states adopting accepted conservation principles. Greeley feared that this would initiate a move to transfer all federal reserves to the states—a policy, he argued, that was "unsound in principle" and likely to precipitate the return of the national forests to the states.[35]

Lumbermen, professional societies, and conservation organizations all supported Greeley's strong defense for the continued federal administration of the national forests. A Seattle correspondent told James Garfield that in Washington, prevailing sentiment opposed the states taking over federal lands. A Kentucky hardwood manufacturer, who evidently interpreted the report differently from Greeley, commended the Public Domain Committee for safeguarding the national forests and preventing the states from "playing cheap politics." *American Forests*, however, joined Greeley in criticizing the report. The journal disapproved of the appointment of state boards with the power to increase or decrease the size of the national forests. These state boards, it feared, would convert national forests into state forests, thus undermining their "integrity and administration." Similarly, the *Journal of Forestry* carried an editorial, "The Public Land Report: A Threat to Conservation," which was critical of turning federal forestlands over to the states.[36] Lumber trade journals had little else to say about the report of the Public Domain Committee.

Although the recommendations avoided explicit mention of relinquishing federal control of the national forests, lumbermen were alarmed. The steadily deteriorating economy convinced many that the return of federal forests to the states would further destabilize an industry already plagued with chronic economic problems. Indeed, most lumber trade spokesmen wanted to expand the federal forests, and some were even suggesting that the government purchase standing timber as a way to help control production and stabilize the market. They feared that turning the national forests over to the states would be the first step in their alienation to private timber holders, thereby worsening the glut in private holdings.

Congressional bills to implement the recommendations of the Public

[35] Greeley to Garfield, January 26, 1931, Hugh A. Brown to Garfield, January 28, 1931, Garfield to Greeley, February 2, 1931, and Greeley telegram to Garfield, February 9, 1931, all in "Public Domain—Reports," PPHP; Dana, *Forest and Range Policy*, p. 235.

[36] Asahel Curtis to James Garfield, March 16, 1931, and H. G. Garret to Garfield, April 1, 1931, both in "Public Domain—Reports," PPHP; "An Editorial—A Dangerous Grant," *American Forests* 37 (May, 1931): 279; "The Public Land Report: A Threat to Conservation," *Journal of Forestry* 29 (October, 1931): 649–51.

Domain Committee got nowhere. Major economic interests, especially in the West, feared that the proposals would worsen an economic situation already verging on chaos. The *Timberman* charged that one of the bills was "the boldest attempt [yet] to weaken the national forest system." In another time and under different circumstances, the bills to return to the states surface rights on the unreserved public domain might have succeeded. But the worsening economy, rampant failure in the private sector, and the refusal of western states to accept public lands unless their mineral rights were included led to the defeat of these proposals.[37]

In 1932, in the midst of despair, Royal S. Copeland of New York introduced a Senate resolution calling for an investigation of the nation's forest resources and of the degree to which reforestation work might be a source of jobs. The Forest Service, under the direction of Earl H. Clapp of the Branch of Research, carried out the work in record time and delivered its report, *A National Plan For American Forestry*, in March, 1933. Although the report is associated with the expanded legislative program of the New Deal, the focus of the Copeland study was on long-standing industrial conditions and forestry problems.[38]

The study was well received. Chief Forester Robert Stuart praised the Copeland Report as "the most comprehensive and exhaustive survey yet made of the forestry situation in the United States." Robert Marshall, a young and left-leaning Forest Service official, thought the Copeland study was "by all odds the best literary production which the Forestry Service has yet gotten out." The executive secretary of the AFA, Ovid Butler, also praised the study, calling it "the most thorough and comprehensive exposure in the history of American forestry." Samuel Trask Dana referred to it as "an encyclopedia of valuable information"; Henry Clepper called it "the most important document on forestry policy up to that time"; and Harold Steen's recent history of the Forest Service labeled it "the New Deal blueprint for forestry."[39]

[37] *Timberman* 33 (April, 1932): 15; Dana, *Forest and Range Policy*, pp. 235–36.

[38] Henry Clepper, *Professional Forestry in the United States*, p. 146; Steen, *U.S. Forest Service*, pp. 199–200; Dana, *Forest and Range Policy*, p. 244.

[39] U.S. Congress, Senate, *A National Plan For American Forestry*, Senate Doc. 12, 73rd Cong., 1st sess., March 13, 1933, p. x; Robert Marshall to Raphael Zon, February 27, 1933, box 7, Zon Papers; Ovid Butler, "Forest Situation Exposed," *American Forests* 39 (May, 1933): 204; Dana, *Forest and Range Policy*, p. 245; Clepper, *Professional Forestry in the United States*, p. 146; Steen, *U.S. Forest Service*, p. 199.

The Copeland Report denounced owners of private timberland for their laissez-faire approach to forestry, which had contributed to the serious deterioration of the nation's timber resources. Moreover, the report continued, lumbermen had shown little interest in reforestation, and their most conspicuous claim to constructive action—fire protection—had largely been publicly financed. This record of failure was juxtaposed with the "progress in American forestry . . . where the public has taken things into its own hands in the ownership and management of lands." The antidote to private mismanagement, therefore, was public control of at least half the national forestry business.[40]

The AFA praised the Copeland Report for pointing out the need for an expanded program to acquire forests. Although the SAF took no official action on the Copeland recommendations, its publication, the *Journal of Forestry*, drew attention to this veritable "forestry encyclopedia which every forester should have at his elbow for ready reference," noting that in normal times, such a report "would be front page news." Raphael Zon, the journal's former editor, told Gifford Pinchot that the Copeland study was a "frank admission of the failure of private forestry." He praised its proposals for an enlarged forest ownership by the public and the regulation of private timberland.[41]

Some foresters, however, had reservations about the Copeland recommendations. Ward Shepard, a former Forest Service assistant to Earl Clapp, thought the federal government was "committing a strategic and moral blunder of the first magnitude" in proposing expanded public acquisition and in rejecting regulation as a solution to the forestry problem. He criticized the Forest Service for using the latest catch phrase—"cooperation" in 1923, and "nationalization" in 1933—and argued that there was no single answer to the forest problem.[42]

From his academy sanctuary at Yale University, Henry Graves welcomed the Copeland Report's bold proposal for public ownership. Although he advised caution and questioned the acquisition of mature timber, Graves praised the report for recommending greater public assistance to

[40] Senate, *National Plan For American Forestry*, 73rd Cong., 1st sess., March 13, 1933, pp. 41, 76, 78.

[41] Ovid Butler, executive secretary, AFA, annual report for 1933, box E-2, American Forestry Association Records, Forest History Society, Santa Cruz, California; Steen, *U.S. Forest Service*, pp. 203–204; "Editorial," *Journal of Forestry* 31 (May, 1933): 507; Raphael Zon to Gifford Pinchot, May 23, 1933, box 7, Zon Papers.

[42] Ward Shepard to Robert Stuart, April 28, 1933, box 7, Zon Papers.

the forest industry. By "removing economic obstacles," he said, the public would make it possible for lumbermen to practice progressive forestry. Graves also favored more stringent public controls of private forestry practices, which he thought could be accomplished by increasing the subsidy to timber owners.[43]

Finally, Wilson Compton added his support for the Copeland recommendations, which he said arraigned "the whole historic land ownership policy of the Federal Government." Whereas in the past the government sought to convert the public domain to private ownership, now it needed to reverse the process. The forest industries, Compton noted, also supported the acquisition of virgin timber, because private owners could not afford to invest in them and were forced by taxes and capital carrying charges to cut unnecessarily. Federal purchase of both virgin and second growth stands would steady the market and prevent "thousands of small sawmills" from "consuming immature forests" and flooding an already overburdened market.[44]

The desperate and chaotic conditions of the Great Depression altered priorities and changed the way industrialists and finance capitalists viewed their world. The struggle for economic survival brought forth an array of nostrums and panaceas and even a few hysterical remedies to restore order and stability to the market. Perhaps because its difficulties antedated the stock market crash, the lumber industry seemed more willing than some to experiment with new measures, many of them centering on production control.

The persistent and widespread distress convinced some lumber trade leaders to consider other means to effect production controls and to stabilize the market. The *American Lumberman* observed that business had deteriorated to the point where its leaders were ready to hear the worst and to adopt whatever remedies would fit their needs. The situation would "require heroic measures for its relief," and lumbermen must show a willingness to change if they were to survive.[45] As conditions became even more acute, industry spokesmen stepped up their recommendations for merging into larger units, government relaxation of antitrust laws, imposition of in-

[43] Henry S. Graves, in "Comments on the Copeland Report," *American Forests* 39 (June, 1933): 258–59.

[44] Wilson Compton in *ibid.*, 259, 284.

[45] *American Lumberman* (April 25, 1931): 26.

dustry-sponsored government controls to limit production, and establishment of uniform standards.

Most of the recommendations, however, centered on production control; the groups that promoted the first voluntary palliatives now turned to newer and headier ventures involving the federal government. In the midst of election year 1932, a Weyerhaeuser executive observed that the Timber Conservation Board's recommendations were "stop-gap" measures and only partially effective—a strong indication that influential leaders were willing to move beyond voluntary and cooperative measures to stabilize the lumber industry.[46]

[46] J. P. Weyerhaeuser address to the U.S. Chamber of Commerce, May 24, 1932, copy in folder 30, box 2, David Mason Papers, Oregon Historical Society, Portland, Oregon.

9

The Great Experiment in
Industrial Self-Government

*"It probably isn't going too far to say that the present effort—new
deal—is the 'last stand of the capitalistic system'—as one man said.
And if we fail to make the new deal work, we'll get rather complete
socialization. We must make it work."—David T. Mason,
August, 1933*

THE policies and programs of the 1920s culminated in an economic disaster of the first order. The marketplace did not effect a smoothly functioning and rationally operating competitive system, and if anything, the dramatic fluctuations of the market served more as an element of discord than as an inducement to cooperation. The rapidly contracting economy of the 1930s undermined voluntary efforts at stabilization, especially in the lumber industry, where circumstances forced operators to keep their mills running in order to try to meet their carrying charges. These disruptive conditions underscored the private sector's inability to control production and achieve a rational and stable economy. Also, these failures became apparent at a time when business and trade associations enjoyed considerable influence in shaping and directing domestic policy.

When Herbert Hoover's New Era failed to usher in the promised utopia, disillusioned business and industrial leaders sought more effective and coercive national programs. The election of Franklin D. Roosevelt, the self-styled "tree-grower," to the presidency in November, 1932, offered if nothing else a change in mood from the gloom and despair that had hovered over the last days of the Hoover administration. What the new administration would offer to speed economic recovery no one knew, but its first legislative fumblings intrigued industrial leaders and quickened their expectations. The largest single lumber organization, the Weyerhaeuser group, agreed that hopes were revived and the country was "on the verge of an era of controlled individualism."[1]

Shortly after Roosevelt's inauguration, the *American Lumberman* reported general enthusiasm and a strengthened lumber market. One lumberman told the trade journal that President Roosevelt would be able to promote cooperation among all interests. An Arkansas lumber sales manager believed the country would witness a prompt advance in business, including lumber. C. C. Sheppard, the president of the Southern Pine Association, predicted that "lumber will advance . . . within the next thirty days," and a Chicago lumberman reflected that the business had "definitely 'turned the corner.'" A Shreveport, Louisiana, lumberman observed "more people with smiles today and . . . more optimists on our streets than we have had for three years."[2]

David T. Mason informed the members of the Western Pine Association in March, 1933, that there were many hopeful signs, but he warned lumbermen to be cautious and to seek cooperative means to control production. He cited the need for greater central coordination and a modification of the Sherman law as prerequisites to effective industry cooperation. Mason, who later took a leading part in writing the lumber code under the National Recovery Administration (NRA), was one of the key proponents of industry and government cooperation to control production. According to Mason, industry either must govern itself or expect to be governed.[3]

Lumbermen anxiously but hopefully watched the unfolding of the Roosevelt administration's program for industrial recovery. The earliest of the New Deal legislation and some proposals still in the rumor and discussion stage embraced controversial recovery measures with the potential to deeply affect the lumber industry. These included inflation of currency, farm and home mortgage relief, limitations on daily and weekly working hours, emergency relief, forestry legislation, a public works program, adjustments in railroad rates, reorganization of the railroads, and tariff adjustments. But until sometime in April, 1933, the administration gave no clear indication that it was intent on an all-inclusive recovery plan. The subsequent decision to adopt a broad industrial recovery program received

---

[1] Quoted in Ralph W. Hidy, Frank Ernest Hill, and Allan Nevins, *Timber and Men: The Weyerhaeuser Story*, pp. 436–37.

[2] *American Lumberman* (March 18, 1933): 17.

[3] Ibid. (April 1, 1933): 32.

wide support from business groups and trade associations, who convinced New Deal managers to draft a recovery policy based on government cooperation with the associations. This "partnership in planning" was a general legislative proposal for industry-government cooperation to achieve industrial recovery. Desperate economic straits and the threat of social upheaval forced the addition of other elements to the final recovery bill.[4]

Franklin Roosevelt's interest in promoting recovery through emergency forestry projects dated at least from the early summer of 1932. At first this took the form of providing employment in forestry programs in Roosevelt's native New York. But by the time he became the Democratic party's nominee for president, the make-work projects of planting and road and trail building had expanded to include, in Roosevelt's words, "a more definite and comprehensive national plan . . . [that] should have among its objectives more efficient stabilization of the forest products industry." By election time, Roosevelt was clearly committed to public acquisition of forestlands east of the Mississippi River in order to provide reforestation work for the unemployed, watershed protection, recreational needs, and perpetuation of forest resources. Thus, Roosevelt embraced the major elements of an aid program for the lumber industry—emergency measures for reforestation and unemployment relief—long before the hastily passed laws of the spring of 1933.[5] His experiences as an amateur forester prompted his support for reforestation and conservation measures; his equally strong commitment to a stable and orderly economic environment for capitalist ventures made him sympathetic to industrial stabilization.

The industrial recovery program that took shape in the first three months of the Roosevelt administration merely elaborated organizational techniques and policies that originated during the First World War and in the trade association movement of the 1920s. Roosevelt's recovery schemes were structured along probusiness lines that bespoke a community of interest between the managers of business corporations and the directors of

[4] Ibid. (April 29, 1933): 12; Robert Himmelberg, *The Origins of the National Recovery Administration: Business, Government, and the Trade Association Issue, 1921–1933*, p. 182; *American Lumberman* (May 13, 1933): 14.

[5] Franklin Roosevelt to Ovid Butler, August 15, 1932, and Roosevelt to Miller Freeman, September 6, 1932, in Edgar B. Nixon, ed., *Franklin D. Roosevelt and Conservation, 1911–1945*, I, 119–20; W. G. Howard to Roosevelt, December 28, 1932, container 1, official file (hereafter cited as OF) 149, Franklin D. Roosevelt Papers (hereafter cited as FDR Papers), Franklin D. Roosevelt Presidential Library, Hyde Park, New York.

government agencies. This shared vision was particularly true of the NRA, which was based on a general consensus among trade leaders that the government should assist them in controlling prices, production, and trade practices. It marked the culmination of a movement rejecting laissez-faire individualism and its wild fluctuations in the business cycle. Because of the increased integration of the national economy and the destructive tendencies so apparent in twentieth-century competitive relations, a few prominent business and industrial leaders now advocated state intervention in an attempt to bring order to otherwise uncontrollable market forces.[6]

The decision of the Roosevelt administration to move in the direction of a wide-ranging industrial recovery program represented a departure from previous federal policy; that policy was new, however, only in its efforts to institutionalize the influence of business and industry in government through trade associations. The NRA tried to legitimize efforts to circumvent the antitrust laws and proposed to use the force of the state to regulate corporate business activity. But little of this was new. In fact, the trade association movement of the 1920s clearly anticipated the forms of industrial self-government outlined in the recovery administration's codes.

In the 1920s the Commerce Department, under Herbert Hoover, promoted voluntary industrial cooperation to cope with excessive competition and volatile economic fluctuations. By the early 1930s, business and industrial leaders agreed that more drastic steps were necessary, and the lumber industry, long plagued by a mercurial market, proved willing to pursue the New Deal objective of regulated self-government. David Mason related later that the National Lumber Manufacturers Association (NLMA) was at work in April, 1933, on legislation to authorize "industrial self-government under Federal supervision."[7] The NRA, then, was a formal attempt to use state influence to institutionalize the cooperative practices of the 1920s.

[6]For a discussion of these ideas, see Himmelberg, *Origins of the National Recovery Administration*, pp. 181–82; Ellis W. Hawley, *The New Deal and the Problem of Monopoly: A Study in Economic Ambivalence*, pp. 36–43; Ronald Radosh, "The Myth of the New Deal," in *A New History of Leviathan: Essays on the Rise of the American Corporate State*, ed. Ronald Radosh and Murray Rothbard, pp. 151–64; Louis Galambos, *Competition and Cooperation: The Emergence of a National Trade Association*, chap. 8; Barton J. Bernstein, "The New Deal: Conservative Achievements of Liberal Reform," in *Towards a New Past*, ed. Barton J. Bernstein, pp. 263–88; and William Appleman Williams, *The Contours of American History*, pp. 343–488.

[7]David T. Mason, "Lumber Code," Lumber Industry Series XI, 1935, Yale University School of Forestry, copy in folder 6, box 7, David Mason Papers (hereafter cited as Mason Papers), Oregon Historical Society, Portland, Oregon.

For a time lumber spokesmen were enthusiastic. The *American Lumberman* praised a Roosevelt "fireside chat" in early May that proposed to cure "sick industries by the excision of certain evils . . . such as overproduction, cut-throat competition and other unfair practices." The trade paper applauded Roosevelt for urging industry "to do its own housecleaning and thus avoid oppressive Federal regulation." Moreover, the journal noted, under the president's program trade associations would be the voice of the industry. Thus, lumbermen should ready themselves through their trade groups in order to express the united concerns of the lumber industry.[8]

Wilson Compton liked the administration's "big push" for industrial recovery. He described it as planned control of "production, prices, wages and employment," begun through the trade associations and supported by the federal government. Compton chastized newspapers that referred to the president's program as socialistic; on the contrary, he argued, the proposal was "a bold effort to see how far it is possible to plan and regulate industry to avoid further economic degeneration, and to avoid socialism." Compton called the Roosevelt plan a conservative, orderly alternative to the pitfalls of radical legislation; it was in accord with the recommendations of the Timber Conservation Board and consistent with the industry's effort to amend the antitrust laws in order to deal effectively with the causes and effects of overproduction. The lumber industry, he said, had a clear duty to draft a proposal for self-regulation, because industry leaders would have government support to force compliance "on the small fringe of chronic non-co-operators."[9]

Trade papers and industry officials offered guarded but supportive commentary as the recovery bill worked its way through Congress. The *West Coast Lumberman* cautioned that the plan was more comprehensive than the policies during the First World War, because production limitations were being added to wage and price restrictions. The Seattle paper, however, recognized a need to establish a proper balance between supply and demand to avoid overproduction and unprofitable market conditions. The *American Lumberman* indicated that the industry was willing to cooperate and was "getting its house in order"; it reported that a group of lum-

[8] *American Lumberman* (May 13, 1933): 14.

[9] Statement of Wilson Compton before the House Judiciary Committee, February 8, 1933, box 108, National Forest Products Association Records (hereafter cited as NFPA Records), Forest History Society, Santa Cruz, California; *American Lumberman* (May 13, 1933): 15.

bermen had met in Chicago under the auspices of the NLMA to work out a code of fair competition. The present circumstances offered the industry its best "opportunity . . . to line up solidly in support of a movement calculated to benefit employer and employee alike." Trade executives were equally supportive. In the Pacific Northwest, William Greeley urged the West Coast Lumbermen's Association to get behind the administration's plan for industrial recovery.[10]

David Mason, who was in Washington, D.C., helping to frame the industrial recovery bill, wrote to a Western Pine associate that recovery legislation "will pass at this session—I believe its passage imperative." Mason was also promoting his broad economic proposal including sustained yield to senators and representatives from the Pacific Northwest; sustained yield, he said, "will give industry a better odor." But Washington politics remained the key attraction. "Altogether there's evidently plenty to do, and this is the place to do things these days. So don't know when I'll be home."[11]

The peripatetic Mason was also active in the effort to formulate a code of practice for the lumber industry. He attended the lumbermen's meeting in Chicago and with other trade leaders put together a preliminary draft of the code, which was adopted without great debate. It was subsequently forwarded to the regional associations for their approval and then back to Chicago, where industry representatives met to formally approve a national code. Mark Reed, who participated in these meetings, commented on the desperate situation. "There doesn't seem to be anything to do but to go along, and in any event it cannot be much worse than it has been for the past three years." These meetings took place while Congress was debating the passage of the National Industrial Recovery Act (NIRA), which Roosevelt signed into law on June 16, 1933.[12]

Foresters interested in regulating cutting practices on private timberlands saw a golden opportunity in the early months of the New Deal. Following its recommendations in the Copeland Report, the Forest Service

[10] *West Coast Lumberman* 60 (May, 1933): 5; *American Lumberman* (May 27, 1933): 10; minutes of the meeting of the Board of Trustees, West Coast Lumbermen's Association, May 16, 1933, folder 4, box 6, West Coast Lumbermen's Association Records (hereafter cited as WCLA Records), Oregon Historical Society, Portland, Oregon.

[11] David Mason to Van Fullaway, May 15, 1933, folder 30, box 2, Mason Papers.

[12] Rodney C. Loehr, ed., *Forests for the Future: The Story of Sustained Yield as Told in the Diaries and Papers of David T. Mason*, p. 100; Herbert C. Berckes, "The Pitch in Pine: A Story of the Traditions, Policies and Activities of the Southern Pine Industry and the Men Responsible for Them" (Unpublished manuscript in the Forest History Society). Reed is quoted in Robert E. Ficken, *Lumber and Politics: The Career of Mark Reed*, p. 207.

urged Secretary of Agriculture Henry A. Wallace to expand the federal acquisition program to about 224 million acres, of which some 134 million should be the responsibility of the federal government. But Ward Shepard, a former Forest Service officer and in 1933 a fellow with the Carl Schurz Foundation, wanted more. He argued against exclusive reliance on federal acquisition and pressed for a composite program of large-scale acquisition, regulation, and cooperation. If the Forest Service put an exclusive emphasis on acquisition, it would "ignore the most favorable political conjuncture in a generation." [13]

Shepard forwarded a letter to Roosevelt, suggesting that the recovery bill was a "providential means for a statesmanlike solution" to the problem of forest devastation. Specifically, Shepard recommended that the president demand, as part of a quid pro quo, a provision to regulate cutting practices on private timberland. The industrial recovery legislation, he suggested, offered a rare opportunity to banish forest destruction in favor of permanent yield forestry. He would include a government policy of "sustained yield forestry as *a minimum basis* for control of lumber production [italics in original]." [14]

The program outlined in Shepard's memorandum attracted support from foresters and conservationists. Raphael Zon, mindful that the Copeland study called for a large public ownership, believed that "stopping forest devastation" was still an integral part of a national forestry policy. The industrial recovery program, he wrote Gifford Pinchot, provided an opportune moment to link cutting restrictions to the industry's proposals. "I cannot conceive of eliminating competition, controlling prices and production, without controlling the timber cut." If the lumber industry were allowed to regulate prices and production and to eliminate small operations without a corresponding requirement for regulating cutting, Zon argued, it "would mean throwing away the greatest opportunity we have to bring the management of private lands under control." And Franklin Reed of the Society of American Foresters advised Roosevelt to give the Shepard idea

[13] Robert Stuart to Henry Wallace, April 18, 1933, container 8, OF 1c, FDR Papers; Henry Clepper, *Professional Forestry in the United States*, p. 147; Ward Shepard to Stuart, April 28, 1933, box 7, Raphael Zon Papers (hereafter cited as Zon Papers), Minnesota Historical Society, St. Paul, Minnesota.

[14] Ward Shepard to Franklin Roosevelt, May 29, 1933, container 8, OF 1c, FDR Papers; Harold K. Steen, *The U.S. Forest Service: A History*, p. 226; Clepper, *Professional Forestry*, pp. 147–48.

very careful consideration. The policy, if adopted, would end forest devastation and "mark one of the greatest victories for forest conservation in the world's history."[15]

After the NLMA drafted its preliminary code in late May, 1933, Shepard fired off another note to the administration stressing the need to exact forestry and silvicultural requirements in exchange for permitting lumbermen to control production and regulate prices. Except for "one vague general statement in the preamble," he charged, the association's document ignored forest conservation. He recommended that the code be overhauled to include sustained yield management as a central feature.[16]

Although he was tucked away in Saint Paul, Minnesota, far removed from the hectic pace of the nation's capital, Raphael Zon kept abreast of national events, especially as they affected the lumber industry and the practice of forestry. Zon advised Earle Clapp, an associate chief forester, to take advantage of the recovery bill to control the timber cut on private lands. To his close friend and confidant, Robert Marshall, Zon suggested taking advantage of "the leverage afforded by the Industrial Recovery Bill for controlling the timber cut." Zon wondered who, apart from Ward Shepard, was cooking up the plan. "Is it Compton, Mason, and Greeley, the same people who balked before at any attempt at regulating the lumber industry?" He warned that advocates of federal cutting regulations should be reassured that the lumber code would not become another Timber Conservation Board.[17]

Secretary Wallace and the chief of the Forest Service advised the president to endorse the "principle of regulation of privately-owned forest lands" as part of the industry's agreement to come under the industrial recovery bill. Roosevelt then instructed Wallace to inform the NLMA that "any code relating to the cutting of timber will contain some provision for the controlling of destructive exploitation."[18] At this stage the administration appeared to be taking a strong stand in favor of imposing cutting re-

[15] Raphael Zon to Gifford Pinchot, May 23, 1933, box 7, Zon Papers; Franklin Reed to Franklin Roosevelt, June 10, 1933, container 8, OF 1c, FDR Papers.

[16] Handwritten note signed by Ward Shepard, June, 1933, container 8, OF 1c, FDR Papers.

[17] Zon to Pinchot, June 16, 1933, box 7, Zon Papers.

[18] Henry Wallace to Franklin Roosevelt, June 15, 1933, container 8, OF 1c, FDR Papers; Wallace to Roosevelt, June 16, 1933, and Roosevelt to Wallace, June 16, 1933, in Nixon, ed., *Roosevelt and Conservation*, I, 181–82; Steen, *U.S. Forest Service*, p. 226.

strictions in return for granting lumbermen freedom to fix prices and set production quotas. Only time would show the long-term resistance of trade leaders to any form of restriction on cutting.

While the administration was lobbying for its version of the industrial recovery bill, Wilson Compton, William Greeley, and David Mason worked vigorously to assure that the program would be acceptable to lumbermen. These three leaders and Laird Bell, associated with the Weyerhaeuser interests, drafted the conservation provision that became Article X of the code. They also served on the Emergency National Committee (appointed by the NLMA in early July, 1933, and eventually incorporated as the Lumber Code Authority) and negotiated with the Forest Service, the American Forestry Association, and the Society of American Foresters. This was a hectic period of intense activity, especially for trade association leaders determined to preserve the principle of industrial self-regulation, yet use the federal regulatory authority to compel adherence to the code.[19]

The Forest Service, assigned the task of negotiating the wording of the conservation provision, wanted a strong regulatory measure to control silvicultural practices on private timberlands. But some service workers, like Raphael Zon, were skeptical that a requirement for sustained yield management, unless emphatically and explicitly worded, could alter cutting practices on private forestland. Zon suspected that lumbermen would favor a mild provision for sustained yield management, "because it is less enforcible [sic], less tangible, and requires a long time to show results." Furthermore, he mused, the industry would be free within two years from government control because the NIRA would expire. George P. Ahern, a long-time critic of timber cutting practices, also doubted that the conservation measures in the code would accomplish anything. The industry, he believed, was "strong for cooperation if they can dictate the kind of cooperation." Lumbermen ruined the forests and took their profits elsewhere. But now that the depression has overtaken them, they "will look to Uncle Sam to put them on their feet with a substantial annuity."[20]

Those who supported industrial self-control, with the federal government serving as the enforcement agency, far outnumbered the skeptics who

[19]Loehr, ed., *Forests for the Future*, pp. 113–19; Hidy, Hill, and Nevins, *Timber and Men*, p. 437; Mason, "Lumber Code," Mason Papers.

[20]Zon to Pinchot, July 15, 1933, George Ahern to Raphael Zon, August 18, 1933, and Ahern manuscript, "The Forest Industries Code Conference: Rugged Individualism Rampant," August 17, 1933, all in box 7, Zon Papers.

raised social and political questions. Lumber trade journals praised the "new system of economic control," emphasizing that some plan was necessary to bring about a better balance between production and consumption. Another journal reminded its readers that the NIRA recognized trade associations as the "natural and logical agency" for implementing industrial control. In addition, the regional groups were praised for readying the preliminary codes and enforcement mechanisms well before the final approval of the lumber code.[21]

The *American Lumberman* applauded the lumber trade for approaching the task of industrial recovery "with a remarkable degree of unanimity and a commendable spirit of cooperation." The industry claimed it could govern itself if freed from antitrust laws, the journal reported. It now had both the opportunity and the leadership: Compton managing the national association and Greeley, Mason, Berckes, and others guiding the regional groups. The industry, so the journal believed, was ready to move forward "in step with the government . . . to a renewed life of service to the country and profit itself."[22] This heady spirit of optimism prevailed among most lumber trade leaders as the associations readied mechanisms for their wage, price, and production quotas.

It was not until August 19, 1933, after considerable haggling between the lumber industry and the administration, that Roosevelt approved Article X of the lumber code. The national association's Emergency National Committee then became the Lumber Code Authority, thus creating a new agency operating at the discretion of the president and empowered to administer the lumber code and to enforce its "rules, regulations and interpretations."[23]

The Code of Fair Competition for the Lumber and Timber Products Industries, with the single exception of Article X, represented the work of industry leaders. Published under the authority of the government, it covered activities that industry leaders considered vital to economic recov-

---

[21] *Timberman* 34 (June, 1933): 7–8; *West Coast Lumberman* 60 (June, 1933): 5–6; *American Lumberman* (June 24, 1933): 12.

[22] *American Lumberman* (June 24, 1933): 12, and (July 8, 1933): 16.

[23] Steen, *U.S. Forest Service*, pp. 226–27. The Emergency National Committee served as the critical coordinating agency for the lumber industry during the formulation and negotiations over the lumber code. The Lumber Code Authority was the clear successor to the Emergency National Committee (see *Lumber Code Authority Bulletin* 1 [August 21, 1933]: 1, copy in folder 30, box 2, Mason Papers).

ery—production control, rules for fair trade practices, minimum wage scales, maximum hours of labor, minimum prices, and the implementation of forest conservation practices and sustained yield management. The *West Coast Lumberman* regarded the code as "the best judgement of a large number of the ablest men in the United States," whose formulation and writing was done within the industry. Moreover, because previous efforts had not revived the industry, there was cause to hope for better things under the code. Although the lumber code went into effect immediately, government and industry officials still had to negotiate the specific recommendations for forest conservation to be included in Article X.[24]

Despite his central role in drafting the lumber code, David Mason was dissatisfied with the early direction of the NRA. According to Mason, the head of the recovery program, General Hugh Johnson, had failed to efficiently organize the overall program and had not delegated enough authority to ensure rapid and smooth cooperation. Johnson's problems included "too much artificial stimulant getting him into public notice in unfavorable way[s]." Mason also feared that the recovery administration would abandon the self-government idea for "bureaucratic autocracy" and that labor groups would gain an inordinate influence and lead the way to complete socialization. Still, he maintained, the effort was necessary, due to a "real danger of very serious collapse—and even serious revolution—this winter." The New Deal, he concluded, might be the "last stand of the capitalist system." If it failed to work, "we'll get rather complete socialization. We *must* make it work [italics in original]."[25]

Although other trade leaders were not verbally as desperate as Mason, some, like the editor of the *Timberman*, cited possible problems. Putting the industrial regulations into effect, even under the code of fair competition, it reported, would wreak hardship on some and dislocate normal operating conditions for others. Problems with wage scales would arise, along with greater difficulties in enforcing uniform prices. The *Timberman* editor cautioned against repeal of the act, however, because the failures of the unregulated market called for new tactics. "We must exercise patience and let these new economic theories . . . have a fair trial," he warned. The *American Lumberman* also praised the willingness of lumbermen to coop-

---

[24] Clepper, *Professional Forestry*, p. 148; *West Coast Lumberman* 60 (September, 1933): 3.

[25] Mason to Fullaway, August, 1933, folder 30, box 2, Mason Papers.

erate in carrying out the principles of the recovery act, but noted difficulties in negotiating cost protection prices and fair trade practices.[26]

The *West Coast Lumberman* was more optimistic and claimed that the codes would benefit the entire industry. Although its provisions might work an occasional hardship through unemployment dislocations, the consensus of opinion was that the industry would prosper under the code. The *American Lumberman* said the code would counteract the work of the chiseler and the price and wage cutter, who flourished under the old laissez-faire system. The trade paper noted that "the constructive leaders in the industry" supported the code, because it would protect the man with a "high-class organization of contented employees and a superior product." Under the code cooperative operators would be protected, "because the price-cutting wage-slasher will be up against the minimum wage." To be effective, the code would require compliance with a minimum wage scale, both minimum and maximum prices, and an effective way to inspect grades of lumber. All agreed that the code would help stabilize the industry.[27]

Article X of the lumber code called for the conservation and sustained yield management of timber resources and required the appointment of a joint committee to draw up formal regulations for achieving these ends. Accordingly, Secretary of Agriculture Wallace convened a preliminary conference in October, 1933, comprised of industry, federal, state, and local representatives, and to this conference he emphasized the critical relationship between conservation and a healthy lumber economy. "Stabilized industry and employment in the natural resource industries," he said, "is impossible without conservation and sustained production of the basic resource." To the extent that such a program could be implemented, lumbermen would be more secure and timber would be grown and harvested on a definite plan rather than as the mere exploitation of the resource. "Individualism, guess-work, and competitive skimming of the cream of natural resources," he claimed, "will give way to team-work, long-term planning, and concerted action to conserve the resources for future use."[28]

---

[26] *Timberman* 34 (September, 1933): 7; *American Lumberman* (October 28, 1933): 14.

[27] *West Coast Lumberman* 60 (August, 1933): 3, and (September, 1933): 3; *American Lumberman* (September 16, 1933): 10.

[28] Clepper, *Professional Forestry*, pp. 148–49; *West Coast Lumberman* 60 (November, 1933): 3–4; Loehr, ed., *Forests for the Future*, p. 127; Forest Conservation Conference on Lumber and Timber Products Industries with Public Agencies, October 24, 1933, pp. 3–4, copy in box 69, NFPA Records.

Wilson Compton, who submitted a series of proposals to the conference, insisted that the entire venture was an industry undertaking and would be administered as such. As a quid pro quo for implementing forestry practices, Compton demanded public cooperation that "must be substantial, dependable and enduring." It should include (1) abandonment of confiscatory systems of taxation; (2) protection of forest properties from fire; (3) protection from foreign lumber imports; (4) capital and credit facilities similar to those extended to agriculture; and (5) the right of the industry to handle these problems with the aid of permanent enforcement mechanisms. Compton attributed the forestry situation to "past unwise public land policies, present unwise state timber taxation policies, and to the destructive competition to which largely these factors have given rise." He specifically avoided any suggestion that lumbermen critically examine their own economic and social environment.[29]

Robert Marshall told the conference that Compton's scheme asked for a public subsidy and offered nothing in return. Marshall suggested balance —"an immense program of forest acquisition" coupled with the regulation of private timberlands and a public board independent of the lumber industry to formulate and enforce standards. Raphael Zon remarked that Compton did not offer "a single clear statement that commits the industry to do anything in the woods." Lumbermen, therefore, were asking a great deal from the public, which already had removed antitrust restrictions on controlling production and fixing prices. The time had come, Zon said, for the industry to "make a dramatic move" of faith in proving that it planned to practice intelligent methods of forest preservation.[30]

The first Article X conference adjourned and divided into interim committees to work out a final agreement. Generally, the proposals supported most of Wilson Compton's suggestions. Specifically, they recommended a public acquisition program that would eventually bring 224 million acres of forestland under federal, state, and local management; transfer of the revested Oregon and California railroad land grant to the Forest Service; federal action encouraging states to rectify their timber taxation policies; an increase in Clarke-McNary expenditures from $2,500,000 to $10,000,000; increased support of forest research (mainly to study forest

---

[29]Forest Conservation Conference (October 24, 1933), pp. 19–44, NFPA Records.
[30]Ibid. (October 24, 1933), pp. 144–46, and (October 25, 1933), pp. 232–36.

insects and diseases); and a policy of extreme conservation in disposing of public timber.[31]

During the interim period (between the preliminary meeting and the convening of the final conference in January, 1934), the lumber industry consolidated its influence over the emerging conservation policy. As the recommendations of the regional code divisions poured into Washington in December, 1933, Ed Munns, a Forest Service official and member of the Article X conference, likened the strength of the lumbermen's proposals to a "babe in arms." In a letter to Raphael Zon he accused David Mason and Arthur B. Recknagel, professor of forestry at Cornell University, of "soft-pedalling [sic] everything really constructive and doing it seriously! Their job has been perfect—from the lumbermen's point of view." Munns reported that Ferdinand Silcox, who had replaced Robert Stuart after the latter's death in November, 1933, was disillusioned. Even though "Mason is exposed," he reflected, it would be virtually impossible "to put over the Code with any real restrictive forestry measures in it."[32]

The final Article X conference elaborated on the proposals made at the first meeting in October. The public commitment, as the conference defined it, included (1) expanding the publicly owned forests; (2) increasing support for protection against fire, disease, and insects; (3) modifying the timberland tax policy; (4) providing for forest fire insurance and extending forest credits; and (5) encouraging greater cooperation between government agencies and private owners. The industry's commitment included the acceptance of an amendment to the lumber code. The president approved the amendment on March 23, 1934, as Schedule C—Forest Conservation Code.[33]

The Schedule C amendment stipulated that each division of the Lum-

[31] "Forest Industry Charts Conservation Course," *American Forests* 39 (December, 1933): 540–41, 572–73.

[32] Samuel Trask Dana, *Forest and Range Policy: Its Development in the United States*, pp. 255–56; Ed Munns to Raphael Zon, December 20, 1933, and January 9, 1934, box 8, Zon Papers.

[33] *West Coast Lumberman* 61 (February, 1934): 11, (March, 1934): 7, and (April, 1934): 5; H. H. Chapman, "Second Conference on the Lumber Code," *Journal of Forestry* 32 (March, 1934): 272–74; "Conference of Lumber and Timber Products Industries with Public Agencies on Forest Conservation," *Journal of Forestry* 32 (March, 1934): 275–307; Dana, *Forest and Range Policy*, pp. 255–56; Clepper, *Professional Forestry*, p. 149; U.S. NRA, "Amendment to Code of Fair Competition for the Lumber and Timber Products Industry," in NRA, *Codes of Fair Competition*, VIII, 693–99.

ber Code Authority should cooperate with state and federal authorities to initiate "measures necessary for the conservation and sustained production of forest resources." It recognized that the industry's ability to carry out these measures depended on the "extent and character of public coopera- tion in each state." Each division was directed to formulate regulations re- garding forest practices appropriate to its locale. The Lumber Code Au- thority would then approve these rules, which were to go into effect June 1, 1934. And they were to be flexible. If the standard procedures seemed un- reasonable to an operator, he could submit an alternate plan for his prop- erty, and with the division's approval he could pursue his own rather than the standard plan.[34]

A careful reading of Schedule C shows that it was weighted heavily toward the industry's determination of what constituted necessary mea- sures to ensure conservation of forest resources. Furthermore, personnel from the private sector dominated the Lumber Code Authority and its re- gional divisions and subdivisions. They were responsible for translating the general guidelines into specific rules adopted by each regional associa- tion. And to assure that no one unfavorably disposed toward the industry would serve in a decision-making capacity, those who drafted the standard practices for each division also acted as judge and jury for management procedures within their jurisdiction. Thus President Roosevelt's determina- tion that a quid pro quo be exacted from the industry in exchange for relax- ing antitrust laws and for other benefits was an empty husk. The forest practice requirements were merely experiments in the industrial regulation of cutting practices, as Samuel Trask Dana and others have noted. The aging and ailing George P. Ahern concluded after reading through the Schedule C amendment, "It is the same old platitudes of the past forty years but still not a tooth in the whole darned thing."[35]

Wilson Compton, on the other hand, informed Roosevelt that the for- est conservation code would provide an "adequate permanent frame-work and machinery for the development of private forestry, if given a chance to work." He outlined four conditions beyond the control of the lumber indus- try but necessary to effective forest conservation: low-interest loans and

[34]NRA, "Amendment to Code of Fair Competition," VIII, 696; *Timberman* 35 (May, 1934): 10.

[35]NRA, "Amendment to Code of Fair Competition," VIII, 693–99; Dana, *Forest and Range Policy*, pp. 456–57. Ahern is quoted in Robert Marshall to Raphael Zon, April 2, 1934, box 8, Zon Papers.

credits, timber tax reform, increased government outlays for forest fire protection, and public acquisition of both mature and second-growth timber. Without these, Compton insisted, the industry's conservation efforts would "be largely a gesture." [36] This argument foreshadowed what was to become the industry's chief propaganda ploy—emphasizing its accomplishments in forest conservation and continually reminding federal officials of the government's responsibility to live up to its part of the bargain (as trade officials defined the agreement).

Compton, as the key leader of the lumber industry, continued to press the Roosevelt administration for a statement of public support. Rexford Tugwell, assistant secretary of agriculture, also advised the president to issue a statement calling for increased public assistance to the industry. This, he believed, would have a favorable psychological effect "in helping to carry the code activities through the difficult initial period of getting rules of forest practice into effect." But Roosevelt's only response was to assure Compton that such a legislative program was under study. [37]

In the summer of 1934, John B. Woods, a Long-Bell forester serving temporarily with the Lumber Code Authority, informed the code officials of his frustrations in attempting to wrest from Roosevelt some support for the conservation program. Woods reported "a complete lack of accomplishment by public agencies in putting forward the agreed legislative program." William Greeley, who served on the Joint Committee of the Article X Conference, also pointed out that the West Coast Division had "taken our Article X and Schedule C very seriously," and the government should do likewise. The forestry provisions were basic to the Industrial Code and such a closely integrated program would only work if each of the parties to the agreement fulfilled its part. [38]

After the dissolution of the NRA in May, 1935, the disbanding agency conducted an inhouse review of its work. The report suggested that the failure of public agencies to carry through their part of the Article X agree-

[36] Wilson Compton to Franklin Roosevelt, May 16, 1934, container 1, OF 148, FDR Papers.

[37] Compton to Roosevelt, May 31, 1934, Rexford Tugwell to Franklin Roosevelt, June 8, 1934, and Roosevelt to Compton, June 13, 1934, all in Nixon, ed., *Roosevelt and Conservation*, I, 285, 291, 292.

[38] John B. Woods to the National Control Committee, Lumber Code Authority, report upon administration of Article X, September 14, 1934, box 69, NFPA Records; William Greeley to Arthur B. Recknagel, November 15, 1934, box 7, William B. Greeley Papers, University of Oregon Library, Eugene, Oregon.

ment "may have seriously interfered with successful administration of the forestry provisions by the Code Authority." This analysis is misleading in retrospect, however. The agency's self-study assumed that the industry "promptly put into effect the forest practice rules" and that a laggard president and Congress caused disheartened lumbermen to break with the spirit of the Article X agreement. The evidence does not support the assumption that forestry practices were promptly implemented. As it had done on previous occasions, the lumber industry sought a scapegoat and ascribed its failures to the unwillingness of Congress to pass the appropriate legislation.[39]

What did the perspective of one year suggest to industrial leaders about the effectiveness of the NIRA? Wilson Compton, who served four months as a volunteer chief of trade associations under the NRA, thought the experiment in "self-regulation" was still worth pursuing. He told the American Trade Association Executives that both industry and government were enjoined in an experiment to see if a system of self-regulation could be established "without converting it into socialism." Compton feared that the NRA was losing confidence in trade associations as administrators of code policy and that associations were becoming suspicious of the expanding bureaucracy of code administrators. But, he conceded, "the vices as well as the virtues" of industrial cooperation were divided between the new Code Authority and the old trade association. The decisive test of the recovery administration would be "its ability to resist pressures for special advantages."[40]

At the annual meeting of the NLMA in June, 1934, Compton expressed gratification for the way the lumber code withstood the rigors of its first year. He praised organized lumbermen for "visualizing the industry's needs and in formulating Code provisions to meet them." Nevertheless, he recognized that vexing problems remained. The code had failed to establish a balance between production and consumption that could sustain a reasonable price level; instead, industrial stability had come to depend on government protection for minimum prices and on the "schedule of trade practices." The long search for production controls had produced a system

[39] Peter A. Stone, et al., "Economic Problems of the Lumber and Timber Products Industry," in U.S. NRA, Division of Review, *Work Materials No. 79*, p. 60. The *Work Materials* included a letter from the NLMA to the review division expressing its "entire accord with the statements of facts and conclusions by the Division of Review" (p. ii).

[40] Wilson Compton, "The Test of Industrial Organization and NRA: An Address Before the American Trade Association Executives," May 1, 1934, box 145, NFPA Records.

of quotas and allotments, but there was little progress toward resolving the critical issue of balancing supply and demand. According to Compton, the industry had to work for more effective controls and an increase in demand for lumber products.[41]

These controls—the wage and price agreements and production quotas—were originally worked out in the regional associations and then forwarded to the Lumber Code Authority for final approval. Neither the regional groups nor the Lumber Code Authority had the power to enforce compliance upon reluctant operators. The system therefore proved unworkable when operators began to ignore the regulations and the NRA, likewise, refused to enforce the code.

Until June, 1934, the work of the recovery administration focused on code formulation and amendments to unfinished codes such as the one for the lumber industry. It was not until June, therefore, that officials paid serious attention to enforcement, and when they did, the situation quickly got out of hand. Because the Lumber Code Authority realized that its minimum price provisions were being violated, it requested through its new executive officer, David Mason, that the NRA begin prosecuting violators who engaged in price-cutting practices. Mason had earlier predicted that noncompliance with the minimum price provision "would wreck the lumber code." The recovery administration eventually did make sporadic efforts to enforce the minimum price mechanism, mostly without success. The practical obstacles to reasonable and effective minimum price requirements were numerous and in the long run proved insurmountable. Small-scale, marginal mill operators persisted in dumping low-quality lumber on the market at prices below code requirements. Moreover, at the slightest indication of business revival, operators tended to produce above their allotted quotas.[42]

By the summer of 1934, noncompliance with the minimum wage and price provisions had become critical. David Mason pointed to the failure of the price controls to include wholesalers and to the NRA's weak enforce-

[41] Compton, "On the Road to Recovery," report of Wilson Compton, 32nd annual meeting, NLMA and American Forest Products Industries, June 12, 1934, box 145, NFPA Records.

[42] Loehr, ed., *Forests for the Future*, pp. 103, 152; Stone et al., "Economic Problems," pp. 4, 108–109. Mason was appointed head of the Lumber Code Authority on June 4, 1934 (Loehr, p. 134).

ment mechanism as the key weaknesses of the code. Finally, in December, 1934, rampant noncompliance with the minimum price provisions led to the suspension of all price controls.[43] The breakdown was attributable, in part, to the code's discrimination against smaller operators and the willingness of others to ignore the code when it was to their advantage to do so.

Indeed, in the hearings that preceded suspension of the code, most grievances concerned the restrictive and costly impositions the requirements placed on small-scale operators, who complained that the code put them at a competitive disadvantage. Compulsory grade marking, for example, favored the more capital-intensive operations with precise and efficient equipment capable of producing standard lumber products. Moreover, certain code amendments made it more difficult for small mills to market their products. One in particular required lumber shipment in sizes too large for small mills.[44]

There also were complaints that large-scale operators had formulated guidelines specifically designed to hamper the ability of the smaller units to carry on their business. Some of these had to do with the maintenance of costly fire equipment while others concerned quotas. One small mill operator in the Pacific Northwest, for example, charged that William Greeley and the West Coast Division were pursuing policies favorable to large lumber mills and had devised production allocations that would put small units out of business. Greeley argued the opposite, insisting that the code had "brought small mills into production," increased their production, and "put the small mills in a more protected division than they occupied for many years."[45] But his critics remained unpersuaded, and similar complaints continued to be voiced at later hearings.

The owner of one small company suggested to Hugh Johnson that the lumber code be abolished because it perpetuated too many injustices. "The intellectuals of the Lumber Manufacturers," he claimed, "slipped a fast one over you when the existing code was adopted . . ." and the best remedy now for the "present mob" in control of the code was to reduce the

---

[43] Loehr, ed., *Forests for the Future*, pp. 101, 103. It is interesting to note that proponents of minimum prices referred to the measure as "cost protection" while its opponents preferred "price fixing."

[44] U.S. NRA, *Hearings on Amendments to the Code of Fair Competition for the Lumber and Timber Products Industry*, deposited in the Code Record Station of the NRA (microfilm copy in University of Iowa Library), April 3, 1934, pp. 433–34, 456–81.

[45] Memo of the Joint Committee on Forest Conservation, April 5, 1934, vol. 160, WCLA Records; NRA, *Hearings on Amendments*, April 12, 1934, pp. 1275, 1282–83, 1290.

price of lumber. These complaints grew in frequency and intensity as more lumbermen became frustrated with the uneven implementation of the lumber code. Donald Bruce, a consultant in the firm of Mason, Bruce, and Stevens, wrote his partner Carl Stevens in the late summer of 1934 that price control was crumbling and all compliance would soon follow unless the NRA began to enforce the lumber code. The *American Lumberman* observed that the code frightened recalcitrants into line for awhile but that slowly this minority "experimented with violations; and if nothing serious happened they went on from there." If the industry was to have rules, they must be quickly and uniformly enforced. The journal noted that for every hundred men who obeyed the lumber code, "one unrestrained pirate can demoralize the market." David Mason was convinced by September that "only a miracle can save us from the abandonment of cost protection minimum prices." And Ellis Hawley, in a study of the NRA, noted that the widespread violation of code prices "made compliance a bad joke."[46]

Besides the small-scale operators who wanted the minimum price provision rescinded, there were others opposed to the federal government serving as a price enforcement agency. One trade journal predicted the government would fail in this capacity because it "was not created to maintain prices." Also, achieving uniform prices in the lumber business was considered to be almost hopeless because of the great variety of production methods, raw material costs, and volume of production. A. W. Clapp of the Weyerhaeuser Sales Company advised the Lumber Code Authority to drop the minimum price requirements because they were not enforceable. It was the price feature of the lumber code that had brought the industry to "industrial and moral chaos." Small-scale mill operators joined Clapp in complaining about production control mechanisms and the imposition of quotas, both of which worked an injustice against small units. A Georgia lumberman protested that the little operator could not carry on his business successfully under the code because its provisions were drawn up by large companies. The big companies, he charged, "make the codes to suit their plants and disregard the small man."[47]

[46]Tri-State Lumber Company to General Johnson, April 12, 1934, in NRA, *Hearings on Amendments*, p. 224; Donald Bruce to Carl Stevens, September 7, 1934, file 312, Mason papers; *American Lumberman* (September 1, 1934): 16–17; David Mason to Stephen MacIntyre, September 28, 1934, container 10, OF 466, FDR Papers; Hawley, *The New Deal and the Problem of Monopoly*, p. 115.

[47]*Timberman* 35 (September, 1934): 9–10; C. F. Reynolds to H. M. Kannee, and

The most reasonable assumption to make from these innumerable complaints is that operators favored or opposed the lumber code in direct proportion to how their competitive position might be enhanced or eroded. But most of the testimony at the September, 1934, hearings still favored the minimum price provisions; therefore, the requirement was maintained. Although code division spokesmen may not have reflected the opinion of the rank and file, trade association leaders still clung to price protection as a workable means of achieving industrial stability.[48]

The large number of complaints from West Coast lumbermen prompted the NRA to conduct more hearings in December, 1934, on the minimum price issue. The West Coast Lumbermen's Association, for example, requested the suspension of all minimum cost requirements. H. W. Bunker of the Coos Bay Lumber Company told the recovery administrators that "the price fixing provision of the Lumber Code was being disregarded as to the sale of at least a majority of the lumber . . . manufactured by the cargo mills in Oregon and Washington." Bunker then asked that the price control requirement be lifted because the code was universally ignored. A. E. McIntosh, representing the Seaboard Lumber Company of Seattle, told the hearing that the minimum price was set too high, because the smaller mills could sell at a lower price and still make a profit. Price requirements in the West Coast division, McIntosh argued, had "completely broken down," and code prices were "the exception rather than the rule."[49]

A spokesman for small-scale lumbermen in Oregon's Willamette Valley told the hearing that his peers were unable to sell when they adhered to code prices. These prices, he claimed, favored the large-scale operators who turned out a better quality lumber. Another lumberman estimated that from 80 to 90 percent of the lumber in the Northwest was sold at less than code price. "Compliance in selling at fixed prices," he insisted, "cannot be

---

[Kannee] to M. H. McIntyre (secretary to the president), November 28, 1934 (NRA Codes, 1933–1935), OF 446, FDR Papers.

[48] This assumption is based on a perusal of U.S. NRA, *Hearings on Applications for Exemption from Code of Fair Competition for the Lumber and Timber Products Industries*, deposited in the Code Record Station of the NRA (microfilm copy in University of Iowa Library), September 17, 1934.

[49] U.S. NRA, *Hearings on the Application for Suspension of the Reasonable Costs and Their Rules and Regulations for their Application under the Code of Fair Competition for the Lumber and Timber Products Industries*, deposited in the Code Record Station of the NRA (microfilm copy in University of Iowa Library), December 11, 1934, pp. 3, 6–9, 12, 16, 23, 27, 32.

secured." A representative of the West Coast Logging and Lumber Division reported that his group would not comply with government prices because the government was either unwilling or unable to enforce the prices. He said that effective cost protection prices were impractical and had been abandoned in practice and that those who adhered to the code were penalized the most.[50]

A. W. Clapp, who represented lumber interests of the Northwest, urged the recovery administration to abandon the minimum price requirement, because enforcing the provision was proving to be a "subversion of justice." It fostered dishonesty and moral chaos and was weakening cooperative effort, according to Clapp, who insisted that the law of supply and demand must prevail. Production quotas, he charged, would have been the perfect remedy, but the quotas were set too high, and this caused people to ignore the price requirements in order to sell their stocks.[51]

The California Redwood Association and the Western Pine Association were the only groups who testified in favor of maintaining cost protection prices at the West Coast hearings. Harry Cole of California Redwood noted that protected prices were "a more reasonable and better answer than unrestrained competition in these critical times." Van Fullaway of Western Pine reported that compliance with minimum prices in his region was good. Abandoning the cost protection feature of the code, he warned, would place a considerable strain on the remaining provisions.[52]

Clearly, the code was not operating rationally or fairly; moreover, it was not ushering in the promised land of industrial stability. Indeed, the force of the market was proving to be the undoing of the code because of its weak enforcement provisions. Rationalizers and modernizers like Compton and Mason were unable to impose the industrial regulatory mechanisms they sought, and small-scale operators were able to avoid controls that threatened to put them out of business.

By the end of 1934, the lumber code was in complete disarray. The NRA finally suspended all price requirements in late December, belatedly recognizing what was largely a fait accompli. Thus, it became increasingly clear to code administrators that a Supreme Court decision was needed to clear the air of legal ambiguities involving major features of the code. Con-

[50] Ibid., pp. 36–40, 44, 62, 66–67, 81, 93.
[51] Ibid., pp. 96, 100–103, 114–15, 157.
[52] Ibid., pp. 391–92, 516, 519.

sequently, from the numerous code violations, the Lumber Code Authority selected as a test case that of William E. Belcher in the northern district of Alabama.[53]

Belcher had openly violated both the wage and hour provisions of the lumber code, but the district court had dismissed the government's indictment against Belcher. The court contended that the NIRA was unconstitutional, because it delegated legislative power to an administrative agency and therefore violated the first article of the Constitution. The Belcher case went nowhere. In a direct blow to the Lumber Code Authority, the Department of Justice announced in late March that it would request the Supreme Court to dismiss the Belcher case. Immediately after the announcement, the executive committee of the Lumber Code Authority advised its regional administrative agencies to request a suspension of the lumber code.[54]

Two days after the Justice Department's decision, David Mason discharged the entire staff of the Lumber Code Authority effective April 15, 1935. Mason obviously was miffed because the government had failed to prosecute the Belcher case, and he most likely believed that dismissal meant the lumber code was null and void. In the ensuing weeks, Donald Richberg, then the most important figure in the collective leadership of the NRA, tried without success to mollify Mason and the malcontents in other code authorities. The Belcher case, therefore, underscored the voluntary nature of the lumber code and forecast its ultimate failure. The technicalities of the Schechter decision, which found key provisions in the NIRA unconstitutional, meant the death of the codes.[55]

When Chief Justice Charles Evans Hughes delivered the Supreme Court's decision in the Schechter case on May 27, 1935, the NRA had already lost much of its credibility. Certainly, the Lumber Code Authority's influence had been considerably diminished long before the Belcher case was trotted forth as a test. The failure of the code authority to effectively enforce the production quotas and complicated price schedules made its provisions unwieldy and ultimately unenforceable. By early 1935, it was widely recognized that the lumber code was a morass of confusion and a jumble of regulations filled with loopholes. And the amendment process

[53] Hawley, *The New Deal and the Problem of Monopoly*, p. 115; Loehr, ed., *Forests for the Future*, pp. 103, 152–53.

[54] Loehr, ed., *Forests for the Future*, pp. 152–53; *American Lumberman* (March 30, 1935): 33.

[55] Loehr, ed., *Forests for the Future*, p. 154; *New York Times*, March 30, 1935; *American Lumberman* (March 30, 1935): 33; *Timberman* 36 (April, 1935): 9.

had merely added more confusion to the mess. The great experiment in industrial self-regulation under the auspices of the federal government came to an end in an outpouring of relief together with considerable anxiety about the future. David Mason reflected that the lumber industry had sought to resolve its problems through industrial self-government under the code. "To a degree far beyond that obtained by any other industry . . . the Lumber Code did grant industrial self-government." But it failed, he asserted, because of inadequate amendments to the code and the failure of the recovery administration to enforce compliance.[56]

For the lumber industry, then, the competitive play of the market had again proven too strong for the limited and weak enforcement arm of its code authority. The trade leaders who drafted the code prejudiced any chance for consensus agreement, because its provisions favored the large, efficient manufacturers who could produce standardized goods in large quantities and who were able to meet standards for fire and safety protection. Furthermore, the minimum price provision would have left marginal millmen who manufactured a lower-quality product without a market. Ellis Hawley concluded that the codes did not strengthen the competitive system, and any claims to that effect were "largely camouflage to begin with."[57]

Organized lumbermen asserted themselves at every step in the drafting of the lumber code, and still they came up empty-handed. Their effort to avoid economic chaos and to return the industry to a semblance of stability under the auspices of the federal government failed. Also, the inability of the Lumber Code Authority to enforce its regulations emphasized the competitive nature of the forest products industry. Lumbermen who sought a more centralized and efficiently operating business climate were unable to achieve adequate cooperation between industries (in an industry that prided itself on its cooperative enterprise), and the continued entry of new competitors made cooperation even more difficult. Moreover, the industry was divided between leaders who wanted to take stronger measures to regulate and stabilize the market and the many small rank and file competitors who wanted a chance to compete in a free and unrestricted market.

The death of the NRA did not end the efforts of lumber trade leaders to control business and to stabilize the market through restraints on competition. These groups still wanted to use the enforcement mechanism of the

[56] David Mason, manager's statement, Western Pine Association Annual Meeting, February 26, 1936, folder 5, box 5, Mason Papers.
[57] Hawley, *The New Deal and the Problem of Monopoly*, pp. 128, 130, 134.

federal government to achieve their objective, but, as before, only on industry terms. The first effort of the business and industrial sector to implement a form of compulsory cartelization ended in failure, however. The
Lumber Code Authority was never able to impose industrial discipline over
the many small-scale operators, and it never constituted itself as an impartial broker speaking for large and small operators alike. The larger capitalized groups dominated the code authority and established policies to
meet their particular needs. And the widespread noncompliance of small
operators underscored the contradictions of a system that claimed to promote free competition for all.

But while large-scale operators were able to dominate the control
mechanism in the codes, they were unable to make these controls strong
enough to serve their purposes. A variety of legal, political, and cultural
constraints kept the more powerful groups from putting the small operators
out of business. The dominant lumber industrialists and trade officials
molded code policy to suit their special interests, but were unable either to
use the authority of the government as they would have liked or to impose
formal barriers against new entrants. The industry's inherent competitive
strength simply undermined the attempt to syndicalize and compel market
behavior.

10

After the NRA: The Tarnished Hope for Stabilization

"The Lumber Code is gone! Some are glad; some are sad; some are
indifferent."—David T. Mason, *Lumber Code Authority Bulletin*
(June, 1935)

ALTHOUGH the National Recovery Administration (NRA) formally integrated and legitimized trade associations as policy-making partners in directing the national political economy,[1] the Schechter decision legally ended that form of syndicalization in most industries. Still, trade associations continued to seek federal assurances and support in their quest for industrial stabilization, and many trade groups wanted to preserve some of the discredited code provisions. But most businesses experienced an extended period of uncertainty as they probed for new ways to resolve their difficulties. The real problem for the larger trade groups was to achieve some form of production control while maintaining their dominant position in the political economy.

In the lumber industry, regional associations encouraged voluntary compliance with most of the code provisions, the major exception being the cost protection feature. Clyde Martin of the Weyerhaeuser Timber Company thought the lumber code had been successful; he noted improved forestry practices, a more cooperative spirit, and better relations between lumbermen and the Forest Service. Others, like A. W. Clapp, another Weyerhaeuser associate, were more critical and questioned the efficacy of self-regulation with or without the lumber code. "I do not believe that

[1] Felix Frankfurter noted in a memo to the president, December 25, 1935, that "the N. R. A. merely formalized the cooperative opportunities for trade associations which the Supreme Court had already permitted by its decisions" (Max Freedman, ed., *Roosevelt and Frankfurter: Their Correspondence, 1928–1945*, p. 297).

there would have been or would be any more compliance with voluntary agreement than there has been with the code provisions."[2]

Henry Clepper, whose long career in forestry embraced the New Deal years, thought the recovery administration had been a positive experience, especially the educational benefits, which continued long after the code was declared unconstitutional. But what Clepper cited as the educational benefits of improved forestry practices lumber trade leaders interpreted to suit a very different purpose. Officials like Wilson Compton and David Mason exploited their experience with the Article X agreement to argue for greater public assistance to the lumber industry.[3] They hammered away so relentlessly at the need for legislative relief that they contributed to a public impression that lumber, like agriculture, would survive only through public aid.

Shortly after the Schechter decision, Mason remarked that most of the lumber code standards would continue to be carried out unless ruinous competition forced their abandonment. He told the National Lumber Manufacturers Association (NLMA) that the code had improved a deplorable economic situation and provided lumbermen with the experience of "what to do and what not to do" under similar circumstances. In the absence of the code, however, Mason recommended greatly strengthening and improving discipline in the existing trade association network, stepping up voluntary agreements to establish industry-wide standards, and eventually seeking federal enforcement to "compel recalcitrant minorities to comply."[4]

Mason was typical of those trade association modernizers who still wanted to use the enforcement mechanism of the federal government to achieve industrial stabilization. The diffuse and complex nature of the industry, with its thousands of operating units spread across the country, undoubtedly contributed to the lingering fascination with coercion. But the root problem for these modernizers was the inability of the larger operators

[2] Samuel Trask Dana, *Forest and Range Policy: Its Development in the United States*, pp. 256–57; Harold K. Steen, *The U.S. Forest Service: A History*, p. 227. Clapp is quoted in Ralph W. Hidy, Frank Ernest Hill, and Allan Nevins, *Timber and Men: The Weyerhaeuser Story*, p. 440.

[3] Henry Clepper, *Professional Forestry in the United States*, p. 149.

[4] David Mason, "Recommendations to the National Lumber Manufacturers Association," *Lumber Code Authority Bulletin* 2 (June 29, 1935): 2–3, copy in folder 32, box 2, David Mason Papers (hereafter cited as Mason Papers), Oregon Historical Society, Portland, Oregon.

to impose their will on the smaller mills and the disruptive influence this had on their ability to control the lumber market.

Some trade leaders, like J. J. Farrell of the Northeastern Lumber Manufacturers Association, wanted to save something from the wreckage of the recovery administration. Farrell thought the industry "was lifted out of the mire that it was in two years ago" and that certain features of the code should be retained. Thus, he reasoned, lumbermen should retain some form of production control, implement the Article X agreement, and vigorously pursue the public support aspects of that agreement. The *Timberman* reported a broad consensus among trade leaders who wanted to retain whatever benefits could be gleaned from the act. The trade paper predicted that voluntary compliance with "essential elements" of the code would be continued.[5]

The defunct recovery act hardened the resolve of some to continue with or without the support of the government. Wilson Compton told the *American Lumberman* that national events had taught lumber operators the futility of seeking their salvation through statutes. No matter what the policy of the government might be, he observed, "the lumber industry must fundamentally rely upon its own continued improvement" in manufacturing, processing, and marketing its product. The president of the National Retail Lumber Dealers Association also reported that his association would not discard the sound principles learned from its close alliance with the code program. In a similar vein, one regional association secretary reported that his organization was trying to "replace the many good things the Supreme Court's decision took away." Another regional trade secretary urged the industry to maintain its competitive practices and standards that had "proven to be economically sound. Let there be no turning back."[6]

Despite expressions of relief that the cumbersome and unmanageable lumber code was a creature of the past, most trade leaders wanted to continue workable cooperative programs. Industry leaders feared a return to the chaotic and demoralizing conditions of 1932, and most of them supported some restrictions on the free market. They differed, however, over the methods to achieve those restrictions. One group, the Southern Pine

[5] J. J. Farrell to John W. Watzek, June 3, 1935, container 1, official file (hereafter cited as OF), 446, Franklin D. Roosevelt Papers (hereafter cited as FDR Papers), Franklin D. Roosevelt Presidential Library, Hyde Park, New York; *Timberman* 36 (June, 1935): 5.

[6] *American Lumberman* (June 8, 1935): 24–25, 47.

Association, lobbied for a modification of the antitrust laws in order to permit cooperative action to control production. But most lumber trade officials worked to pass the laws they claimed were part of the Article X agreement and vital to a healthy private forestry program.[7]

Lumber trade associations continued to maintain a rump group known as the Joint Committee of the Article X Conference. While the committee described itself as an objective fact-finding group comprising industry and public representatives, it was in fact the handmaiden of the lumber trade, trying its best to give a luster of neutrality and objectivity to the quest for public subsidies. Trade leaders frequently invoked the name of the committee to gain public support for industry programs.

Complaints about the government's failure to carry out the public component of the Article X recommendations were by this time an old story. From the time Article X went into effect in June, 1934, trade leaders complained that public agencies were dragging their feet. Before the Schechter decision these complaints had an aura of official sanction, because association spokesmen dominated the regional conservation committees under the Lumber Code Authority. The Joint Committee on Forest Conservation in the West Coast Logging and Lumber Division, for instance, included fifteen representatives, nine from the lumber industry and six representing the public. But only industry representatives had voting privileges—the others served as "advisory, non-voting" members. Consequently, it is not surprising that these committees, and their post-Schechter extensions, emphasized the accomplishments of lumber operators and chastised federal and state governments for failing to provide economic relief.[8]

After the lumber authority was disbanded, the West Coast Lumbermen's Association (WCLA) and the Pacific Northwest Loggers Association had one of the more active and aggressive committees working to resolve the old production and marketing problems. And because the Pacific Northwest was the dominant lumber-producing region, it provided most of the industry's prominent leaders. These trade officials controlled the internal politics of the NLMA and moved with ease between public and private employment.

As a result, general guidelines were framed for what the Northwest's

[7] Ibid., pp. 42–43.

[8] "Order Creating the Joint Committee on Forest Conservation in the West Coast Logging and Lumber Division," March 16, 1934, vol. 160, West Coast Lumbermen's Association Records (hereafter cited as WCLA Records), Oregon Historical Society, Portland, Oregon.

regional joint committee called a "public" forestry policy. These were measures that did not "subject industry to the competition of production by public agencies and which, as true measures of cooperation, are free from unnecessary public regulation." The list included (1) state and federal acquisition of forestlands to stabilize holdings and prevent premature liquidation; (2) tax measures to permit long-term holding of timberlands; (3) increased public support for fire protection; and (4) forest credits legislation to provide low interest rates. Of these measures the fire protection subsidy attracted the most attention, and in the following months the West Coast committee pressured congressmen to increase fire protection funds under the Clarke-McNary authorization.[9]

During these months, the industry was confronted with another fearsome threat of government regulation. In January, 1935, Chief Forester Ferdinand Silcox dropped a bomb in an address to the Society of American Foresters calling for a strengthening of the conservation items in the lumber code with "the enforcement of these provisions . . . entrusted to public agencies, rather than left to the industries." In the midst of the lumbermen's self-congratulatory accounts of their accomplishments under the Article X mandate, he argued that the practice of industrial self-control provided "for no public approval of forest practices . . . and no means of enforcement except within the industry itself."[10]

The reaction to the Silcox speech was immediate, and, in the estimation of the Article X committee, fraught with danger. The committee chairman, David Mason, called a special meeting to discuss the alarm and concern over the chief forester's remarks. Mason feared that Silcox had led the public to believe that the lumber code was not effectively bringing about the conservation of forest resources. He reported that "some of our most temperate elements" had complained about the speech, and he wondered if the Roosevelt administration was discarding the recommendations of the Article X conference. If such were the case, Mason thought, it might be necessary to reconvene the conference, because the Silcox statement would

---

[9] "A Statement of Objectives and a Program of Activities of the Joint Conservation Committee," WCLA, Pacific Northwest Loggers Association, June, 1934, vol. 160, and untitled petition, March 22, 1935, both in WCLA Records.

[10] Ferdinand Silcox, "Foresters Must Choose," address before the annual meeting of the Society of American Foresters, January 29, 1935, copy in box 10, William B. Greeley Papers (hereafter cited as Greeley Papers), University of Oregon Library, Eugene, Oregon. This is a reproduction of Silcox's speech published in the *Journal of Forestry* 33 (March, 1935): 198–204.

poison public opinion of private industry. A southern member of the joint committee argued that federal acquisition policy was going astray and that the government was delaying credits and "other helpful things possibly to force us out. And we don't like it." Mason agreed that lack of credit would hamper the retention of timberland by industry and make it easier for the government to acquire timberland.[11]

When the Lumber Code Authority came to a formal end in the late spring of 1935, the Article X joint committee considered ways to redirect the conservation agreement in order to preserve its gains. David Mason told one member that most of the lumber code divisions had "already planned to go as far as practicable with Article X work on a voluntary basis," but all were waiting to see what Roosevelt proposed. By midsummer, however, it became clear that the joint committee was little more than a public relations and lobbying adjunct to the NLMA and that its primary objective would be legislative programs. Although the committee emphasized its virtues of public service, it spent most of its energy in single-minded pursuit of the industry's objectives.[12]

John B. Woods, who literally wore a different association or federal agency hat each month, praised Senator Duncan Fletcher for sponsoring a forest credits measure permitting loans to private operators in order to encourage the practice of sustained yield management. The industry, he said, wanted long-term loans at low interest rates to perpetuate a forest crop. Such loans, he argued, would provide hard-pressed owners with the capital necessary to meet carrying charges and thereby keep the timber off an already overburdened market. In effect, he wanted a low-cost federal subsidy as a prop to production control, a plan somewhat similar to the assistance provided to agriculture under the Farm Credit Act.[13]

Woods also reminded Senator Fletcher that the credits bill was only part of a program lumber operators were seeking "to change over from quick liquidation—cut and get out—to permanent sustained yield operations." Although there was no machinery to compel private industry to keep up its part of the program, it was determined to do so if it could secure appropriate public support. The American Forestry Association and

[11] Minutes of meeting of Joint Committee of Conservation Conferences, February 28, 1935, folder 32, box 2, Mason Papers.

[12] Arthur B. Recknagel to David Mason, May 29, 1935, Recknagel to J. W. Watzek, Jr., May 29, 1935, and Mason to Recknagel, May 31, 1935, all in folder 32, box 2, Mason Papers.

[13] John Woods to Duncan Fletcher, July 3, 1935, folder 32, box 2, Mason Papers.

its executive secretary, Ovid Butler, backed the forest credits bill as part of the public program agreed upon through the Article X conferences. The industry had done its part, he declared, and now it was the government's turn to help maintain this industrial conservation program.[14]

The forest credits bill, according to Secretary of Agriculture Henry A. Wallace, was similar to a recommendation in the Copeland Report and was part of the Article X agreement. In his view, it would be a "constructive, necessary feature of the Administration's forest conservation program." But despite the support of both the Forest Service and the secretary of agriculture the bill made no headway, because it conflicted with the president's budgetary program. Although such a bill continued to be one of the legislative objectives of lumbermen, it was not until 1953 that federal credit was available for forest management.[15]

The joint committee had limited success with another piece of legislation, the Fullmer bill, which appropriated money to the states to expand their timberlands. Representative Hampton Fullmer of South Carolina sponsored the bill, which had the support of the Association of State Foresters, the Society of American Foresters, and the American Forestry Association. It also enjoyed wide support in the South and was in general accord with the Article X conference recommendation for enlarging the public timberlands. Secretary Wallace enthusiastically backed the bill, as did the president, although the latter wanted to delay appropriations. The Senate subsequently reduced the original House authorization from twenty million dollars to five million, and although the bill became law, Congress never appropriated money to put it into effect.[16]

The threat of government regulation of the lumber industry, which had lain dormant for nearly a decade, raised its skeletal frame once again in the form of Chief Forester Silcox's address to the Society of American Foresters in January, 1935. Most lumbermen were aware that as long as they held the initiative in determining the character of regulation, all was

[14] Ibid; Ovid Butler to Franklin Roosevelt, July 5, 1935, in Edgar B. Nixon, ed., *Franklin D. Roosevelt and Conservation, 1911–1945*, I, 390–91.

[15] Henry Wallace to Daniel W. Bell, June 26, 1935, and Bell to Wallace, June 4, 1935, both in Nixon, ed., *Roosevelt and Conservation*, I, 395–96, 396–98; Dana, *Forest and Range Policy*, p. 286.

[16] Dana, *Forest and Range Policy*, pp. 263–64; Henry Wallace to Franklin Roosevelt, July 8 and 11, 1935, and Roosevelt to Wallace, July 13 and 26, 1935, all in Nixon, ed., *Roosevelt and Conservation*, I, 392–93, 398–99, 403–404.

well. Such had been the case through most of the preceding decade and well into the 1930s. Indeed, when economic problems worsened in the later 1920s, trade leaders sought federal enforcement of production controls and price support mechanisms.

The NRA marked the peak of the industry's influence over regulation during these years, and then, perhaps due to the confused circumstances of the last year under the Lumber Code Authority, it lost the initiative. Organized lumbermen did not regain this momentum and reassert their hegemony in shaping policy until the days of the Joint Congressional Committee on Forestry, beginning in 1938. Like other business sectors, lumber appears to have been adrift—a period in which, as Ellis Hawley said, it is "difficult to discern any over-all pattern or integrating theme." [17] Operators spent much energy and paperwork during this time fighting the threat of federal regulation, with much of their rhetoric directed against Chief Forester Ferdinand A. Silcox.

In the years just before he was appointed to head the Forest Service, Silcox had been working in the field of labor relations. He was not new to forestry, however, because he had worked his way up under Pinchot and Graves and was assigned to work on labor problems during the First World War. When the war ended, Silcox remained in labor relations, perhaps due to policy differences with William Greeley, who served as chief between 1920 and 1928. Henry Clepper characterized Silcox as "handsome, personable, articulate, and withal a forester's forester who . . . personified for that heady era the new and satisfying status of the professional forester as a man of action." [18]

Although Clepper exaggerated Silcox's commitment to social change, many lumber officials were convinced that the latter was leading the industry to socialism. What alarmed his opponents most were his personal qualities—articulateness, persuasiveness, and sense of good will. William Greeley, who later clashed with Silcox over the regulation issue, at first applauded his "savoir-faire and political instinct" and expected Silcox to wield more political influence than anyone since Pinchot's days. "Silcox," Greeley remarked, "is open-minded; he is not wedded to any fixed theories or conceptions." [19]

[17] Ellis W. Hawley, *The New Deal and the Problem of Monopoly: A Study in Economic Ambivalence*, p. 276.
[18] Clepper, *Professional Forestry*, pp. 149–50.
[19] Steen, *U.S. Forest Service*, pp. 198–99; William Greeley to Austin Cary, April 25, 1934, box 7, Greeley Papers.

But Silcox marked a change. He insisted that forestry had to be considered "in its social relation to our industrial life." In his famous address of January, 1935, Silcox accused foresters of placing too much emphasis on timber production without considering its effects on nearby towns. Lumbermen, on the other hand, were concerned with the extraction of logs for profit, but without giving appropriate attention to the "social consequences of timber depletion." The chief forester believed the public no longer had confidence that private timber owners could satisfy the needs of the industry and of those who depended on it. As a consequence of this failure, Silcox speculated that the government would have to expand the areas under the public ownership and institute effective public regulation of private timberlands.[20]

Organized lumbermen immediately sensed that Silcox presented a threat to their autonomy. His address was the first unequivocal statement by any chief forester proposing the federal regulation of private timberlands. Although his views echoed the earlier declaration for federal regulation outlined in the Pinchot committee report of 1919, Silcox was an active figure in the Forest Service and Pinchot was not. Moreover, the chief forester's plea for regulation came at a time when lumbermen enjoyed great influence in federal policymaking; thus, it is likely that trade leaders were uncertain of Silcox and worried that his use of federal authority might diminish their influence.

The industry's reaction to the Silcox initiative was harsh. George F. Jewett, an executive with the Weyerhaeuser Potlatch operations in northern Idaho, informed President Roosevelt that the proposal to have the federal government undertake logging and milling where it was necessary to maintain existing communities was distinctly socialistic and would destroy private industry. The forest industries, he continued, were "all at sea because of the Government's attitude." While he shared Silcox's ideals and goals for forestry, he believed they could be attained through "private enterprise under enlightened governmental leadership."[21]

The *American Lumberman* expressed a similar view, arguing that the chief forester's pillorying of the lumber industry was doing great harm.

---

[20] Silcox, "Foresters Must Choose," Greeley Papers. Silcox is quoted in Steen, *U.S. Forest Service*, p. 199.

[21] George Jewett to Franklin Roosevelt, February 14, 1935, Western Forestry and Conservation Association Records, Oregon Historical Society, Portland, Oregon. In a handwritten note at the bottom of the copy of this letter to E. T. Allen, Jewett remarked: "I sure hit the roof when I read Silcox speech. I was not the only one. I sent Compton a copy of this, I don't suppose it will do any good, but somebody had to write like this."

And the normally cooperative Wilson Compton referred to "chiliastic conservationists . . . in the saddles of a potent government" who had done
nothing to extend to the forest products trade the kinds of credit made
available to other businesses. While the government procrastinated, Compton remarked that the lumber industry had done everything expected of it.[22]

Trade leaders, however, persisted in their effort to "educate" the chief
forester about their accomplishments in conservation and silviculture. John
B. Woods, the national association's director of forest conservation, informed Silcox that 75 percent of the industry was cooperating voluntarily
to carry on Article X work. Lumbermen now were awaiting federal and
state action considered vital in removing recognized obstacles to progress.
He told Silcox that the trade was "pretty well through the reorganization-
after-code phase," and where skepticism existed, "it springs . . . from the
belief that the promise of public aid is a hoax." In a letter to David Mason,
Woods speculated that Silcox would keep harping on the devastation issue
until he had something equally dramatic to catch the public's attention.
Woods assured Mason that he would continue a dialogue with Silcox as
often as he could reasonably do so and that he would urge him not to keep
the industry stirred up with "unfair statements."[23]

Before he returned to his private consulting practice in Portland,
Oregon, Mason met privately with the chief forester and assured Silcox of
the conservation strides lumber operators had made since the code was
dropped. In his diary Mason recorded that Silcox "was much impressed,
had no idea industry had done so much—said this was exactly [the] kind of
industry action he had wanted." At Mason's invitation, Silcox agreed to
attend the annual meeting of the Western Forestry and Conservation Association in December, 1935.[24]

At the western forestry meeting, George F. Jewett, the presiding
officer, emphasized that the most critical issue to the lumber industry was
the government's failure to "remove artificial barriers" to progress in forestry. Conservation, he insisted, could not otherwise be attained. Silcox,
as the guest of honor, then assured the mildly hostile audience of nearly

[22] *American Lumberman* (March 16, 1935): 20–21. Compton is quoted in this same
article.
[23] John Woods to Ferdinand Silcox, November 6, 1935, and Woods to David Mason,
November 1, 1935, folder 33, box 2, both in Mason Papers.
[24] Rodney C. Loehr, ed., *Forests for the Future: The Story of Sustained Yield as Told in
the Diaries and Papers of David T. Mason*, entry for October 30, 1935, p. 181.

two hundred lumbermen that the government had no intention of engaging in business or regulatory activity where "private business can do the job and . . . recognizes public interests and protects those interests." The Forest Service, he noted, was taking steps to carry out the Article X provisions. Finally, Silcox praised the cooperation of groups like the Western Forestry and Conservation Association, which enabled opposing sides to sit down and confer, resolving any problems between them. The *West Coast Lumberman* remarked that Silcox "did not speak as radically as he has been quoted."[25] More to the point was the chief forester's unique ability to disarm otherwise hostile audiences.

Throughout this period David Mason and John Woods exchanged an extensive correspondence, most of it concerning efforts to gain public support for stabilization programs and the industry's worries over government regulation. Woods kept the national and regional associations informed about new government plans and worked closely with Mason, Franklin Reed (editor of the *Journal of Forestry*), and Ovid Butler of the American Forestry Association to promote cooperative forestry and to discredit proposals for federal regulation. Mason also agreed that the government's program of cooperation with industry inspired fairly general agreement. But suspicions about Silcox persisted. David Mason wondered if the Forest Service was "giving its secret moral support and encouragement" to the regulatory proposals that kept reappearing.[26]

Despite the mutual suspicion between trade leaders and the Forest Service, the two groups collaborated on specific legislative proposals. Compton, Silcox, Woods, and Mason plotted strategies to gain increased appropriations for fire protection, continue the forest survey, fight blister rust, and support the research of the forest products laboratory. Regional association leaders worked with congressional delegations to urge adequate funding for the Forest Service and for its "cooperative activities." And the old joint committee of Article X days still maintained its paper existence, with John Woods and David Mason using committee stationery to publicize the trade association's legislative program. By this time the "committee" had dropped its pose of neutrality and was openly an adjunct of the NLMA's Department of Conservation, headed by Woods. There were occasional

[25] *Timberman* 36 (December, 1935): 55–57; *West Coast Lumberman* 63 (January, 1936): 24.

[26] Woods to Mason, August 9, 1935, and Mason to Woods, August 14, 1935, both in folder 33, box 2, Mason Papers.

suggestions to reorganize the committee, mostly during the spring and summer of 1936, but these ideas were dropped in favor of other options to publicize the lumber trade program.[27]

One of the key industry recommendations in the early New Deal years was an expanded federal program to acquire timberland. An enlarged public ownership, lumbermen believed, would stabilize land ownership, help control production, and fund federal reforestation programs. After the dissolution of the lumber code, federal acquisition continued as a high priority among the industry's legislative proposals. The arguments at the McNary hearings in 1923 had been repeated before the Timber Conservation Board, in the recommendations of the Copeland Report, and in the debates at the Article X conferences. William Greeley remained the foremost champion of acquisition. His proposals included sufficient federal purchase of marginal and commercial timberlands to really help stabilize timber values and to facilitate the development of sustained yield management.[28]

As in the past, when economic distress plagued the lumber industry, lumbermen pushed harder for federal purchase of timberland. Public acquisition was popular in the early 1920s, lost favor at mid-decade, and then gathered momentum in the late 1920s as economic conditions worsened. At first, federal acquisition efforts focused on cutover and abandoned lands, primarily to promote reforestation. During the depression, however, lumbermen expanded federal purchase programs to include second growth areas in the South (to keep the "peckerwood mills" from cutting premature timber) and both second and old growth stands in the Pacific Northwest. Some industry leaders promoted more aggressive acquisition programs than others, but all looked at federal purchase as a way to stabilize forest ownership and to control the market availability of standing timber.[29]

[27] Mason to Woods, February 29, and March 16, 1936, folder 34, box 2, Mason Papers. For suggestions to reactivate the joint committee, see Woods to Mason, April 2 and 7, 1936, George F. Jewett to Woods, June 1, 1936, and Jewett to Mason, June 1, 1936, folders 21 and 34, box 2, Mason Papers.

[28] David Mason to Ralph S. Hosmer, November 7, 1934, box 7, Greeley Papers.

[29] For the earlier appeal to expand federal purchases, see *Timberman* 19 (August 23, 1918): 27–28, and 21 (April, 1920): 29; *Lumber* 64 (October 27, 1919): 43; Royal S. Kellogg, "A Discussion of Methods," *American Forests* 25: 1282–83; *Lumber World Review* (January 25, 1925): 43, and (October 25, 1925): 23–24; Wilson Compton, "Who Shall Absorb Lands Present Owners Cannot Carry?" address to the annual meeting of the Western Forestry and Conservation Association, March 19, 1931, box 146, National Forest Products Association Records (hereafter cited as NFPA Records), Forest History Society, Santa Cruz, California.

Chief Forester Silcox placed more emphasis on expanding the national forest system than did his predecessors. His enthusiasm for a larger public ownership alarmed conservative foresters like Austin Cary, who saw "strong socialistic tendencies" in the program. It also worried John B. Woods, who supported a selective policy of enlarging the national forests, but feared that excessive federal ownership would lead to regulation because the government would control the disposal of raw materials. On the other hand, Greeley, a thoroughgoing industry modernist, thought federal purchase should be flexible. "Where private ownership of timber lands can carry on, it should not be disturbed. Where it can not, the Government should step in with a sufficient purchase program to stabilize the situation." [30]

Because of the latent productive capability of Pacific Northwest mills and their tendency to gear up at the slightest indication of an improved market, support for an expanded federal forest system persisted in this region long after it had dissipated in others. Some of the region's trade leaders, like William Greeley, even supported public acquisition of limited amounts of old growth timber; the idea was to remove such stands from the threat of premature liquidation. As late as 1935, when support for federal purchase was lessening elsewhere, Greeley told Chief Forester Silcox that the "undertaking of greatest importance" in the Pacific Northwest was federal purchase of forestlands. The federal government, he said, should buy enough timberland "to reasonably stabilize stumpage values and remove from the industry the menace of destructive liquidation." He singled out for immediate purchase those undeveloped holdings in danger of quick liquidation. [31]

While Greeley emphasized the importance of federal acquisition to stabilize the lumber industry in the Northwest, the idea was becoming less popular in other parts of the country. A. G. T. Moore, an official with the Southern Pine Association, noted that improved cutting practices, better transportation, more adequate fire protection, and the development of second growth timber had increased the prospects for profitable reforestation. Southern timberland owners, he contended, were less willing to sell their cutover land because of its increasing value. Moore called federal acquisi-

---

[30] Austin Cary to William Greeley, November 18, 1935, box 7, and Greeley to Cary, November 29, 1935, box 9, Greeley Papers; and John Woods memo to J. C. Nellis, "Government Ownership of Forest Lands," July 8, 1935, box 61, NFPA Records.

[31] William Greeley to Ferdinand Silcox, December 19, 1935, box 33, NFPA Records; *Timberman* 36 (December, 1935): 57.

tion an "insidious method of effectuating eventual control of the lumber industry." [32]

We can only speculate about this gradual change in the industry's attitude toward further additions to the national forests. Revised state tax laws, improved fire protection, and rising stumpage prices offered the prospect that the private ownership of timberland would prove valuable in the long run. Although tax-delinquent lands made up much of the acreage already added to the national forest system, lumbermen grew increasingly restive about the New Deal acquisition program. In his annual report for 1935, Ovid Butler, executive secretary of the American Forestry Association and a man with close industry ties, questioned the large allocations for federal purchase. President Roosevelt, in his turn, appeared receptive to a more conservative federal purchase program, despite the protestations of Agriculture Secretary Wallace. In fact by early 1937, even Greeley had dropped public acquisition as a priority. [33]

The lumber industry literally was adrift and seemed to lack central coordination as the Roosevelt administration neared the end of its first term. John B. Woods, in a long letter to David Mason, blamed this indifference and want of direction on a general malaise in the lumber trade. There was a lack of industry solidarity, according to Woods, with many of the regional affiliates preferring to go their own way. But as conservation officer for the national organization he could do little, "because the regionals resent being told anything by the National." Moreover, Woods feared that the joint program of the Article X conference was headed for disaster, because certain groups in the lumber industry considered the threat of public regulation as past. [34]

Woods was concerned that once the joint program broke down, the next step would be a drive for regulatory laws. Hence, he argued, the industry should place "more emphasis on the Joint Committee," because

[32] A. G. T. Moore, "Federal Policy Jeopardizes Private Lumber Industry," *Manufacturers Record* (March, 1936), reprint in folder 34, box 2, Mason Papers.

[33] Hidy, Hill, and Nevins, *Timber and Men*, p. 445; Steen, *U.S. Forest Service*, p. 218; Ovid Butler, annual report, American Forestry Association (1935), box E-2, American Forestry Association Records, Forest History Society, Santa Cruz, California; Wallace to Roosevelt, October 10, 1936, container 9, OF 1c, FDR Papers; "The Lumber Picture," annual report of W. B. Greeley, secretary-manager, WCLA, box 7, Greeley Papers.

[34] Woods to Mason, March 22, 1936, folder 21, box 2, Mason Papers.

senators and congressmen were more receptive when they were approached in its name. This was something the industry should capitalize upon, and he speculated that the government might even support half the expenses of a reconstituted committee whose chief objective would be to advance the "joint program."[35]

In a revealing note to David Mason, Woods discussed his growing differences with Wilson Compton. The latter, he believed, intended to keep the national association's conservation work under his personal control. Furthermore, friends informed him that Compton wanted to pursue increased trade promotion because it would bring direct returns. Woods feared that Compton would slight conservation efforts because they did not "ring the cash register." This, he believed, was the motive behind Compton's desire to have his "own man" as the national's conservation officer. Unless the industry favored the joint committee's recommendations, Woods could not imagine himself continuing to be effective.[36]

Despite his bitterness Woods was an astute observer of Washington politics, and he stayed very much in the center of most activities. He advised lumbermen to make "a declaration of faith . . . reaffirming the industry's intention to go forward with the joint program." A strong stand on conservation, he thought, would impress Silcox. When Woods suggested to the chief forester that the joint committee be reorganized, Silcox offered to support half the committee's office expenses. But the personal conflict between Woods and Wilson Compton seemed to inhibit such a move.[37]

In spite of the confusion in the national association's policy-making apparatus, trade leaders frequently discussed reconvening the old Article X conference as a preliminary step to a national forestry meeting. Even here there was disagreement. The conservative George Jewett thought the lumber industry would be short-changed again, as he believed it had been under the Article X proposals. He also opposed inviting public representatives to a general forestry meeting, because they had criticized the industry in the past and thereby gave impetus to the "movement to socialize our forests." Therefore, he advised, the national association must ensure that its members outnumbered the public representatives. In Jewett's view, an

[35] Ibid.
[36] Ibid.
[37] Loehr, ed., *Forests for the Future*, p. 185; Woods to Mason, April 2 and 7, 1936, folders 21 and 34, Mason Papers.

industry conference would be more appropriate, especially if it were arranged through the NLMA. Then lumbermen could avoid the appearance
of "supporting the socialist crowd," because their interests were "diametrically opposed to the public ownership crowd." [38]

The extended correspondence carried on by industry leaders convinced David Mason to propose that the Article X conference be recon-
vened. In a memorandum to the regional associations, Mason cited the industry's need to counter social disruption and to protect its public image;
all businesses, he argued, should take constructive action to resolve differences between themselves and the public. Forest conservation was another major issue requiring the consideration of lumbermen. Finally, because the lumber industry could pit its achievements against the failures of
the federal and state governments to meet their commitments, Mason argued that reconvening the Article X conference would "put more power
into accomplishing the program of public action." It would reaffirm the old
agreement, because no new program was proposed; it would press for laws
dealing with the public commitment; and it would dispel "fears of possible
new, oppressive proposals for industry action, against which the Conference itself is the best defense." Therefore, a general meeting was considered
an ideal way to emphasize the industry's efficacy in its program of action
and the need for public representatives to "cooperate more effectively with
industry." [39]

While John Woods counseled his colleagues to cooperate with government agencies in order to organize the forestry conference, a few association officials (including those representing Western Pine) wanted the
gathering to represent lumber interests only. As a compromise, Woods proposed an industry meeting immediately preceding the joint session of public and private agencies. He warned, however, that a preliminary session
should not be construed as "a pep rally or secret practice," and he insisted
that all representatives to the discussion should take the joint program of
cooperation seriously. Wilson Compton also cautioned the organizers to
"know just what we are wading into," because the industry was assuming
full responsibility for all the arrangements. Compton, Woods, and David

[38] Jewett to Woods, May, 1936, folder 34, box 2, Mason Papers. Jewett said the lumber
industry should "stand apart as far as possible" from the "contamination" of the Roosevelt
administration.

[39] David Mason to Wilson Compton, September 17, 1936, box 22, NFPA Records.

Mason did just that. They carefully and meticulously assured the predominance of lumber representatives, but assured state and federal agencies and conservation groups that each would be fairly represented. Because past experience suggested that the industry's viewpoint would prevail among the "public" representatives, the conference organizers were confident that a consensus could be achieved and that any recommendations would have the general support of most lumbermen.[40]

As part of the planning strategy, John Woods suggested that lumbermen should be prepared to offer a substitute for the NRA, because Silcox was going to exact a "quid pro quo of premiums for good management and penalties for bad." Woods proposed a three-point program: "industry action, state forest codes and the use of Federal funds predicated upon the adequacy of . . . state codes." In considering such a program, he cautioned trade leaders to remember that the government expected the regulation of forest use; the main question was, Who will do the regulating?[41]

Woods and his colleagues worked hard to assure that the recommendations of the proposed conference would be acceptable to lumbermen. The leaders of the NLMA coordinated and planned the forestry conference much as they did for the hearings and congressional debates leading to the passage of the Clarke-McNary Act of 1924. The meticulous arrangements for the meeting, like the effort of the early 1920s, assured the outcome.

In a response to a questionnaire sent to its members, the national association drafted a proposed Joint Program of Forest Conservation to be Undertaken by Public and Private Agencies. The recommendations reiterated the Article X conference agreement, except for public acquisition, which was de-emphasized. It proposed a program that would "rely to the maximum extent practicable upon *private* forest ownership, management and operation, with *public* action to the extent necessary." To attain the objec-

[40] John Woods to Wilson Compton, December 5, 1936, box 22, NFPA Records; memo to Members Executive and Economics Committee, Western Pine Association, December 17, 1936, folder 31, box 2, Wilson Compton to David Mason, December 29, 1936, folder 28, box 2, Woods to Mason, January 27, 1937, folder 21, box 2, and Woods to Mason, February 23, 1937, folder 1, box 3, all in Mason Papers. By early 1937 most references to the Joint Committee of the Article X Conference were dropped, and even David Mason spoke as chairman of the NLMA's Committee on Conservation and not the old Article X joint committee.

[41] Woods to Mason, February 23, 1937, folder 1, box 3, Mason Papers. In this letter Woods outlined the national association's general strategy and the rationale for pursuing that plan.

tive of continuous forest production, it urged cooperation with all levels of government, "including the enactment of needed legislation recommended by the [Article X] Forestry Conference."[42]

The Forestry Conservation Conference, which met in Washington, D.C., from April 7 to 9, 1937, was the first national gathering of private and public forestry groups since the last assembly of the Article X representatives in January, 1934. Again the conferees approved the policy of "the continuous production, or sustained yield, of forest resources as the ultimate object of our industries." Lumbermen agreed, as a voluntary act of cooperation with government agencies, to leave cutover lands "in restocking condition," to continue their fire protection work, and to maintain regional conservation committees to carry out the recommendations of the conference. The federal role, similiar to that outlined in 1934, was to include increased appropriations for fire protection; establishment of a system of forest credits; better financing for insect and disease research; continuing the policy of withholding federal timber from sale (except to carry on existing operations); and pooling of public and private timberlands into sustained yield units. The conference then directed the president of the NLMA to appoint a standing committee to carry out its proposals.[43]

The forestry conference revealed nothing startlingly new or innovative. It reaffirmed previous policy, and, perhaps more important, it energized the industry and increased its cohesiveness and sense of self-confidence. In retrospect, the conference was little more than a public relations extravaganza and morale booster. But it did provide organized lumbermen with the opportunity to flex their muscle, rail against government despotism, and praise the virtues of government-industry cooperation.

In 1937, the lumber industry also resolved to its satisfaction one other vexing issue. In cooperation with the Forest Service, the state of Oregon, and local government agencies, it worked out a management agreement for the vast timber stands on the revested Oregon and California railroad land grant. Since 1916, the year of revestment to the federal government of a grant of about 2,600,000 acres (including the remaining Coos Bay Wagon

[42]John B. Woods to W. B. Nettleton, March 25, 1937, and "Summary of Recommendations," memo dated March, 1931, in folder 1, box 3, Mason Papers.

[43]Dana, *Forest and Range Policy*, pp. 272–73; Steen, *U.S. Forest Service*, p. 230; "Forest Industry Will Do Its Part," *American Forests* 43 (May, 1937): 232–33, 262–63; Forest Conservation Conference Report, April 7–9, box 17, NFPA Records; Loehr, ed., *Forests for the Future*, p. 197.

Road grant of 93,000 acres), the Department of the Interior had administered the holding under a congressional directive that provided for the liquidation of the timber and the eventual reversion of the land to private ownership. This policy, however, had contributed to chaotic exploitation, wasteful logging, and, as the problem of overproduction became more apparent in the late 1920s, easy availability of cheap stands of public timber.[44]

Beginning with its recommendations to the Timber Conservation Board, the lumber industry had supported a policy of controlled management of the Oregon and California lands. William Greeley also advised this in his testimony to a 1932 Senate hearing, and subsequently the Article X conference had proposed that the revested lands be placed under sustained yield management. In March, 1934, the *West Coast Lumberman* warned that the welfare of the lumber industry in Oregon's Willamette Valley depended on the intelligent management of the grant lands. George T. Gerlinger, a Willamette Valley lumberman and one of the leaders in the effort to implement sustained yield management on the revested grant, told a meeting of the Western Forestry and Conservation Association in late 1935 that the lands should be turned over to the Forest Service and the timbered sections sold, with the provision that the lands be managed on a sustained yield basis.[45]

By 1936, several other groups were pressing for laws to rationalize management practices on the revested lands. The lumber industry's public relations apparatus, the Joint Committee of the Article X Conference, supported a recommendation to amend the Chamberlin-Ferris Act, the organic law administering the Oregon and California grant. Ovid Butler of the American Forestry Association thought the lack of congressional action

---

[44]Dana, *Forest and Range Policy*, p. 265; Clepper, *Professional Forestry*, pp. 109–10; W. H. Horning, "Sustained-Yield Program of the O and C Lands," *Oregon Business Review* 5 (April, 1946): 1–2; Richard C. Ellis, "The Oregon and California Railroad Land Grant, 1866–1945," *Pacific Northwest Quarterly* 39 (1948): 274–76; Wesley C. Ballaine, "The Revested Oregon and California Railroad Grant Lands," *Land Economics* 29 (August, 1953): 226.

[45]U.S. Congress, Senate, "Amendment of Federal Trade Commission Act and Establishment of a Federal Court," *Hearings before a Subcommittee of the Committee on the Judiciary*, 72nd Cong., 1st sess., March 31, 1932, p. 244; David Mason, "The Effect of O and C Management on the Economy of Oregon," *Oregon Historical Quarterly* 64 (March, 1963): 58; *West Coast Lumberman* 61 (March, 1934): 7, 35, 62 (January, 1935): 7, and 63 (January, 1936): 31–32. For background to the idea of sustained yield, see Roy O. Hoover, "Public Law 273 Comes to Shelton: Implementation of the Sustained-Yield Management Act of 1944," *Journal of Forestry* 22 (April, 1978): 86–101.

would continue the waste of the timber resource on the old railroad lands. The Society of American Foresters shared his concern and requested Congress to investigate the administration of the lands and to end "what is now probably the most outstanding case of waste and mismanagement of timber resources in the United States."[46]

In the summer of 1936, in an effort to canvass local opinion on proposals for managing the grant, Louisiana Congressman Rene DeRouen conducted a two-day hearing in Portland. William Greeley told the hearing committee that lumbermen favored a sustained yield management policy, because it meant the "stabilization" of the lumber industry and its dependent communities. Others, however, suggested limiting the annual cut on the revested lands and postponing action until the Department of the Interior had conducted further studies. Although the Portland hearing was a preliminary inquiry and purposefully avoided the issue of administrative jurisdiction, the session adjourned with the recommendation that the WCLA present a sustained yield bill to the next session of Congress.[47]

In the Seventy-fifth Congress, DeRouen introduced another bill to manage the Oregon and California lands (H.R. 5858), evidently with input from the Interior Department and the WCLA. William Greeley advised the House Committee on Public Lands that most Oregon lumbermen wanted the federal government to administer the lands on a permanent basis to assure their continued productivity. He recommended that the laws include a provision for a standing committee consisting of timberland owners to advise the government in managing the lands. Others who testified at later hearings on the proposed bill argued either for or against amendments to shift management of the lands to the Forest Service.[48]

Following the hearings, Congressman DeRouen introduced a substitute bill (H.R. 7618), which was divided into two sections. The first provided sustained yield management of the lands under the Department of the Interior, and the second distributed receipts from timber sales to the eighteen counties where the grant lands were located (the latter provision

[46] "Forest Legislation to be Urged," *American Forests* 42 (March, 1936): 128; Ovid Butler, "The Oregon Checkmate: How the Federal Government is Blocking Conservation of the Nation's Greatest Remaining Forest," *American Forests* 42 (April, 1936): 157–62, 196–97; "Investigations of O and C Lands Urged," *American Forests* 42 (July, 1936): 325.

[47] "Conference on O and C Lands Held in Portland," *American Forests* 42 (September, 1936): 436; *Timberman* 37 (August, 1936): 63–64.

[48] G. H. Collingwood, "Forestry in Congress," *American Forests* 43 (January, May, and July, 1937): 43, 255, 370.

was necessary to appease the counties). President Roosevelt signed the bill into law on August 28, 1937.[49]

Samuel Trask Dana referred to the act of 1937 as a complete reversal of previous policy. Paul Wallace Gates, in his monumental *History of the Public Land Law Development*, described the act as "a landmark in the development of forestry in the Department of Interior. . . . Most important, the Secretary of the Interior was required to manage the lands on a sustained yield basis." Another writer called the act "the most important occurrence for forestry and the lumber industry during 1937." Public Law 405 was also important in other respects; it indicated the growing receptiveness of the lumber industry to the progressive ideas of David Mason. The WCLA praised the legislation for providing a permanent supply of timber, along with steady and dependable revenue to the counties. The association also commended William Greeley, John Woods, and especially George Gerlinger and Charles Snellstrom, who represented western Oregon lumbermen, for their persistence and hard work in getting the bill through Congress. Greeley admitted later that "the lumber industry . . . wrote the bill that was substantially followed in the final legislation."[50]

The Oregon and California sustained yield legislation helped stabilize a volatile situation in the lumber economy of western Oregon. It rationalized the process of liquidation and reforestation in one of the richest forest-growing regions in the United States. The act also established a practice that favored the owners of large timberland acreages. It created sustained yield management units that were organized as partnerships between private holders and public agencies. As the system developed, it would become increasingly difficult for smaller competitors to secure sustained yield agreements. The law ultimately helped lumber trade leaders stabilize and control the availability of timber. It limited access to standing timber for operators with insignificant stands of their own, and it set up an administrative apparatus highly responsive to those who dominated the lumber business.

[49] Ibid. (August, 1937): 406, 412.

[50] Dana, *Forest and Range Policy*, p. 265; Paul Wallace Gates, *History of Public Land Law Development*, pp. 603–604; Loehr, ed., *Forests for the Future*, p. 195; WCLA, *Annual Report and Reference Book* (1937): 13–14, copy in Oregon State University Library; William B. Greeley, "Forty Years of Forest Conservation," *Journal of Forestry* 38 (May, 1940): 388. I received Elmo Richardson's *BLM's Billion-Dollar Checkerboard: Managing the O&C Lands* while this manuscript was in press. Richardson's analysis, however, does not differ appreciably from the argument presented here.

Despite a period of equivocation after the Schechter decision, the lumber industry muddled through its conflicting objectives and ambitions and continued to assert itself at both the state and the federal level. Although relations between Chief Forester Silcox and lumber trade officials continued to simmer, both parties cooperated to support Forest Service appropriations and various forms of public subsidies to lumbermen. And despite the public pronouncements of the chief forester, the federal government did not seriously threaten to regulate private timberlands. Instead, lumber association leaders pressed ahead to implement the "public" aspects of the Article X agreement, fought against government proposals to harvest and mill its own lumber, and skillfully maneuvered the association's public relations forces to gain public support for its programs.[51]

When it became obvious to lumber entrepreneurs that private forestlands were valuable assets, the industry retreated from a decade of support for federal acquisition. By 1936, trade leaders supported federal ownership of timberland only where it contributed to the formation of sustained yield management units. The Fullmer Act of 1935, which provided federal assistance to purchase land for state forests, proved a dismal failure, because Congress never appropriated money to put it into effect.[52] One suspects that the lumberman's diminishing enthusiasm for public ownership had something to do with the ineffectiveness of the act. By the time the industry convened a major policymaking conference in the spring of 1937, support for public acquisition was limited to pooling arrangements for sustained yield units.

Despite the unpopularity and failure of much of the NRA, the general principle of allocating great influence and power to the private sector lived on but without formal name and structure. Herbert Berckes of the Southern Pine Association reflected years later that various forms of the recovery program "lingered on through all legitimate and practical means" long after the National Industrial Recovery Act was declared unconstitutional. In his important book *The Limits of Legitimacy*, Alan Wolfe concludes that "what was an extremely conspicuous failure during its lifetime became a

---

[51]For instance, see Wilson Compton to John McSweeney, March 10, 1937, T. V. Larsen to Charles McNary, May 12, 1937, William Greeley to McNary, May 14, 1937, and Greeley to Frederick Steiwer, May 15, 1937, all in box 68, NFPA Records; *Timberman* 36 (April, 1935): 9.

[52]Dana, *Forest and Range Policy*, pp. 264–65.

model of business-government relations in later years."[53] Although lumber trade associations did not gain the influence over government policy attained in the oil industry, its leadership shrewdly adjusted policy in accord with expected economic trends and changes in federal programs. Skilled public relations men like David Mason and John Woods emphasized the industry's conservation accomplishments to allay public concern and to gain federal support for its stabilization programs. When word spread that the Roosevelt administration contemplated a major reappraisal of national forest policy, lumber trade leaders immediately began to coordinate and orchestrate the character of that reassessment.

[53] Hawley, *The New Deal and the Problem of Monopoly*, pp. 142–46; Herbert C. Berckes, "The Pitch in Pine: A Story of the Traditions, Policies and Activities of the Southern Pine Industry and the Men Responsible for Them" (Unpublished manuscript in the Forest History Society), p. 164; Alan Wolfe, *The Limits of Legitimacy: Political Contradictions of Contemporary Capitalism*, pp. 130–31; Robert Engler, *The Politics of Oil*, p. 141.

11

The Regulation Dilemma and the War Crises

"In regard to the forestry legislation, I think that at this time, and
until the war is over . . . there shall be no Federal legislation
providing for Federal regulation of forestry practices on private
lands."—Franklin D. Roosevelt, 1942

WITH the support of his superiors, Chief Forester Ferdinand Silcox moved
aggressively during the second term of the Roosevelt administration to establish government regulation over private timberlands as one part of a
comprehensive federal forest policy. The work of Silcox and Earle Clapp,
who became acting head of the Forest Service when Silcox died in late
1939, represented the most concerted attempt to effect federal regulation
since the early 1920s. Organized lumbermen supported some elements in
the new forestry program, but they fought the regulatory proposals through
their trade publications, in testimony before committee hearings, and in
the subsequent debates over congressional legislation. Trade leaders raised
the specter that the socialist tendencies apparent in regulating private enterprise would stifle the lumber business. This ploy served as effective
propaganda to cloak their real fear—loss of autonomy over forestry policy
and a distrust of both Silcox and Clapp. The persistence of depressed conditions in the lumber industry increased this sense of uneasiness.

The aggressive moves of national socialism in Europe and the growing conflict between Japan and the United States for Pacific rim markets
and raw materials complicated the efforts of the Roosevelt administration
to formulate and implement a comprehensive forest policy. Moreover, the
president and some congressmen vacillated between policies to stabilize
the lumber industry and a desire to relieve rural poverty through programs
like the Farm Security Administration and a similar plan to aid small
woodlot farmers. But large agricultural interests represented by the American Farm Bureau Federation, lumber trade executives, and the leaders of

the Forest Service opposed these attempts to assist smaller competitors. The lumber associations ignored this neopopulist move to help small operators and concentrated their efforts instead on the traditional proposals favored by the major forest products groups. Not least among their priorities was an all-out fight against the threat of federal regulation.

Most lumber officials viewed the Forest Service regulatory proposal as a threat to industrial self-government. John Woods, forester for the National Lumber Manufacturers Association (NLMA), circulated a statement highly critical of the chief forester's annual report for 1937. Silcox, he argued, ignored facts and studded his statement with "half-truths" to discredit private enterprise. The debate continued. When Forest Service representatives attended regional association meetings, lumbermen challenged them to outline specifically their program for regulation. Lumber trade leaders, in turn, pointed to the achievements of self-regulation and the many successful forest practices being translated into state law. The associations also set out to educate the public about its responsibility to help support fire protection.[1]

Through most of the dialogue over federal regulation, the more cautious lumber executives counseled a cooperative attitude with the Forest Service and other government officials. While he believed some form of regulation was inevitable, John Woods argued that it should begin on a trial basis at the state level, where the lumber industry could "guide the legislation along right lines." This tactic would increase the chances of blocking "such cure-all Federal legislation" as the Forest Service favored. He advised the acerbic George F. Jewett to emphasize government-industry cooperation in his presidential address to the Western Forestry and Conservation Association (WFCA). Jewett, he said, should adopt "the role of provocateur instead of prosecuting attorney" and ask questions rather than offering a bill of particulars. Woods also advised Jewett to praise the enactment of the "O and C Bill" as a public relations measure. Despite these words of caution, Jewett, who was normally more reserved in public, threw restraint to the winds and railed against socialistic tendencies in Washington and dictatorial policies of the Forest Service.[2]

---

[1] John B. Woods to Federated Associations, December 17, 1937, file 312, David Mason Papers (hereafter cited as Mason Papers), Oregon Historical Society, Portland, Oregon.

[2] John Woods to George F. Jewett, July 15 and December 1, 1937, box 33, National Forest Products Association Records (hereafter cited as NFPA Records), Forest History Society, Santa Cruz, California; Harold K. Steen, *The U.S. Forest Service: A History*, p. 231.

The chief forester, who was also more conciliatory in his public discussions, wrote to George Jewett disputing the industry's claim that it had made significant progress in the practice of forestry. Frankly, Silcox said, these were faint murmurs. The industry expended most of its energies crying for public aid, yet loudly protesting any government interference. Citing a recent WFCA resolution asking for greater federal assistance, Silcox accused lumbermen of seeking a " 'one way' proposition, pure and simple." On another occasion, he charged the industry for lacking initiative and being unduly reactionary and too insistent upon receiving cooperative aid. Such sentiments prompted the *Southern Lumberman* to observe that the chief forester "burns with the unquenchable fire of the zealot, and he never overlooks an opportunity" to promote government control of private timber.[3]

Because of these attacks on the lumber industry, George Jewett advised the NLMA to hire a full-time forester "to combat the unreasonable charges made against us." He specifically urged that John Woods be given the power to deal more authoritatively with legislators and government officials. Jewett contended that President Roosevelt's message in March, 1938, which requested an investigation of the nation's forest resources, demanded that the industry have a "central clearinghouse" to present the strongest possible case.[4]

Chief Forester Silcox and Secretary Wallace submitted a joint memorandum to the president in January, 1938, calling attention to the "critical situation" in the South. The memorandum recommended use of sustained yield forestry practices, public regulation of private forestlands, extension of public assistance to private operators, and increases in public ownership. Regulatory controls, it stated, would protect the public's interest and would shield the more progressive owners from irresponsible competitors. Roosevelt acted upon the recommendation and requested Congress to appoint a joint congressional committee to propose redemptive legislation aimed specifically at the southern states.[5]

The call for a congressional inquiry pleased lumber trade leaders like

[3] Ferdinand Silcox to George Jewett, [February], 1938, and conference with Chief Forester Silcox, February 23, 1938, box 22, NFPA Records; *Southern Lumberman* 156 (April 15, 1938): 24.

[4] George Jewett to Executive Committee, NLMA, January 31, 1938, file 312, Mason Papers; Jewett to Executive Committee, NLMA, April 12, 1938, box 22, NFPA Records.

[5] "The Forestry Situation in the South: Graphic Portrayal," memo from Secretary Wallace to President Roosevelt, January 5, 1938, and Roosevelt to Wallace, January 28, 1938,

David Mason, who thought that a well-organized congressional committee would give lumbermen an opportunity to present an effective case. The Supreme Court packing defeat, Mason noted, had forced Roosevelt to follow the "very much milder course" of recommending legislation rather than issuing a regulatory order. The industry "was ready for such a committee" because of the impressive record it had established since "Code days." To Mason's friend, John Woods, the appointment of a congressional committee was a splendid opportunity for the lumber groups to present a well-rounded picture of their problems. In the past, he observed, Congress let the Forest Service make these reports, and they usually led to "more or less secret and 'Star Chamber'" investigations. Although it detected the "radical influence" of the chief forester in the president's message, the *Southern Lumberman* concurred that lumbermen had nothing to fear, because the inquiry would deal only with facts and dispel misconceptions about the lumber industry.[6]

In the next few months, trade leaders exchanged a flurry of correspondence to plot strategy on acceptable proposals. George Jewett thought it would be "sound tactics to play around with the President" so that the industry could emphasize its need to permanently and profitably invest capital. He observed that Wilson Compton should use his influence with Secretary Wallace to ensure the appointment of a sound committee. John Woods also recommended that the national association's conservation committee serve as a "directing and coordinating agency" with the joint committee to formulate a "cooperative national forestry program." The industry, Woods believed, had the opportunity to obtain congressional appropriations that otherwise might be delayed for years.[7]

There were some parallels between the congressional investigations that led to the passage of the Clarke-McNary Act of 1924 and the joint congressional inquiry of 1938. In the hearings leading to the 1924 act, lumbermen worked closely with the Forest Service and Chief Forester William Greeley to coordinate testimony. The industry's lobby, the National For-

---

container 10, official file (hereafter cited as OF) 1c, Franklin D. Roosevelt Papers (hereafter cited as FDR Papers), Franklin D. Roosevelt Presidential Library, Hyde Park, New York.

[6] David Mason to George Jewett, with copies to James McNary, Wilson Compton, and John Woods, March 16, 1938, and Woods to Mason, March 17, 1938, box 36, NFPA Records; *Southern Lumberman* 156 (April 1, 1938): 22.

[7] George Jewett to C. S. Chapman, March 21, 1938, Jewett to John Woods, March 21, 1938, and Woods to Jewett, March 29 and April 8, 1938, all in box 36, NFPA Records.

estry Program Committee, also cooperated with Greeley to provide expert testimony and technical information. Although the industry was better equipped to present a united front to Congress in 1938, its ability to influence the Forest Service was less certain. John Woods thought he detected "a joker in the President's message" when Roosevelt suggested that the technical agencies of the federal government serve as interpreters of information. Woods feared that the Forest Service would be the only interpreting agency and would push its program of "outright regulation." But if the industry handled its case properly, he believed it could pound home the vital details and recommendations of the 1937 forestry conference.[8]

The officers of the NLMA approached the congressional inquiry with considerable confidence. They recognized that the association had successfully fought regulatory attempts in the past and that it had dominated the writing of the forestry code under the National Recovery Administration. And there was no one with the stature of a Gifford Pinchot to deliver emotional tirades against forest devastation. The industry's leaders based their self-assuredness on at least two decades of modest success in molding forest policy.

They also were aggressive, but tactful. Wilson Compton told Secretary Wallace that lumbermen had made great strides in their cooperative plan, begun in 1934, to promote forest conservation and welcomed the opportunity to present their problems to the congressional committee. The association's conservation committee also advised against a public confrontation with the Forest Service or an attack on Silcox. Compton suggested instead that the committee emphasize "research, cooperation, extension of markets, economic stability for forestry, more consideration in tariffs and foreign trade." Above all, he warned, "Don't let Silcox bait the industry into playing his game." Other members urged those testifying to concentrate strictly on the business before the joint congressional committee, because Silcox would try to "cover the whole field of human affairs."[9]

Not all lumber trade leaders, however, wanted to drop the idea of attacking the chief forester. Potlatch's George Jewett, who seemed to be at the vanguard of attacks on the federal government, suggested an all-out

[8] John Woods to I. N. Tate, April 1, 1938, box 36, NFPA Records.

[9] Wilson Compton to Henry Wallace, June 1, 1938, box 36, and notes on meeting of NLMA Conservation Committee, July 19–20, 1938, box 27, NFPA Records; George Jewett to Compton, June 23, 1938, file 312, Mason Papers.

crusade against Silcox. The issue was clearly "how we shall battle the menace of socialism in our forests." Although he was willing to accept the judgment of the conservation committee, Jewett doubted that Congress could turn back the tide of socialism, and a policy of educating the public in the virtues of private enterprise would take too long. At the same time, Jewett delighted in telling Wilson Compton that Silcox and Robert Marshall had been mentioned before the congressional committee on subversive activities, with "evidence tending to prove . . . that Silcox is fundamentally a Socialist."[10]

Despite Jewett's belligerence, most industry leaders urged lumbermen to take a higher ground. David Mason, who was a member of the national association's conservation committee, told a correspondent that if regulation became necessary, "the nearer we get to the business man's method, the better." Again he insisted that the public remove obstacles to the practice of forestry before any form of regulation was considered. Progressive lumber operators, he argued, would join with the public to regulate the laggards if conditions were more favorable. Although lumbermen opposed federal control, Mason indicated that they would support a step-by-step approach to state regulation. John Woods also thought the issue of regulation should be left in the background until the "public has done its duty," but he advised lumbermen to "work like the devil for a workable system."[11]

Finally, E. T. Allen, now in semiretirement on the northern Oregon coast, offered his sage advice to the WFCA. The organization, he said, should avoid repeated mutual criticism with Silcox and focus its energies on cooperation and dealing with practical problems. Heady advice, complimented John Woods, because this strategy concentrated on "forestry principles and not . . . baiting public foresters . . . Those things had their value, but there are other matters . . . which are more important nowadays." In a letter to Wilson Compton, Woods noted that Western Forestry was finally "dispensing with the Billingsgate and trying to discuss among themselves the problems of putting forest practices into the forests."[12]

---

[10] Jewett to Compton, August 18, 1938, box 63, NFPA Records.

[11] David Mason to Charles Boyce, August 11, 1938, box 63, NFPA Records; Woods to Mason, August 16, 1938, file 312, Mason Papers; Emanuel Fritz to E. T. Allen, September 15, 1938, Western Forestry and Conservation Association Records (hereafter cited as WFCA Records), Oregon Historical Society, Portland, Oregon.

[12] E. T. Allen to George Jewett and C. S. Chapman, September 7, 1938, box 4, WFCA Records; John Woods to Allen and Woods to Wilson Compton, October 18, 1938, box 33, NFPA Records.

Except for an occasional criticism of Silcox in private correspondence or an infrequent outburst in a trade editorial, the industry closed ranks to defuse the regulation issue. Association leaders emphasized the virtues of cooperation, underscored the need for greater federal support to make private forestry profitable, and generally avoided personalizing their opposition to Silcox. By adopting this strategy, industry spokesmen presented a united front to the congressional committee and were able to drive home their forestry proposals with convincing testimony.

Senator John H. Bankhead of Alabama chaired the Joint Congressional Committee on Forestry, appointed in June, 1938. The committee members included Senators William G. McAdoo, Ellison D. Smith, James P. Pope, and Charles McNary, and Congressmen Hampton Fulmer, Wall Doxey, Walter Pierce, Daniel Reed, and Harry Englebright. With the exception of McAdoo and Pope, all appointees served for the duration of the committee. John Woods, who was carrying on the industry's public relations work, praised the makeup of the committee, remarking that Alabama's Senator Bankhead was "a realist and practical business man with a desire to be helpful"; South Carolina's Senator Smith was "interested in all phases of the [forestry] problem"; Reed of New York was "apt to be matter-of-fact and conservative"; and Wall Doxey had "a national viewpoint . . . [and] is willing to learn." McNary, Pierce, Englebright, and McAdoo, he noted, were all well-known and acceptable. South Carolina Congressman Hampton Fulmer, however, who was vice-chairman of the committee, might present a problem. Although Fulmer wanted to help state forestry, Woods feared that he was "even more anxious to protect the small mill man against the wicked big operator."[13]

The work of the joint committee progressed slowly. A subcommittee conducted a two-day hearing in Sun Valley, Idaho, in early September, and another subcommittee held a two-day hearing in Jacksonville, Florida, in November. The testimony at these two hearings revealed a common pattern—praise for the industry's effort to carry on forest conservation and reforestation, praise for the increase in selective logging, and praise for the close cooperation between industry and state foresters in fire protection. Trade leaders stressed the need for increased appropriations under Clarke-

[13] Woods to Mason, August 16, 1938, file 312, Mason Papers. For an account of Fulmer's suspicions about large-scale lumbermen, see William B. Greeley, *Forests and Men*, pp. 213–14.

McNary, the extension of the national forest survey, and an end to public acquisition—the latter because excessive federal holdings, especially in the Northwest, were increasing the tax burden on private timberland.[14]

These early hearings reiterated the lumberman's plea for a greater "public responsibility" and revealed little that was new. Trade spokesmen emphasized the industry's accomplishments and eschewed any attacks on the Forest Service or other federal agencies. This initial testimony established a pattern of reciprocity, good will, and mutual cooperation that was repeated at each successive hearing. During the summer of 1939, the Forest Service released a "short range" forestry program that would be part of its forthcoming testimony to the Joint Congressional Committee. Wellington Burt, the new assistant forester with the NLMA, thought the report was reasonable, with the exception of its ambitious acquisition program. The report lacked the "socialistic" tendencies that, he suspected, would be part of the "long-range" report still in preparation.[15]

Burt's fears about the "long-range" Forest Service report were unfounded. Circulated confidentially as "The National Interest in Forestry," the study urged that the public regulation of forest practices be developed "through wide experimentation in the States as well as by gradual extension of Federal laws." Intended as a draft for the joint committee, the Forest Service report contemplated no drastic action from Washington and insisted that "laws of this kind must grow with public opinion."[16] Except for the recommendation for an expanded acquisition program, the Forest Service proposal was similar to those adopted at the industry-sponsored forestry conference in April, 1937.

Even these assurances did not ease the industry's suspicions about the recommendations coming out of Washington, D.C. The *Southern Lumberman* reminded its readers that although "the subject has not been recently agitated," timberland owners were constantly threatened by government regulation. And Chief Forester Silcox, the paper warned, was under the influence of a "radical fringe" in the Forest Service. Other trade leaders

---

[14] U.S. Congress, *Hearings before the Joint Committee on Forestry. Forest Lands of the United States*, 75th Cong., 3rd sess., pt. 1, 1939; *West Coast Lumberman* 65 (October, 1938): 34.

[15] Wellington Burt to Federated Associations, NLMA, August 29, 1939, box 78, NFPA Records.

[16] "The National Interest in Forestry," second draft of a report to the Joint Committee of Congress, labeled confidential and not for publication, October, 1939, pp. 34–35, in box 27, NFPA Records.

like Charles W. Boyce, an executive with the American Paper and Pulp Association, disapproved of the Forest Service acquisition program. Some segments of his industry, Boyce told Earle Clapp, were "approaching the stage of violent opposition" to federal acquisition.[17]

The Joint Congressional Committee held one of its last field hearings in Portland, Oregon, in December, 1939. National association officials provided northwestern trade leaders with descriptions and character sketches of the prejudices and interests of the committee members. During the committee's tour, Congressman Hampton Fulmer lived up to his advance billing as the champion of small-scale mill operators and timberland owners. John Woods reported that Fulmer was "rank poison" at both the San Francisco and the Portland hearings. Woods also complained that Oregon Congressman Walter Pierce "was always messing things up" and that Earle Clapp dominated the program at both hearings. But despite these private grumblings, Woods, Wellington Burt, and other industry leaders were conciliatory and diplomatic.[18]

Perhaps the most important of the Joint Congressional Committee hearings was held in Washington, D.C., in January and February, 1940. Repeating the pattern of the McNary hearings seventeen years earlier, the NLMA chose its most influential and best-known spokesmen to represent the industry. George Jewett emphasized the need for increased fire protection funds, with "the public contributing in proportion in which it creates hazards." He also urged the committee to speed changes in the system of taxing timberland, because the large acreages in federal ownership placed an undue tax burden on private owners.[19]

Most of Wilson Compton's presentation to the joint committee reiterated the Forestry Conservation Conference recommendations of April, 1937. He insisted on the maximum retention of forestland by private owners and argued that any further public acquisition should be limited and at the state level. He also praised the accomplishments of forest management

[17] *Southern Lumberman* 159 (September 1, 1939): 20; Charles Boyce to Earle Clapp, September 5, 1939, carton 4, box 3, Record Group 95, National Archives, Washington, D.C. (hereafter cited as RG 95, NA).

[18] A. G. T. Moore to G. F. Jewett, and Moore to C. S. Chapman, November 25, 1939, box 91, NFPA Records; Greeley, *Forests and Men*, pp. 213–14; Woods to Compton, December 16 and 23, 1939, box 36, Wellington Burt to Henry [?], December 17, 1939, box 91, and Burt to Federated Associations, NLMA, December 18, 1939, box 91, all in NFPA Records.

[19] Congress, *Hearings: Forest Lands of the United States*, 75th Cong., 3rd sess., pt. 1, 1939, pp. 1599–1600.

under the old lumber code and applauded state achievements in regulating forest practices, noting that good forestry was a local concern. Compton further insisted that regulation should occur at the state level "by gradual extension as experience accumulates and as the need develops." He reminded the committee that the late chief forester (Silcox died in December, 1939) had never explicitly stated how his regulatory program would be implemented. Finally, Compton asked for "public understanding and public cooperation," and, above all, help in preserving "the fundamental pattern of private enterprise."[20]

Earle Clapp, acting head of the Forest Service, outlined to the joint committee a specific plan for the federal regulation of private timberlands, specifying that the requirements be tailored to fit individual needs and circumstances and be based on a quid pro quo. If the public provided "cooperative assistance" to the industry, it was "not unreasonable for the public to insist that private owners safeguard the public investment by reasonable forest practices." The people, Clapp argued, "should not be left holding the bag." Federal regulation, he believed, was necessary because the "liquidation philosophy" was so deeply embedded that voluntary cooperation was not enough to ensure prudent forest practices. The acting chief advised a system of state regulation with the federal government establishing the minimum requirements. But if a state failed to set up an acceptable program, "then the Federal Government would step in and do the job." The Forest Service plan, Clapp observed, had "more teeth in it" than the Clarke-McNary policy and was therefore more likely to succeed.[21]

The NLMA mailed copies of Clapp's testimony to all its regional affiliates, and the administration's emerging forestry program aroused a storm of protest. George Jewett thought the proposals, if adopted, would destroy democratic processes and lead to a "regimented society." Under the Forest Service plan, he feared, private forestry would perish, economic independence would break down, and liberty and democracy would be undermined. Jewett warned that the United States had embarked on "so many socialistic enterprises that our private enterprises are seriously hampered." To a member of the joint committee, he complained that the acquisition program would give the Forest Service control of the forest products market and from there the power to regulate industry. William Greeley later

[20] Ibid., pp. 1715–18, 1731.
[21] Ibid., pp. 1956–59, 1966–67.

observed that although Earle Clapp was straightforward and honest, he was also "wholly sincere and forthright in wanting forest regulation and single-minded in pursuit of it." [22]

The Joint Congressional Committee on Forestry did not publish its findings until March, 1941, in the midst of the European conflagration and the growing crisis in the Pacific. The report blamed private owners, the general public, and the federal government for perpetuating the uninhibited exploitation of forests and other natural resources. The neglect of forestlands in many parts of the United States, the document read, "has resulted in receding land value, loss of employment and earning power, tax delinquency, and a declining tax revenue." This, combined with a depressed economy, had worsened unemployment, decreased salaries, and created idle lands and ghost towns. Testimony at the hearings, the report noted, pointed particularly to the South and the northern lakes states, where the industry had moved away after leaving in its wake "ruthless destruction" and poverty. It was further contended that the states of Washington and Oregon also had many areas "where destructive liquidation is rapidly running its course." [23]

The report pointed to private forestlands as the country's most critical problem; any measures to correct the failures of previous policy, therefore, must focus on restoring and maintaining these lands in a condition satisfactory for production. The committee's study cited the most serious difficulties facing forest owners: fire damage, insects and diseases, uncertain markets, importation of foreign forest products, tangled patterns of land ownership, oversized plants and excessive mill capacity, and overextended investment and heavy carrying charges that increased the pressure to liquidate. Because forestlands were closely integrated with the nation's economic health, the ownership of forestland carried with it certain obligations to the public. The heavy public funding that benefited private owners, the document pointed out, "accentuated the responsibilities of private ownership." For its part, the public also had to recognize its obligation to the well-being of forestlands. [24]

[22] Forest Service testimony before Joint Congressional Committee on Forestry, box 91, George Jewett to Earl Clapp, February 28, 1940, box 36, Jewett to Charles McNary, March 4, 1940, box 36, and Jewett to Senator E. D. Smith, March 4, 1940, box 36, all in NFPA Records; Greeley, *Forests and Men*, p. 212.

[23] U.S. Congress, *Report of the Joint Committee on Forestry. Forest Lands of the United States*, 77th Cong., 1st sess., 1941, pp. 5, 15–19.

[24] Ibid., pp. 20, 24, 26–27.

The committee's report listed sixteen recommendations to restore the productivity of forestlands and to assure the stability of communities dependent on timber resources. The more important of these included an increase in cooperative protection funds under Clarke-McNary from $2,500,000 to $10,000,000, provided certain guidelines were adopted by the cooperating states. The report suggested that federal assistance be withdrawn if compliance with these guidelines was unsatisfactory. Other recommendations advised increased subsidies to protect against insects and disease, aid to reforest private lands, and financial help for forest products and forest management research. The study also proposed legislation to authorize cooperative sustained yield units, a forest credit system, and the expansion of the national forests. Of the committee's sixteen recommendations, only the first mentioned regulation; its diluted wording satisfied neither the lumber industry nor the Forest Service.[25]

The reaction of trade journals to the committee's report was only mildly critical. The *West Coast Lumberman* faulted it for pointing to every extreme example of forest liquidation and ignoring progress in private forestry. The trade paper praised the study for recommending an increase in the Clarke-McNary authorization and noted that it did not call for direct federal intervention. The *American Lumberman* remarked that some of the committee's findings were "studded with half truths and inconsistencies," but that its general recommendations were notable. The Chicago journal praised the study for urging state responsibility to achieve a balanced forest economy. The keynote to federal forestry, it argued, "continues to be largely one of Federal cooperation rather than Federal domination."[26]

The Portland-based *Timberman* told its readers that lumbermen had been apprehensive about the joint committee's report, with "their feet braced for something of a shock or at least a suggestion for federal regulation." But the published report proposed no formal legislative program, and its recommendations were based on the tested and proven principle of federal cooperation. Stuart Moir, a forester with the Western Pine Association, said he found no quarrel with the report, because it contained "no proposals of direct federal regulation of private forest lands and from that standpoint is satisfactory." Wilson Compton was also pleased, noting that the report adhered "to the proven policy of Federal co-operation." The

---

[25] Ibid., pp. 28–33; Steen, *U.S. Forest Service*, pp. 235–36.
[26] *West Coast Lumberman* 68 (April, 1941): 85; *American Lumberman* (April 5, 1941): 64.

joint committee, Compton observed, has conducted itself "in an atmosphere friendly to the forest industries."[27]

Although William Greeley thought the joint committee "painted a black picture and prescribed strong medicine," its recommendations were far less drastic than some of the committee's findings might have warranted. The final document followed Forest Service recommendations for regulating private timberlands, but most of the proposed measures followed the pattern of increased subsidies, more research appropriations, and sustained yield policies that the lumber industry had been seeking for years. George Jewett's shrill blast at Earle Clapp's regulatory measure ignored the convoluted and exceedingly modest nature of the Clapp proposal. And even the recommendation for an expanded federal forest system followed the dominant thinking in the lumber industry until at least the mid-1930s. Thus, the criticisms of federal acquisition reflected hindsight and the mood of the later 1930s, when forest products officials opposed further expansion of the federal forests.[28]

While George Jewett ranted privately (and sometimes publicly) about preserving American institutions and values, William Greeley, Wilson Compton, and other less volatile leaders emphasized cooperation with the federal government and the state regulation of forest practices. If lumbermen would support minimal forestry requirements at the state level, modernizers like Greeley and Compton argued, it would undermine the effort to impose federal regulation. E. T. Allen told Greeley to push "hard on the states, especially receptive governors, to assume more responsibility" in regulating forestry practices. Allen also had no objection to reciprocal relations with the federal government, if they were safeguarded. When states adopted progressive forestry policies, he argued, "it is the obligation of the Government to help bear the cost, and this without having in any way dictated such policies or methods."[29]

William Greeley also urged the lumber industry to "move aggressively for State legislation." The adoption of forestry codes in the Northwest, he believed, would keep state regulatory policy in accord with the techniques of the more progressive 60 percent of private owners. This ap-

---

[27] *Timberman* 42 (May, 1941): 9, 48; *American Lumberman* (April 5, 1941): 64.

[28] Greeley, *Forests and Men*, p. 214; Steen, *U.S. Forest Service*, p. 235. For a criticism of the federal forest acquisition policy, see Ralph W. Hidy, Frank Ernest Hill, and Allan Nevins, *Timber and Men: The Weyerhaeuser Story*, p. 445.

[29] E. T. Allen to William Greeley, June 14, 1940, box 61, NFPA Records.

proach, he suggested, would extend cutting regulations "from the grass roots upward." Greeley insisted that "the future development of . . . forestry policy will turn largely around that point" and that the industry should meet the challenge in a positive and aggressive way.[30]

Essentially, Greeley was pursuing an ideological view similar to his arguments in support of the Snell legislation of the early 1920s: lumbermen should act responsibly to keep their lands productive through "localized regulation." With minor exceptions, this thesis bore a striking resemblance to the recommendations in the joint committee report of 1941. Reforestation was a necessity in parts of the country, Greeley indicated, and if private owners failed to replant their logged-off lands, "public regulation or public ownership will—sooner or later—take over." Because most of the cutover land in the Pacific Northwest could be easily restocked, he urged lumbermen to demand compulsory reforestation from their state legislatures. Moreover, the region would have the opportunity to set the standard for the rest of the country, because the Northwest was the " 'melting pot' of forest policy."[31]

During this period of protracted public and private debate, the Forest Service assured lumber trade leaders that the government was not proposing straight federal regulation. Moreover, government officials kept lumber trade officials informed about federal laws relating to the forest products trade, and Acting Chief Forester Earle Clapp praised regional leaders in the Pacific Northwest who were pushing for state regulations. Clapp urged regional forester Lyle Watts to use his influence to make these bills effective. But even while he encouraged such measures, Clapp feared that the industry-sponsored laws would "accomplish nothing in the woods, and . . . tend to mislead the public." Watts informed his chief that he would never recommend the widespread adoption of the bills before the state legislatures in Oregon and Washington as a basis for federal cooperation. Both Watts and Clapp seemed convinced that the state legislative proposals were weak and lacked provisions for enforcement.[32]

The furor over regulation and the potential for federal interference

---

[30] William Greeley to E. T. Allen, June 20, 1940, box 61, NFPA Records.

[31] William Greeley to Karl Swenning, October 21, 1940, and Greeley to Philip T. Coolidge, January 28, 1941, box 7, William B. Greeley Papers (hereafter cited as Greeley Papers), University of Oregon Library, Eugene, Oregon; Lawrence Hamilton, "The Federal Forest Regulation Issue," *Journal of Forest History* 9 (April, 1965): 10.

[32] C. M. Granger to Earle Clapp, September 20, 1940, RG 95A, NA; notes on the proposed forest regulation bill as submitted and discussed by Mr. Earle Clapp at the meeting of

with the management of private timberlands prompted the Oregon legislature to pass a forest practices act in 1941. William Greeley, who was closer to the Oregon situation than most lumber trade leaders, praised the Oregon act for imposing "minimum requirements for commercial cutting" and because it was based on the industry's own interests. Greeley, who hoped the Washington legislature would follow the Oregon example, advised keeping "the interest and initiative localized and . . . the power of private initiative and enterprise in play."[33]

But many lumber trade leaders would broach no compromise with federal officials. Clyde S. Martin, associated with the Weyerhaeuser interests, confided to Earle Clapp that his policies threatened progressive industries providing steady employment, good wages, and reasonable prices to the consumer. Martin likened Clapp's plan to a "local soviet," where private industry would turn over control of cutting practices without recourse to appeal. Although he approved of cutting regulations to bring irresponsible operators into line, he doubted that this was possible under the present government, where "upright men are prosecuted." Martin, in effect, let Clapp have the full brunt of his anger over the Justice Department's investigation of the Weyerhaeuser combine for price fixing and other trust activities. George Jewett, who received a copy of Martin's letter, also fired off a note to Clapp, castigating the government's "socialistic enterprises" and urging the acting chief to "foster legislation which will make private forestry practical."[34]

Through this verbal bombardment, Clapp held fast to his belief that an essential feature of the Forest Service plan was a minimum federal requirement for forest practices on private timberland. He also assured H. G. Collingwood, the new forester with the NLMA, that the Forest Service supported expanded public cooperation. But with equal conviction, he insisted that the "cut-out-and-get-out philosophies . . . are still prevalent among most operators," and this required a greater public presence. If the states were left alone, he feared, some of them "might not go ahead."[35]

the Forest Industries Conference, June 27, 1940, box 61, NFPA Records; Clapp to Lyle Watts, February 5, 1941, RG 95A, NA.

[33] Samuel Trask Dana, *Forest and Range Policy: Its Development in the United States*, p. 280; William Greeley to Henry Graves, July 21, 1941, box 7, Greeley Papers.

[34] Clyde Martin to Earle Clapp, March 4, 1941, and Jewett to Clapp, March 7 and April 29, 1941, box 63, NFPA Records. In his April letter Jewett told Clapp, "The leadership of the United States Forest Service is socialistic." He recommended that Clapp "realign" the goals of the service.

[35] Earle Clapp to H. G. Collingwood, March 27, 1941, box 61, NFPA Records.

The major issue in this rhetorical maneuvering was the disposition of the Joint Congressional Committee's recommendations. Ward Shepard, who was employed with the Bureau of Indian Affairs, thought the committee's report was a weak compromise, particularly with respect to regulation. Shepard told Interior Secretary Harold Ickes that much more should be expected from the administration than the mild proposals in the joint committee's study. The recommendations, he reasoned, closely fit "the strategy of the lumbermen in opposing effective Federal intervention," because they would make it possible for lumber interests to "hamstring effective State legislation." Shepard called for a renewal of executive leadership. In a memorandum to the secretaries of agriculture and interior, President Roosevelt concurred that the recommendations were "on the whole pitifully weak." Therefore, he suggested a further investigation to differentiate between the problems of small woodlot owners and commercial lumbermen.[36]

While the Roosevelt administration seemed to favor some form of federal regulation, lumbermen's groups were seeking ways to redirect the implications of the joint committee report. The forest conservation committee of the influential West Coast Lumbermen's Association urged its members to accept state regulation as a quid pro quo for an increase in Clarke-McNary funds to $10,000,000. The committee also favored extending the cooperative principle to include protection against forest insects and diseases and recommended the retention of the maximum amount of timberland by private owners. Where private lands could not be kept in production, states should assume the responsibility. With only a few exceptions, however, the conservation committee was favorably disposed toward the joint committee's recommendations.[37]

Wilson Compton also thought lumbermen should confront the forest conservation problem "squarely and affirmatively." In a May, 1941, report to his association, he noted that most lumber operators were aware of forest conservation problems and had requested public cooperation to resolve the worst abuses. Although the industry had outlined those policies it opposed, it had not stated clearly what it favored. Compton counseled the lumber trade to move quickly to lessen public suspicions. He recom-

[36] Ward Shepard to Harold Ickes, March 27, 1941, and Franklin Roosevelt to Claude R. Wickard, May 14, 1941, both in Edgar B. Nixon, ed., *Franklin D. Roosevelt and Conservation, 1911–1945*, II, 495–96, 509–10.

[37] Minutes of meeting, Joint Committee of Forest Conservation, West Coast Lumbermen's Association, May 1, 1941, vol. 160, West Coast Lumbermen's Association Records, Oregon Historical Society, Portland, Oregon.

mended the adoption of a "simple system of State legislation" to improve
public understanding and to serve as a barrier against federal regulation.
Like most industry leaders, he feared that "drastic Federal regulation"
would be the alternative to moderate state regulation.[38]

Although the new secretary of agriculture, Claude Wickard, favored
federal regulation of private timberlands, he had his department prepare
alternative bills, one defining strict federal requirements and the other requiring regulation only if the states failed to do the job. The legislative
dilemma, Wickard told the president, was to "induce the Congress to modify and strengthen the report of its own committee." As the summer wore
on and defense considerations became increasingly important, Wickard
continued to remind Roosevelt of the urgent need for federal regulation.
And war-related increases in timber cutting convinced the agriculture secretary that the problem was becoming worse. Therefore, Wickard wanted
the president to "fall back on the last defensive line—Federal leadership
and Federal action." To bring an end to destructive cutting practices and to
assure the permanence of rural communities, he advised Roosevelt to support public regulation and a greatly increased acquisition program. The
White House took no action.[39]

When the Bureau of the Budget declared against federal regulation, it
compounded the difficulties of the Forest Service and Secretary Wickard.
Harold Smith, the bureau's director, warned Roosevelt that regulating forest practices would be costly and that he had reservations "concerning the
whole program of public regulation of private forestry." James E. Scott, a
bureau officer in charge of agriculture and natural resources, thought the
Forest Service proposal for regulation was filled with propaganda, and, although it recommended state action, he believed its ultimate objective was
federal control. He also accused Earle Clapp and the Forest Service of attempting to bypass the administration and lobby directly with Congress on
the issue.[40]

The four years of intense debate over federal forest policy reached a
climax in late 1941 when Alabama's Senator Bankhead introduced the Co-

[38] Wilson Compton, "We Have More Problems Than We Have Answers; But We Are
Finding the Answers," report to Executive Committee, NLMA, May 14, 1941, p. 8, box 145,
NFPA Records.

[39] Claude Wickard to Franklin Roosevelt, June 18 and August 11, 1941, in Nixon, ed.,
Franklin D. Roosevelt and Conservation, II, 518–19, 523–24.

[40] Harold Smith to Franklin Roosevelt, April 10, 1941, container 2, OF 149, FDR Papers; Henry Clepper, *Professional Forestry in the United States*, p. 155.

operative Forest Restoration Bill (the Omnibus Forestry Bill), which was designed to implement most of the recommendations in the Joint Congressional Committee report. The lumber trades opposed the bill, because they feared it involved federal dominion over the states and ultimately the regulation of private timberland. The omnibus bill got nowhere—the Forest Service failed to support it, and it eventually died in committee.[41]

Roosevelt's prepossession with national defense failed to dampen the enthusiasm of the proponents of federal regulation. In late December, 1941, when Secretary Wickard informed the president that legislation was urgently needed to keep the forests productive, Roosevelt still seemed only mildly interested. Acting Chief Forester Earle Clapp then tried to convince the president to impose federal regulation through the use of his emergency war powers. This proposal was killed when industry leaders convinced Donald Nelson, the director of the War Production Board, that federal controls would hamper the war effort. Any further attempts to impose regulation by executive decree ended when Wayne Coy, assistant director of the Bureau of the Budget, told Roosevelt that the need for federal regulation of private forestry practices "has not been convincingly demonstrated." The president responded firmly. Until the war was over, he declared, "There should be no Federal legislation providing for Federal regulation of forestry practices on private lands."[42]

William Greeley, who led the fight for state regulation, thought the New Deal's "enthusiasm for regimentation" was beginning to ebb as the nation turned its energies to war production. In an *American Forests* guest editorial in the spring of 1942, Greeley advised the adversaries in the regulation debate to look beyond the issue to the more pressing challenge of protecting the forests from enemy incendiarism. To an old friend, Greeley confided that the war had "strengthened timber values" and thereby made everyone aware of the importance of fire protection.[43]

Despite the president's opposition to federal regulation on private for-

[41] Dana, *Forest and Range Policy*, pp. 279–80; Steen, *U.S. Forest Service*, p. 236; Clepper, *Professional Forestry*, p. 156; Hamilton, "Federal Forest Regulation Issue," p. 10.

[42] Wickard to Roosevelt, December 26, 1941, and Roosevelt to Wickard, December 29, 1941, Wayne Coy to Roosevelt, May 16, 1942, and Roosevelt to Harold Smith and Coy, May 19, 1942, all in Nixon, ed., *Franklin D. Roosevelt and Conservation*, II, 543–44, 550–54; Clepper, *Professional Forestry*, p. 158.

[43] Greeley, *Forests and Men*, p. 214; William Greeley, "The War Job for Foresters," *American Forests* 48 (April, 1942): 175; Greeley to Barrington Moore, March 17, 1943, box 7, Greeley Papers.

estlands, his advisers occasionally put forward programs that involved some form of government control. Secretary of Agriculture Wickard, at the insistence of the Forest Service and Donald Nelson of the War Production Board, presented a plan to increase lumber production, especially among small mills in the South and the East. The proposal would have placed all private lumber operations under the control of the Forest Service, which would exercise its authority through the president under the Second War Powers Act. Secretary Wickard assured Roosevelt that the plan would stimulate production and help end destructive timber-cutting habits. He recognized that timber owners would not be "too enthusiastic about public regulation of cutting practices on their lands," but he thought the president could change their outlook.[44]

Like other schemes to implement forest regulation by executive fiat during the war, this plan fell victim to the cost-conscious head of the Bureau of the Budget. Harold Smith, the director, reminded Roosevelt that the Forest Service had ignored the president's directive and had tried to enlist the support of the War Production Board in yet another regulatory proposal. The budget director said the new measure would not assist idle mills in the South, because most of the targeted operations were small and inefficient. Then the crux of the issue—even if it did stimulate small mill production, the plan would intensify competition between small-scale operators and the larger, more efficient manufacturers. Smith told the president that the "forest devastation scheme is rather overworked" and that the shortage of lumber was not due to idle "teakettle" mills, but rather to the shortage of labor, equipment, and transportation affecting the large mills as well. Moreover, lumber tradesmen opposed the recent regulatory proposal, fearing that the Forest Service was trying to regulate forest practices under cover of a response to meet war needs. The budget director's appeal was successful. Roosevelt did not act on the Forest Service proposal and instructed Donald Nelson to seek "a simpler and more generally acceptable plan."[45]

The feverish pace of activity associated with war production gave American industry an opportunity to fully reassert itself after the confusion following the National Recovery Administration. Lumbermen who had

[44] Wickard to Roosevelt, October 23, 1942, container 1, OF 446, FDR Papers.

[45] Smith to Roosevelt, December 4, 1942, and Franklin Roosevelt to Donald Nelson, February 26, 1943, container 1, OF 446, FDR Papers.

survived the demoralized market conditions of the 1930s successfully fought Forest Service efforts to impose federal regulation in the early 1940s. Then the wartime crisis provided the opportunity to press for the legislative program they had sought since the days of the Lumber Code Authority. Congress reciprocated and passed four pieces of forestry legislation at the peak of the war effort in 1944. Three of the new laws had been recommended ten years earlier as part of the Article X agreement: (1) increased appropriations to carry on the forest survey; (2) authorization to raise the annual Clarke-McNary fund to $9,000,000; and (3) the Sustained-Yield Forest Management Act.[46]

The sustained yield act permitted the Forest Service and lumber companies to enter into long-range agreements to provide mills with a constant supply of timber without resorting to competitive bidding. The rationale for the act, according to its supporters, was community stability; it authorized the pooling of federal and private timberlands into cooperative sustained yield units and allowed the creation of similar units from federal land when the stability of a community depended upon federal stumpage. Another major milestone of 1944 was an amendment to the federal income tax law allowing lumbermen to report profits from timber sales as capital gains rather than as conventional income.[47] In the long run, the act promoted vertically integrated operations and hastened the merger of the production and manufacturing sectors of the industry.

According to the biographers of the Weyerhaeuser company, the forestry laws passed in 1944 benefited all lumbermen. The most important of these was the sustained yield act, which offered new encouragement to many of the Weyerhaeuser subsidiaries. Overall, this "new constructive policy" included improved methods of fire control, implementation of "skillfully constructed forest management plans," revision of tax laws, and other instances of government encouragement for advanced forestry techniques.[48]

The industry was waxing fat in the war-stimulated environment and had achieved a position in the national political economy rivaled only perhaps by its successes in the first Clarke-McNary measure in the mid-1920s.

[46] Steen, *U.S. Forest Service*, pp. 250–53.
[47] Ibid., pp. 252–53; Dana, *Forest and Range Policy*, pp. 284–85.
[48] Hidy, Hill, and Nevins, *Timber and Men*, pp. 506–507.

The wartime laws conferred great social and economic influence on the industry, especially in the broader implications of the sustained yield legislation. And in 1941 the American Forest Products Industries, a subsidiary of the NLMA, set out on an aggressive public relations effort to improve the industry's image. Through magazine articles, newspaper coverage, syndicated features, movies, and reading material for children, the organization sought to convince the public that lumbermen no longer carried on the exploitive practices of old.[49]

Clearly, the Roosevelt administration's reaction to these initiatives was ambivalent. This ambiguity was particularly apparent in Roosevelt's equivocation on the renewed antitrust activities of the late 1930s. Beginning in 1938, the Anti-Trust Division of the Justice Department brought several suits against trade associations and corporations for violating the Robinson-Patman Antitrust Act of 1936. Five lumber trade groups and numerous lumber corporations and individual operators were among those indicted. Most of those charged signed consent decrees, paid nominal fines, and did very little to alter their trade practices.[50]

The *Timberman* remarked that associations "accepted the . . . fines without contesting the validity of the charge, simply as a matter of expediency." But, the trade paper argued, lawyers should be trained in economics as well as the study of "abstract and abstruse fine spun legal precedents." Antiquated laws, the *Timberman* continued, should be abolished to keep in step with modern conditions. Wilson Compton viewed the consent decree signed by the NLMA in 1941 as a reasonable conclusion to its differences with the Department of Justice. The national association, he said, would observe the decree "in letter, in spirit and in detail," but it did "not propose to waste time in a post mortem."[51] The lumber industry obviously handled the Thurman Arnold antitrust indictments more confidently and with greater assuredness than it had the Justice Department prosecutions of the early 1920s.

Although the Second World War is beyond the scope of this study, it should be recognized that many industry leaders with first-hand knowledge

[49] Clepper, *Professional Forestry*, pp. 163–64; Greeley, *Forests and Men*, p. 224; Hidy, Hill, and Nevins, *Timber and Men*, p. 505.

[50] Ellis W. Hawley, *The New Deal and the Problem of Monopoly: A Study in Economic Ambivalence*, pp. 411, 456, 470; Hidy, Hill, and Nevins, *Timber and Men*, pp. 445–48.

[51] *Timberman* 41 (June, 1940): 66; Compton, "We Have More Problems Than We Have Answers," p. 6, NFPA Records.

about government-business relations during the previous war were still active in 1941. Thus, industrial leaders entered the war confident that they could influence and shape policy to their advantage. The relative lack of alarm about antitrust indictments and the industry's legislative successes in 1944 were testimony to that confidence.

Epilogue:

The Consequences of Market Control

FOR nearly half a century, lumbermen have been engaged in a sometimes turbulent scramble for survival in the marketplace economy. The struggle destroyed marginal operations and strengthened the stronger competitors. Despite the strenuous efforts of far-sighted trade leaders, too many operators ignored the essential character of the market and proceeded to act in single-minded fashion to meet their immediate needs. The appeals to support voluntary and cooperative trade associations failed to create a collective effort to stabilize the cyclical gyrations in the lumber economy. Such private attempts at social cooperation were destroyed during the depression in the early 1930s. Even so, in the midst of these persisting difficulties, the industry did not lack corrective proposals. Forest Service studies in 1917 and 1920, the technical expertise brought to bear in the Timber Conservation Board investigation of 1930–1932, and the Copeland Report of 1933 all expanded the information available to decision makers and offered a variety of proposals to stabilize the lumber market. These studies went for naught. The failure, however, lay not in the inability of a prescient trade leadership to draft a coherent and carefully thought-out program, but rather in the contradictions of a competitive system that discouraged the application of the proposals.

Those contradictions were impressive. The perennial desire to liquidate standing timber to meet the carrying charges associated with over-capitalized land and mill investments contributed to a periodically saturated market. And organized lumbermen never were able to resolve or compromise their differences to cope with rampant overproduction. The consequences included endemic economic instability, a colossal waste of resources, and a badly managed forest environment. The run of the market remained supreme, and only the better-financed operations were able to survive the periodic downturns.

The history of the lumber industry is a story of unbalanced production, economic fluctuations and dysfunctions, new institutional arrangements dictated by changing competitive conditions, and an alarming toll in social and human costs. Conventional accounts of lumber and forest history do not confront the issue of social costs. For a more comprehensive understanding of these matters, we need to know the effects of the lumber business on local communities, the work force, and the forest environment. The account presented here assesses only one aspect of the lumber world in the first half of the twentieth century. It focuses on the dominant figures in the industry—the large-scale plant, mill, and timberland owners whose decisions were shaped by the profit motive. But much more of the story lies beyond the scope of this study. Others—men and women who worked in the mills and woods, suffered through seasonal layoffs, endured reduced wages when the market was down, and moved on each time the timber operator shifted to the next stand—also shaped this history. For this was a social system dominated by one segment of society, which reaped a grossly disproportionate share of the benefits.

As with other natural resource industries, lumbermen enjoyed leaders who worked through highly politicized private associations and public agencies and lobbied with congressional committees to shape and control an orderly future. Lumber trade leaders sought what they considered enlightened and progressive approaches and recommended programs to stabilize and then resolve the industry's problems. They successfully limited the annual harvest in the national forests in order to keep federal timber off the market, then liquidated their own stands with little regard to the diminishing volume. In contrast, when an active market after 1945 surpassed the ability of private holdings to meet demand, trade leaders pressured the Forest Service to increase the annual cut on the national forests.

Today, industry officials are working vigorously to raise the allowable federal cut in order to meet their marketing needs. They argue that an increased harvest in the national forests is necessary to satisfy domestic demand, at least until private stands of second-growth timber can be harvested. Private lumber spokesmen insist that these are technical and scientific decisions and that they are acting in the long-range public interest.

When opposition to these recommendations arises, the industry is able to muster an extensive public relations network and an impressive political clout to defend its proposals.

The industry also manipulates information and myths about the nation's timber supply. The illusive "timber famine" of the late nineteenth and early twentieth centuries was used by lumbermen as a scapegoat for many of their difficulties. For years trade leaders blamed conservationists for perpetuating a belief in an impending timber famine, which, they argued, had caused rampant overspeculation and the buying up of excess acreages of timberland. Then, during the late 1920s, lumber officials embarked on an aggressive advertising campaign to convince the public that the famine argument was false. This effort obviously was related to a demoralized market and was not an accurate assessment of the true volume of standing timber. By the 1970s, however, the industry had come full circle. It sought to modify the Sustained Yield Act of 1960 to enable the Forest Service to increase the annual cut of national forest timber to guard against an expected "timber famine" of the future.

The dominant corporations in the forest products business today are multinational and include such units as Boise Cascade, Georgia-Pacific, and the Weyerhaeuser Corporation (the largest holder of commercial forestland in the world).[1] The Weyerhaeuser empire embraces about 5,800,000 acres of prime timber in the Pacific Northwest and in the pine forests of the southeast; it also has cutting rights to another 10,700,000 acres, most of them in Canada. The company reported net sales of $2.4 billion in 1978 from about seventy-five subsidiaries in the United States, Canada, Japan, Australia, and Indonesia. These investments sometimes range far from the company's woods products base. Moreover, Weyerhaeuser and its corporate allies are skilled masters of public relations and are able to exert great political influence at the federal level.[2]

The presence of these major corporations extends far beyond the trees

---

[1] With increasing frequency in the 1930s, the term *forest products* began to be used to describe the wide range of manufacturing activities of the wood-using industries. The symbolic (and formal) transition took place in the mid-1960s, when the National Lumber Manufacturers Association was rechristened the National Forest Products Association.

[2] Michael Harris, "News From Timber Country: On Tour With the American Forest Institute," *The Progressive* 44 (May, 1980): 48–49; Lloyd C. Irland, "Do Giants Control Timber-Based Industries in North America?" June 29, 1976, p. 14 (copy in possession of Charles Sutherland, Department of Forest Management, Oregon State University).

they control. Industry economists claim that the concentration of land-ownership among the major forest products companies is modest, with the eight largest firms in the United States owning only 23 percent of all forested lands. This is still a sizable chunk. Furthermore, they control the best timber-growing land in the most productive regions in the country. This is particularly true in states like Oregon and Washington, where these eight firms control 34 percent of the timberland. If one looks at the highly productive Douglas fir subregion alone, the eight leaders hold 62 percent of all privately owned acreages. Those economists, therefore, who claim that the lumber industry is still a model of competition ignore the real world, where a few corporations exert a disproportionate influence on the market. Moreover, large-scale owners are in a favored position to bid on Forest Service timber, whereas firms without their own stands *must* bid for federal contracts.[3]

The structure and character of the lumber and forest products industry have changed considerably since 1945. The sustained momentum in the American economy toward merger and consolidation has been dramatically revealed in wood products; mergers there have exceeded those of most other industries.[4] Even so, these postwar economic developments merely mark the culmination of a decades-long effort in the lumber trade to eliminate the excesses of competition through carefully planned financial consolidations.

The bright hope, of course, was to stabilize the marketing of lumber. Wilson Compton had long counseled the industry to eliminate its overly competitive tendencies through business merger. A number of forced consolidations occurred during the 1930s, but the lumber trade still lagged behind other business sectors in degree of concentration. What happened after 1945 suggests that this once highly competitive trade was catching up with the rest of the economy in its move toward greater economic concentration. This was still a haphazard affair, however, because of the disparate size of the units being merged.

All financial consolidations, of course, were not economically signifi-

---

[3] Irland, "Timber-Based Industries in North America," p. 12; Walter J. Mead, *Competition and Oligopsony in the Douglas Fir Lumber Industry*, pp. 1, 88; Thomas P. Clephane, "Ownership of Timber: A Critical Component in Industrial Success," *Forest Industries* 105 (August, 1978): 32.

[4] Walter J. Mead, *Mergers and Economic Concentration in the Douglas-Fir Lumber Industry*, pp. 75–76.

cant. Indeed, most forest products mergers pale beside the financial empire that Georgia-Pacific has created during the last thirty years. Beginning with a small financial base in Georgia, the firm branched out across the country and purchased the Coos Bay Lumber Company and 120,000 acres in 1955 for $70,000,000; the Hammond Lumber Company and 127,000 acres in 1956 for $75,000,000; and the rich 200,000 acres, production facilities, and operating railroad of the Booth-Kelly Lumber Company in 1959 for $93,000,000. That was only the beginning. About half of the mergers between 1950 and 1970 came about between 1965 and 1970.[5]

Changes in federal tax law during the 1940s provided a major inducement for many of these mergers. Section 631(a) of the Internal Revenue Code allowed timber owners to use the difference between the market value of cut timber and its cost as a capital gain, providing that the timber was manufactured by the same corporation that owned the timber. Corporations today that hold title to and manufacture their own timber have a decided tax advantage over firms lacking either a manufacturing capacity or their own forest resource. Such vertically integrated businesses are in a much stronger marketing position than those who sell timber only, or who limit their services to manufacturing lumber products.[6]

Investment analysts predict that owning timberland will be increasingly critical to success in the forest products industry for the foreseeable future. Timber ownership now means greater profits for most companies because of the diminishing stands of privately owned mature stocks. The Weyerhaeuser Corporation, still the preeminent leader in forest ownership despite the growth of combines like Georgia-Pacific, dominates the companies that own and process their lumber. According to one recent study, Weyerhaeuser is 88 percent self-sufficient in supplying its raw material. The rising value of forestland, the study argues, "make[s] timber ownership appealing for corporate investors both within and outside of the existing industry."[7]

Another post–World War Two phenomenon has been the sharp increase in the annual harvest of national forests. The lumber industry earlier opposed any sizable expansion in production of federally owned timber, because it would tend to glut the market and lower stumpage prices on pri-

[5]Dennis C. LeMaster, *Mergers Among the Largest Forest Products Firms, 1950–1970*, p. 1.
[6]Ibid., p. 3.
[7]Clephane, "Ownership of Timber," pp. 30–31.

vate lands. Trade leaders lobbied successfully for more than forty years to keep the federal harvest at a relatively low level. The national forests supplied only 1.4 percent of the total volume harvested in the United States in 1920, and even as late as 1940 the federally owned forests supplied only 3.2 percent of the nation's timber. But the rapid cutting of privately owned stock in excess of its ability to reproduce has diminished these stands and prompted lumbermen to bring pressure on the Forest Service to increase the federal harvest. As a consequence, by 1970 the national forests accounted for 18 percent of the harvest. The Forest Service acknowledged in 1967 "the increasing dependence industry is placing on the National Forests to supply their roundwood requirements" and noted that "pressures in the timber resources management program . . . are becoming increasingly difficult to contain." [8]

The forest products industry is now vertically integrated, to the point that many of the largest manufacturers produce everything from two-by-fours to tissue paper. Moreover, the multinational conglomerates have established a foothold in the industry through the purchase of both land and manufacturing plants, and indications are that major oil and resource corporations will become more active in the woods products field in the future. [9]

The dynamic of capitalism demands accumulating capital and resources and wielding influence over an ever-increasing share of the market. These truths are clearly apparent in the lumber industry. Banking and investment groups vastly increased their influence throughout the lumber trade in the 1920s and the 1930s. After 1945, the power shifted to diversified, heavily capitalized multinational corporations and is now revealed in the recent investments in forest products of ITT, Gulf and Western, Mobil, and Tenneco. [10]

There is more. Communities dominated by the lumber trade remain victims of the whims of forest products corporations. The increasing acreages of harvestable second-growth timber in the South have attracted capital from corporations whose major financial interests had once been in the lush forests of the Pacific Northwest. Those diminishing stands have prompted some corporations to look elsewhere for more lucrative operations. Cheaper labor costs and a weakly unionized work force probably add

[8] Ralph R. Barney, *The Last Stand: The Nader Study Group Report on the U.S. Forest Service*, pp. II-2, II-4, II-25.
[9] Clephane, "Ownership of Timber," p. 31.
[10] Ibid.

to the attractions of the southland. Georgia-Pacific's recent announcement that it would move its corporate headquarters from Oregon to Georgia is perhaps the most striking example. In response to these changes, people are understandably alarmed that the old pattern of disrupted communities, unemployment, and a diminished tax base will be repeated.

Since World War Two the industry has been increasingly sensitive to political tamperings with the prime interest rate, an obvious indication of the thoroughly integrated character of forest products economic activity. There is an old saying among loggers in the Douglas fir country that when the Federal Reserve board raises the prime rate in the morning, timber fallers can expect the pink slip that evening. Plants cut back on production, extra shifts are laid off, and smaller operations are sometimes forced to shut down. The people who suffer, however, are not the plant owners and managers: they can wait out the slump in building activity. The loggers and mill hands, though, are reduced to unemployment and welfare, and the corporations once again tap the taxpayer for the profits.

Bibliography

Bibliographic Note

THIS study of the integration of politics and economics in the lumber resource sector of the American economy is based largely on industry and federal government sources. Because lumber trade leaders worked primarily through private organizations to resolve their market problems, one must look to repositories of trade association documents, personal papers of influential industry officials, and related government agencies to understand the integrated political economy in which they operated.

Any study of lumber and forest history should begin by consulting Ronald J. Fahl, *North American Forest and Conservation History: A Bibliography* (Santa Barbara, Calif.: ABC-Clio Press, 1977). Equally comprehensive for unpublished materials on the same theme is Richard C. Davis, *North American Forest History: A Guide to Archives and Manuscripts in the United States and Canada* (Santa Barbara, Calif.: ABC-Clio Press, 1977). Three important journals associated with professional societies also cover a wide array of topics dealing with the subject: *American Forests* (American Forestry Association), *Journal of Forestry* (Society of American Foresters), and *Journal of Forest History* (Forest History Society).

For an understanding of the function and changing structure of the lumber industry in the twentieth century, the National Forest Products Association (NFPA) Records contain a wealth of material on virtually every issue of national importance. The records include correspondence between the leaders of the National Lumber Manufacturers Association and its regional affiliates, correspondence between government and lumber industry officials, mimeographed copies of important private and public papers, and most of the significant materials on government-industry cooperation. The latter include the First World War, the regulation debate of the early 1920s, the standardization and wood utilization movement of the same decade, President Hoover's Timber Conservation Board, volumes of material on the National Recovery Administration, the Lumber Code Authority, and the series of forestry conferences following the demise of the recovery administration. The NFPA Records also contain extensive correspondence on the regulation furor of the late 1930s, the work of the Joint Congressional Committee on Forestry, and the strategies that lumber trade leaders used to defuse the threat of federal regulation. Finally, the records include the important correspondence, memos, speeches, and articles of Wilson Compton, secretary-manager of the National Lumber Manufacturers Association from 1918 to 1944.

Two major regional collections, both in the Pacific Northwest, also hold valuable sources for understanding the national lumber picture. The records of the Western Forestry and Conservation Association (WFCA) contain position papers, correspondence, and documents that relate to national forest policy issues. The association's key executive official, E. T. Allen, held equally influential positions with the national association. In this respect, he was one of several lumbermen from the region who were important at the national level. The WFCA Records reveal an organization committed to educating the public about the virtues of cooperation between government and industry—in short, a skilled public relations force for lumbermen at both the regional and national levels. The West Coast Lumbermen's Association Records are especially useful for the period after 1928 when William Greeley became its chief executive officer. The holdings include important correspondence from the 1930s and the National Recovery Administration era.

The collections of the American Forestry Association, the oldest "conservation" organization in the United States, provide insight into most of the major controversies involving the lumber industry. Much of the correspondence and petitioning of the association reflects the ideas of elite groups outside the industry. The Society of American Foresters Records are useful for understanding the sometimes radically divergent views of professional foresters, especially on the issue of federal regulation of private timberlands.

The Herbert Hoover Presidential Library holds important documents and papers on lumber politics and economics in the 1920s and the early 1930s. Most useful are the extensive trade association papers from Hoover's eight years as Commerce Secretary, the significant reports and correspondence of the Hoover-appointed Timber Conservation Board, and the papers of the Committee on the Conservation and Administration of the Public Domain. These collections reveal Hoover as a progressive capitalist who believed that antitrust laws hindered "cooperation" and individual efforts to bring order to the economy. Most of the important materials in the Franklin D. Roosevelt Presidential Library on lumber industry matters in the 1930s and the early 1940s are available in Edgar B. Nixon, ed., *Franklin D. Roosevelt and Conservation, 1911–1945*. Three days of searching through Forest Service and lumber-related files in the Roosevelt Library turned up little that is not already available in print.

The National Forestry Program Committee Records focus primarily on the extensive public relations and lobbying of important lumber and forest products interests in the early 1920s. The correspondence in the collection is useful for understanding how the industry fought proposals to implement the federal regulation of private timberlands. The committee was a significant factor in pressing for the industry-backed Clarke-McNary Act of 1924.

The papers of four activists prominent in national lumber politics for much of the first half of the twentieth century were indispensible to this study: E. T. Allen, William Greeley, David Mason, and Raphael Zon. All of them were trained foresters; all served as expert witnesses in congressional testimony; and all contributed important articles to professional journals. Allen, Greeley, and Mason left federal employment for the private sector and, in this capacity, spoke persuasively for the lumber industry in matters of national concern. The Allen papers are important for the period from 1910 to the late 1930s, as are the Greeley and Mason collections for the era between the two world wars (the careers of Greeley and Mason extend well beyond the period covered in this study). The Raphael Zon correspondence offers a different perspective. Zon was an early employee of the Forest Service, but unlike his three contemporaries, he remained with the agency for the remainder of his career. An outspoken man with decidedly progressive leanings, Zon invariably opposed the industry-oriented proposals of the major trade associations.

Unpublished Material

ARCHIVES

Eugene, Oregon. University of Oregon Library.
　　William B. Greeley Papers.
Hyde Park, New York. Franklin D. Roosevelt Presidential Library.
　　Franklin D. Roosevelt Papers.

Ithaca, New York. Cornell University Libraries.
    Ralph S. Hosmer Papers.
    National Forestry Program Committee Records.
Portland, Oregon. Oregon Historical Society.
    David Mason Papers.
    John Minto Papers.
    West Coast Lumbermen's Association Records.
    Western Forestry and Conservation Association Records.
St. Paul, Minnesota. Minnesota Historical Society.
    Raphael Zon Papers.
Santa Cruz, California. Forest History Society.
    American Forestry Association Records.
    Wilson Compton Papers.
    Royal S. Kellogg—Letter File.
    National Forest Products Association Records.
    Society of American Foresters Records.
Washington, D.C. National Archives.
    Record Group 95.
West Branch, Iowa. Herbert Hoover Presidential Library.
    Herbert Hoover Commerce Papers.
    Herbert Hoover Presidential Papers.
    Edgar Rickard Diaries.

MANUSCRIPTS AND DISSERTATIONS

Berckes, Herbert C. "The Pitch in Pine: A Story of the Traditions, Policies and Activities of the Southern Pine Industry and the Men Responsible for Them." Manuscript. Forest History Society, Santa Cruz, California.

Hawley, Ellis. "Neo-institutional History and the Understanding of Herbert Hoover." Paper presented to the Symposium on Herbert Hoover, April 26, 1980, George Fox College, Newberg, Oregon.

Irland, Lloyd C. "Do Giants Control Timber-Based Industries in North America?" June 29, 1976. Copy in possession of Charles Sutherland, Oregon State University.

Meany, Edmund. "The History of the Lumber Industry in the Pacific Northwest to 1917." Ph.D. dissertation, Harvard University, 1935.

White, Roy Ring. "Austin Cary and Forestry in the South." Ph.D. dissertation, University of Florida, 1960.

Published Material

PUBLIC DOCUMENTS

Dixon, A. C. "Efforts of the Lumber Industry at Production Controls Prior to NRA." In U.S. National Recovery Administration, Division of Review. *Work Materials No. 79*. Appendix 1.

Fairchild, Fred Rogers. "Taxation of Timberlands." In *Report of the National Conservation Commission*. Washington, D.C.: Government Printing Office, 1909.

Gates, Paul Wallace. *History of Public Land Law Development*. Washington, D.C.: Public Law Review Commission, 1968.

Greeley, William B. *Some Public and Economic Aspects of the Lumber Industry*. Washington, D.C.: U.S. Forest Service, 1917.

Stone, Peter, et al. "Economic Problems of the Lumber and Timber Products Industry." In U.S. National Recovery Administation, Division of Review. *Work Materials No. 79.*

U.S. Bureau of Foreign and Domestic Commerce. *Services Available to the Lumber Industry Through the Department of Commerce*. Washington, D.C.: Government Printing Office, 1930.

U.S. Bureau of Forestry. *Annual Reports*. 1900–1905.

U.S. Congress. *Congressional Record*.

———. *Hearings before the Joint Committee on Forestry. Forest Lands of the United States*. 75th Cong., 3rd sess., pt. 1, 1939.

———. *Report of the Joint Committee on Forestry. Forest Lands of the United States*. 77th Cong., 1st sess., 1941.

U.S. Congress, House. *Forestry: Hearings Before the Committee on Agriculture*. 66th Cong., 3rd sess., January 26 and 27, 1921.

———. *Forestry: Hearings Before the Committee on Agriculture*. 67th Cong., 2d sess., January 9 and 12, 1922.

U.S. Congress, Senate. "Amendment of Federal Trade Commission Act and Establishment of a Federal Trade Court." *Hearings before a Subcommittee of the Committee on the Judiciary*. 72nd Cong., 1st sess., March 31, 1932.

———. *A National Plan For American Forestry*. 73rd Cong., 1st sess., March 13, 1933, Senate Doc. 12.

———. Select Committee on Reforestation. *Hearings*. 67th Cong., 4th sess., March 26, April 4, November 22–23, 1923.

U.S. Department of Agriculture. *Reports of the Chief of the Forestry Division*. 1883–1892.

U.S. Department of Commerce. *Annual Reports*. 1924–1928.

———. Bureau of Corporations. *Report on the Lumber Industry*. 1913.

U.S. Federal Trade Commission. *Report on Lumber Manufacturers Trade Associations*. Washington, D.C.: Government Printing Office, 1922.

U.S. Forest Service. *Annual Reports*. 1907–1941.

———. *Lumber Production, 1869–1934*. Washington, D.C.: Government Printing Office, 1936.

———. *Timber Depletion, Lumber Prices, Lumber Exports, and Concentration of Timber Ownership*. Washington, D.C.: Government Printing Office, 1920.

U.S. National Recovery Administration. "Amendment to Code of Fair Competition for the Lumber and Timber Products Industry." In National Recovery Administration, *Codes of Fair Competition*. Vol. 8. Washington, D.C.: Government Printing Office, 1934.

———. *Hearings on Amendments to the Code of Fair Competition for the Lumber and Timber Products Industry*, April 3, 1934. Microfilm copy in the University of Iowa Library, Iowa City, Iowa.

————. *Hearings on Applications for Exemption from Code of Fair Competition for the Lumber and Timber Products Industries*, September 17, 1934. Microfilm copy in the University of Iowa Library, Iowa City, Iowa.

————. *Hearings on the Application for Suspension of the Reasonable Costs and Their Rules and Regulations for their Application under the Code of Fair Competition for the Lumber and Timber Products Industries*, December 11, 1934. Microfilm copy in the University of Iowa Library, Iowa City, Iowa.

BOOKS AND PAMPHLETS

Ambrose, Stephen E., ed. *Institutions in Modern America*. Baltimore: Johns Hopkins University Press, 1967.

Barney, Ralph R. *The Last Stand: The Nader Study Group Report on the U.S. Forest Service*. Washington, D.C.: Center for the Study of Responsive Law, 1972.

Bradley, Joseph F. *The Role of Trade Associations and Professional Business Societies in America*. University Park: Pennsylvania State University Press, 1965.

Brown, Nelson C. *The American Lumber Industry: Embracing the Principal Features of the Resources, Production, Distribution, and Utilization of Lumber in the United States*. New York: John Wiley and Sons, 1923.

Bryant, Ralph C. *Lumber: Its Manufacture and Distribution*. New York: John Wiley and Sons, 1922.

Burner, David. *Herbert Hoover: A Public Life*. New York: Knopf, 1979.

Burns, Arthur Robert. *The Decline of Competition: A Study of the Evolution of American Industry*. New York: McGraw-Hill, 1936.

Chittenden, Alfred K. *The Taxation of Forest Lands in Wisconsin*. Madison: Democrat Printing Co., 1911.

Clepper, Henry. *Professional Forestry in the United States*. Baltimore: Johns Hopkins University Press, 1971.

Cochran, Thomas. *The Inner Revolution*. New York: Harper and Row, 1964.

Cochran, Thomas, and William Miller. *The Age of Enterprise*. New York: Macmillan, 1942.

Cohen, G. A. *Karl Marx's Theory of History: A Defence*. Princeton, N.J.: Princeton University Press, 1978.

Compton, Wilson. *The Organization of the Lumber Industry*. Chicago: American Lumberman Press, 1916.

Cox, Thomas R. *Mills and Markets: A History of the Pacific Coast Lumber Industry to 1900*. Seattle: University of Washington Press, 1974.

Dana, Samuel Trask. *Forest and Range Policy: Its Development in the United States*. New York: McGraw-Hill, 1956.

Dubofsky, Melvyn. *We Shall Be All: A History of the Industrial Workers of the World*. Chicago: Quadrangle, 1969.

Engler, Robert. *The Politics of Oil*. New York: Macmillan, 1961.

Fairchild, Fred Rogers; A. C. Shaw; and B. E. Fernow. *Forest Taxation*. Columbus, Ohio: Reprinted from the Addresses and Proceedings of the International Conference on State and Local Taxation, Toronto, Canada, 1908.

Faulkner, Harold U. *From Versailles to the New Deal*. New Haven, Conn.: Yale University Press, 1955.

Ficken, Robert E. *Lumber and Politics: The Career of Mark Reed*. Seattle: University of Washington Press, 1979.

Fickle, James E. *The New South and the "New Competition": Trade Association Development in the Southern Pine Industry*. Champaign: University of Illinois Press, 1980.

Forty Years of Western Forestry: A History of the Movement to Conserve Forest Resources by Cooperative Effort, 1909–1949. Portland, Oreg., 1949.

Freedman, Max, ed. *Roosevelt and Frankfurter: Their Correspondence, 1928–1945*. Boston: Little, Brown, 1967.

Galambos, Louis. *Competition and Cooperation: The Emergence of a National Trade Association*. Baltimore: Johns Hopkins University Press, 1966.

Greeley, William B. *Forests and Men*. New York: Doubleday, 1951.

Hawley, Ellis W. *The Great War and the Search for a Modern Order, 1917–1933*. New York: St. Martin's Press, 1979.

———. *The New Deal and the Problem of Monopoly: A Study in Economic Ambivalence*. Princeton, N.J.: Princeton University Press, 1966.

Hays, Samuel P. *Conservation and the Gospel of Efficiency: The Progressive Conservation Movement, 1890–1920*. Cambridge, Mass.: Harvard University Press, 1959.

Hicks, John D. *The Republican Ascendancy, 1921–1933*. New York: Harper and Row, 1960.

Hidy, Ralph W.; Frank Ernest Hill; and Allan Nevins. *Timber and Men: The Weyerhaeuser Story*. New York: Macmillan, 1963.

Himmelberg, Robert. *The Origins of the National Recovery Administration: Business, Government, and the Trade Association Issue, 1921–1933*. New York: Fordham University Press, 1976.

Holbrook, Stewart. *Holy Old Mackinaw: A Natural History of the American Lumberjack*. New York: Macmillan, 1938.

———. *Yankee Loggers: A Recollection of Woodsmen, Cooks, and River Drivers*. New York: International Paper Co., 1961.

Hurst, James W. *Law and Economic Growth: Legal History of the Lumber Industry in Wisconsin, 1836–1915*. Cambridge, Mass.: Belknap Press, 1964.

Ise, John. *The United States Forest Policy*. New Haven, Conn.: Yale University Press, 1920.

Jensen, Vernon. *Lumber and Labor*. New York: Farrar and Rinehart, 1945.

Kirkland, Edward C. *Industry Comes of Age*. New York: Holt, Rinehart and Winston, 1925.

Kolko, Gabriel. *The Triumph of Conservatism: A Reinterpretation of American History, 1900–1916*. New York: Macmillan, 1963.

Lasch, Christopher. *The Culture of Narcissism: American Life in an Age of Diminishing Expectations*. New York: W. W. Norton, 1978.

LeMaster, Dennis C. *Mergers Among the Largest Forest Products Firms, 1950–1970*. Pullman: Washington State University, College of Agriculture Research Center, Bulletin 854, 1977.

Loehr, Rodney C., ed. *Forests for the Future: The Story of Sustained Yield as Told in the Diaries and Papers of David T. Mason*. St. Paul: Minnesota Historical Society, 1952.

McGeary, M. Nelson. *Gifford Pinchot: Forester*. Princeton, N.J.: Princeton University Press, 1960.

Mason, David. *Timber Ownership and Lumber Production in the Inland Empire*. Portland, Oreg.: Western Pine Association, 1920.

Mead, Walter J. *Competition and Oligopsony in the Douglas Fir Lumber Industry*. Berkeley: University of California Press, 1966.

———. *Mergers and Economic Concentration in the Douglas Fir Lumber Industry*. Portland, Oreg.: Pacific Northwest Forest and Range Experiment Station, 1964.

Miller, William, ed. *Men in Business*. Cambridge, Mass.: Harvard University Press, 1952.

Morgan, George T. *William B. Greeley, A Practical Forester*. St. Paul: Forest History Society, 1961.

Nash, Roderick. *Wilderness and the American Mind*. Rev. ed. New Haven, Conn.: Yale University Press, 1967.

National Conservation Congress. *Proceedings of the Fourth Conservation Congress*. Indianapolis, Ind.: The Congress, 1912.

National Industrial Conference Board. *Trade Associations: Their Economic Significance and Legal Status*. New York: The Board, 1925.

National Lumber Manufacturers Association. *Annual Report*. 1910–28.

———. *Highlights of a Decade of Achievement*. Washington, D.C.: The Association, 1929.

Nixon, Edgar B., ed. *Franklin D. Roosevelt and Conservation, 1911–1945*. 2 vols. Hyde Park, N.Y.: Franklin D. Roosevelt Library, 1957.

Noble, David. *America By Design: Science, Technology and the Rise of Corporate Capitalism*. New York: Oxford University Press, 1977.

Perkins, Edwin J., ed. *Men and Organizations*. New York: Putman's, 1977.

Pinchot, Gifford. *Breaking New Ground*. New York: Harcourt, Brace, 1947.

Pinkett, Harold T. *Gifford Pinchot, Private and Public Forester*. Champaign: University of Illinois Press, 1970.

Richardson, Elmo. *BLM's Billion-Dollar Checkerboard: Managing the O&C Lands*. Santa Cruz, Calif.: Forest History Society, 1980.

———. *The Politics of Conservation: Crusades and Controversies, 1897–1913*. Los Angeles: University of California Press, 1962.

Rodgers, Andrew. *Bernard Fernow: A Story of North American Forestry*. Princeton, N.J.: Princeton University Press, 1951.

Schlesinger, Arthur M., Jr. *The Crisis of the Old Order, 1919–1933*. Boston: Houghton Mifflin, 1957.

Smith, J. Russell. *North America: Its People and the Resources*. New York: Harcourt, Brace, 1925.

Southern Pine Association. *Economic Conditions in the Southern Pine Industry.* The Association, 1931.

Steen, Harold K. *The U.S. Forest Service: A History.* Seattle: University of Washington Press, 1976.

Tyler, Robert. *Rebels of the Woods: The I.W.W. In the Pacific Northwest.* Eugene: University of Oregon Press, 1967.

Wagner, Susan. *The Federal Trade Commission.* New York: Praeger, 1971.

Weinstein, James. *The Corporate Ideal in the Liberal State.* Boston: Beacon Press, 1968.

West Coast Lumbermen's Association. *Annual Report and Reference Book.* N.p., 1937.

Wiebe, Robert. *The Search for Order, 1877–1920.* New York: Hill and Wang, 1967.

Williams, William Appleman. *The Contours of American History.* New York: World Publishing Co., 1961.

Wilson, Joan Hoff. *Herbert Hoover: Forgotten Progressive.* Boston: Little, Brown, 1975.

Winters, Donald L. *Henry Cantwell Wallace as Secretary of Agriculture.* Champaign: University of Illinois Press, 1970.

Wolfe, Alan. *The Limits of Legitimacy: Political Contradictions of Contemporary Capitalism.* New York: Free Press, 1977.

ARTICLES

Allen, E. T. "Economics of Timber Supply in Relation to Production and Consumption." In *Proceedings of the Fifth National Conservation Congress.* St. Paul, Minnesota, 1913.

"American Forest Congress." *American Forests* 11: 9–20.

Appleman, Roy E. "Timber Empire From the Public Domain." *Mississippi Valley Historical Review* 26: 193–208.

Ballaine, Wesley C. "The Revested Oregon and California Railroad Grant Lands." *Land Economics* 29: 219–32.

Bates, J. Leonard. "Fulfilling American Democracy: The Conservation Movement, 1907–1921." *Mississippi Valley Historical Review* 44 (1957): 29–57.

Bernstein, Barton J. "The New Deal: Conservative Achievements of Liberal Reform." In *Towards A New Past,* ed. Barton J. Bernstein. New York: Pantheon, 1968.

Bruncken, Ernest. "Private Forestry and Taxation." *American Forests* 9:509–12.

Butler, Ovid. "Forest Situation Exposed." *American Forests* 39: 204–206.

———. "The Oregon Checkmate: How the Federal Government is Blocking Conservation of the Nation's Greatest Remaining Forest." *American Forests* 42: 157–62, 196–97.

Carrott, M. Browning. "The Supreme Court and American Trade Associations, 1921–1925." *Business History Review* 44: 320–28.

Cary, Austin. "How Lumbermen in Following Their Own Interests Have Served the Public." *Journal of Forestry* 15: 279–85.

Chapman, H. H. "Second Conference on the Lumber Code." *Journal of Forestry* 32: 272–74.

Clephane, Thomas P. "Ownership of Timber: A Critical Component in Industrial Success." *Forest Industries* 105: 30–33.

Compton, Wilson. "Forest Economics: Some Thoughts on an Old Subject." *American Forests* 25: 1337–39.

———. "How Competition Can Be Improved Through Association." *Proceedings of the Academy of Political Science* 11: 32–38.

———. "The Price Problem in the Lumber Industry." *American Economic Review* 7: 582–97.

———. "Recent Tendencies in the Reform of Forest Taxation." *Journal of Political Economy* 23: 971–79.

"Conference of Lumber and Timber Products Industries with Public Agencies on Forest Conservation." *Journal of Forestry* 32: 275–307.

"Conference on O and C Lands Held in Portland." *American Forests* 42: 436.

Cox, John H. "Trade Associations in the Lumber Industry of the Pacific Northwest, 1899–1914." *Pacific Northwest Quarterly* 41: 285–311.

Defebaugh, J. E. "Relation of Forestry to Lumbering and the Wood-Working Industries." *Proceedings of the American Forestry Association* 1893: 150–52.

"An Editorial—A Dangerous Grant." *American Forests* 37: 279.

"Editorial: Cut-over Lands a National Problem." *American Forests* 23: 304–306.

"Eighteenth Meeting of the American Forestry Association." *American Forests* 6: 9.

Ellis, Richard C. "The Oregon and California Railroad Land Grant, 1866–1945." *Pacific Northwest Quarterly* 39: 253–83.

Fernow, Bernard E. "Letter to the Editor." *American Forests* 2: 45.

———. "Principles Underlying the Taxation of Forests." In *Taxation of Forests*. Concord, N.H.: Society for the Protection of New Hampshire Forests, 1912.

"Forest Industry Charts Conservation Course." *American Forests* 39: 540–41, 572–73.

"Forest Industry Will Do Its Part." *American Forests* 43: 232–33, 262–63.

"Forest Legislation to be Urged." *American Forests* 42: 128.

Galambos, Louis. "The Emerging Organizational Synthesis in Modern American History." *Business History Review* 44: 279–90.

Gaskill, Alfred. "How Shall Forests Be Taxed?" *American Forests* 12: 119–22.

Gillett, Charles A. "Citizens and Trade Associations Dealing With Forestry." In *Fifty Years of Forestry*, ed. Robert K. Winters. Washington, D.C., 1950.

Goetz, C. H. "Why Americans Cut Their Forests." *American Forests* 13: 282–84.

Graves, Henry S. "The Advance of Forestry in the United States." *American Review of Reviews* 41: 461–66.

———. "Comments on the Copeland Report." *American Forests* 39: 258–59.

———. "Private Forestry." *Journal of Forestry* 17: 113–21.

———. "Public Regulation of Private Forests." *Annals of the American Academy of Political and Social Science* 33: 497–509.

Greeley, William B. "Forty Years of Forest Conservation." *Journal of Forestry* 38: 386–89.

————. "Self-Government in Forestry." *Journal of Forestry* 18: 103–105.

————. "The War Job for Foresters." *American Forests* 48: 175.

Guff, Robert D. "American Historians and the Organizational Factor." *Canadian Review of American Studies* 4: 19–31.

Hamilton, Lawrence. "The Federal Forest Regulation Issue." *Journal of Forest History* 9: 2–11.

Harris, Michael. "News From Timber Country: On Tour With the American Forest Institute." *Progressive* 44: 48–49.

Hawley, Ellis W. "Herbert Hoover, the Commerce Secretariat, and the Vision of an 'Associative State,' 1921–1928." *Journal of American History* 61: 116–40.

Heilbroner, Robert. "The New Economics." *New York Review of Books* 27 (February 21, 1980): 19–22.

Hoover, Roy O. "Public Law 273 Comes to Shelton: Implementation of the Sustained-Yield Management Act of 1944." *Journal of Forest History* 22: 86–101.

Horning, W. H. "Sustained-Yield Program of the O and C Lands." *Oregon Business Review* 5: 1–2.

Hosmer, Ralph S. "The National Forestry Program Committee." *Journal of Forestry* 45: 627–45.

Hough, Franklin B. "On the Duty of Governments in the Preservation of Forests." In *Conservation in the United States: A Documentary History*, ed. Frank E. Smith. Vol. 1. New York: Chelsea House, 1971.

"Investigations of O and C Lands Urged." *American Forests* 42: 325.

Kellogg, Royal S. "A Discussion of Methods." *American Forests* 25: 1282–83.

————. "The Rise in Lumber Prices." *American Forests* 12: 68–69.

Knappen, Theodore M. "The West at Washington." *Sunset Magazine* 55: (June, 1913): 47–48.

Kolko, Gabriel. "Intelligence and the Myth of Capitalist Rationality in the United States." *Science and Society* 44: 130–54.

"Letter from J. Sterling Morton." *Proceedings of the American Forestry Congress* 1888: 12–13.

"Lumberman's Views on Reforestation." *American Forests* 14: 35–36.

"Lumbermen Favor Forestry." *American Forests* 9: 202–204.

McCarthy, G. Michael. "Colorado Progressives and Conservation." *Mid-America: An Historical Review* 57: 213–26.

Mason, David. "The Effect of O and C Management on the Economy of Oregon." *Oregon Historical Quarterly* 64: 55–67.

Mohr, Charles. "The Interest of the Individual in Forestry in View of the Present Condition of the Lumber Interest." *Proceedings of the American Forestry Congress* 1889: 36–38.

Norcross, Charles P. "Weyerhaeuser—Richer than John D. Rockefeller." *Cosmopolitan* 42: 252–59.

Pinchot, Gifford. "Forestry on Private Lands." *Annals of the American Academy of Political and Social Science* 33: 487–96.

————. "The Frontier and the Lumberman." *American Forests* 9: 176–77.

"The Public Land Report: A Threat to Conservation." *Journal of Forestry* 29: 649–51.

Radosh, Ronald. "The Myth of the New Deal." In *A New History of Leviathan: Essays on the Rise of the American Corporate State*, ed. Ronald Radosh and Murray Rothbard. New York: E. P. Dutton, 1972.

Rakestraw, Lawrence W. "Uncle Sam's Forest Reserves." *Pacific Northwest Quarterly* 44: 145–51.

Russell, Charles Edward. "The Mysterious Octopus: Story of the Strange and Powerful Organization That Controls the American Lumber Trade." *World Today* 21: 1735–50.

Saley, M. L. "Relation of Forestry to the Lumbering Industry." *Proceedings of the American Forestry Association* 1893: 147–50.

Schmaltz, Norman J. "Forest Researcher." *Journal of Forest History* 24: 24–39, 86–97.

Shepard, Ward. "Editorial: Forest Leadership." *Journal of Forestry* 31: 631–32.

———. "The Necessity for Realism in Forestry Propaganda." *Journal of Forestry* 25: 11–26.

Silcox, Ferdinand A. "Foresters Must Choose." *Journal of Forestry* 33: 198–204.

Silver, James W. "The Hardwood Producers Come of Age." *Journal of Southern History* 55: 427–53.

Society of American Foresters. "Forest Devastation: A National Danger and a Plan to Meet It." *Journal of Forestry* 17: 900–45.

Sussman, Warren. "The Persistence of American Reform." In *American Reform: The Ambiguous Legacy*, ed. D. Walden. Yellow Springs, Ohio: Ampersand Press, 1967.

"Take off the Taxes." *American Forests* 14: 122–23.

Vietor, Richard H. K. "Businessmen and the Political Economy: The Railroad Rate Controversy of 1905." *Journal of American History* 64: 47–66.

White, Henry Gilbert. "Forest Ownership Research in Historical Perspective." *Journal of Forestry* 48: 261–64.

Woods, John B. "The Forestry Situation in the U.S. Today and a Simple Workable Remedy." *Journal of Forestry* 28: 928–32.

PERIODICALS

American Lumberman
Lumber
Lumber Manufacturer and Dealer
Lumber World Review
National Lumber Bulletin

Pacific Lumber and Trade Journal
Salem (Oregon) *Statesman*
Southern Lumberman
Timberman
West Coast Lumberman

Index